# COLLISION OF WILLS

# COLLISION
## of WILLS
### JOHNNY UNITAS, DON SHULA,
### AND THE RISE OF THE MODERN NFL

## JACK GILDEN

UNIVERSITY OF NEBRASKA PRESS | LINCOLN & LONDON

∞

Library of Congress Cataloging-in-Publication Data
Names: Gilden, Jack, author.
Title: Collision of wills: Johnny Unitas, Don Shula,
and the rise of the modern NFL / Jack Gilden.
Description: Lincoln: University of Nebraska Press, [2018] |
Includes bibliographical references and index.
Identifiers: LCCN 2017056784
ISBN 9781496206916 (cloth: alk. paper)
ISBN 9781496210388 (epub)
ISBN 9781496210395 (mobi)
ISBN 9781496210401 (pdf)
Subjects: LCSH: Baltimore Colts (Football team)—History. |
Unitas, Johnny, 1933–2002. | Shula, Don, 1930– | Football—
Maryland—Baltimore—History. | Football—United States—
History. | National Football League—History.
Classification: LCC GV956.B3 G456 2018 |
DDC 796.332/64097526—dc23
LC record available at https://lccn.loc.gov/2017056784

Set in Scala OT by E. Cuddy.

For Jerry Gilden, because he alone gave me every valuable thing I have. And for Miriam Ann Bransky Gilden, who brought beauty to marriage, motherhood, and, especially, to the canvas.

If you can meet with Triumph and Disaster
And treat those two impostors just the same;
. . .
Yours is the Earth and everything that's in it.

—RUDYARD KIPLING, "If—"

# CONTENTS

# ILLUSTRATIONS

# COLLISION OF WILLS

# Prologue

Entombed within a sprawling South Florida manse with a sweep of shimmering turquoise water behind him, and a lavish, manicured lawn and golf course in front, sits Don Shula, the most frequent winner in the history of professional football.

The trappings of his unprecedented success surround him: elegant furniture, magnificent statues, and original masterworks of the canvas. He is in a room deep within his huge home, and his home is deep within the heart of the community where he elevated football to higher levels than anyone else knew existed. But on this day he is no longer a choreographer of wild men; he's white haired and enfeebled. Wherever he sits, his walker sits beside him. Despite his infirmities he is kind and friendly; he offers cold drinks and polite conversation. He is a comfortable and satisfied man.

And, perhaps, he also holds the answer to one of the few mysteries still extant in the overcovered, overanalyzed National Football League (NFL).

Today, mighty networks and their online affiliates follow the league around the clock, bringing more probing investigation to a felonious running back than any enterprising journalist in the world applies to Iran's nuclear weapons program. There's not much that happens in the league, has ever happened in the league, that the public doesn't know.

But Shula's secret is buried deep, and it comes from a city that's so distant, it's half a century away. Back then the coach wasn't decrepit; he was ferocious, a young man with ambitions that were as red-hot as his volcanic temper. Because of his later success with the Miami Dolphins, where he lasted almost thirty years, coached two Hall of Fame quarterbacks, went to five Super Bowls, and led his team to football's only undefeated season, few remember his first job. They don't recall that Don Shula was once the brilliant young head coach of the mythic Baltimore Colts.

Some of the details are fuzzy even to him.

I asked him: "Who had a higher winning percentage? The Packers under Vince Lombardi or the Baltimore Colts under Don Shula?"

"I don't know," he said, smiling, the old competitive fires glinting behind his tired eyes. "Who?"

The answer is Shula's Colts, by a single percentage point. From 1963 to 1969 they won more than 75 percent of their games against the likes of Halas and Butkus and Sayers, Jim Brown and Paul Warfield, the Fearsome Foursome, and, of course, Lombardi's Packers, with whom the Colts shared a rivalry of unmatched intensity.

Yet the Packers won five championships in that tumultuous decade; Shula and the Colts, for all their success, didn't win a single one. Twice they qualified for the big game. Both times they lost in spectacular upsets. The mystery of this success-failure dynamic only deepens if you know that Shula's business partner in these pursuits was Johnny Unitas.

Since George Halas drafted Sid Luckman and aimed the quarterback's Semitic right arm at the rest of the league, the coach-and-quarterback combination has been the most consistent indicator of success in football. That's roughly been true from World War II to Brady and Belichick.

Unitas and Shula should've been the greatest of these duos. Shula's coaching career would last more than thirty years, fueled by his unmatched success. Unitas would one day be eulogized on the cover of *Sports Illustrated* as "The Greatest There Ever Was." Separately, they achieved as much as Lombardi and Starr, winning five world championships. Unitas won two, under Weeb Ewbank, before Shula arrived on the scene and one under Don McCafferty, the first season after Shula departed. As the Don of the Dolphins, Shula quickly went to three straight Super Bowls and won two of them.

They appeared, to the public, to be in perfect sync—two young and intelligent men, deeply competitive, and extraordinarily driven. But that was merely a facade. Behind the scenes there were tensions between them that few others knew or understood.

So what was their issue?

What is it usually between two men who are at odds, money, power, or, maybe, a woman?

Sitting on his sofa I asked Shula directly, "Why was it so difficult between you and Unitas?"

"Difficult!" Shula laughs as he responds. "We won a hell of a lot of games together."

True enough. But his answer is so polished, so at the ready, it was as if he knew back in the mid-'60s that some swaddling baby was out there who would one day appear on his twenty-first-century doorstep with that embarrassing question. In the old days, by all accounts, an uncomfortable question like that one would have provoked an indignant answer.

But he's not that guy anymore. Years of professional success and domestic bliss have softened what was once very coarse. He has had forty-five years, a lifetime, to work on his diplomacy.

Unitas died on September 11, 2002, but he remained, to the end, entertainingly bitter. He started his career by facing Shula on the practice fields of Baltimore when both were hard-nosed young players. His emerging success came at the expense of exposing Shula's shortcomings. The quarterback soon ascended to the top of the profession, while the cornerback faded into obscurity.

Just a few short years later, in a turn of events that could happen only in the highest reaches of the military or the government, the inept player became the great player's boss.

After leaving Baltimore Shula leads Miami to the only undefeated season in league history and is feted as one of the greatest coaches of all time. Meanwhile, an aging Unitas loses his footing as a player, surrenders his five children to end an unhappy marriage, and fails over and over again in business.

"Johnny U came here to visit me just a few years before he died," one old Colts coach said, "and when Shula's name came up he said, 'If Shula was standing here right now, and he was on fire, I wouldn't piss on him to put it out.'"

That unambiguously angry statement was delivered only about

thirty years after Unitas last laid eyes on Shula in person. The anger of Unitas, much like the talent, knew no bounds.

That Unitas and Shula would square off in personal combat was not unusual, considering their time and place. They lived, operated, prospered, fell, and rose again in a universe of attack, conflict, and collision. That's the world of football, but, more poignantly, it was also the state of the world in their era.

In the 1960s the United States was engaged in a Cold War with the Soviet Union and a red-hot war in the jungles of Southeast Asia. Conflicts in Cuba and wars between the Arabs and Israelis both brought the world to a nuclear high alert. At home the culture wars raged between the so-called Greatest Generation and their own offspring, the boomers. The kids had longer hair and looser morals, to the horror of their parents. Music went from crooners like Sinatra to the weird dreamers of psychedelic rock, a musical journey that washed over the listener like a hit of acid.

Americans argued and fought about civil rights, exporting freedom at the point of a bayonet, and sexual awakening that uncloaked the beauty of the female form and unleashed the once repressed and "dirty" desires of American men.

It was an era in which domestic terrorists, like the Ku Klux Klan, lynched and bombed black Americans. Police officers, in a perversion of their mission to maintain law and order, turned fire hoses and nightsticks on peaceful citizens marching for equality. The old thought of the young as dirty, dumb, and lazy. The young were convinced that the old were venal, racist, and violent.

The '60s began with the infectious enthusiasm of John F. Kennedy, a man who overcame his Irish Catholic roots to rise to the highest office in the white Anglo Protestant land. But Kennedy, too, had a dark side. He blundered at the Bay of Pigs, where he secretly and unsuccessfully tried to overthrow Fidel Castro. Soon after that he embarrassed himself and the nation at a disastrous meeting in which Soviet leader Nikita Khrushchev dominated him. As a consequence of his missteps, he stumbled into Vietnam, the original quagmire. He did so, he said, in order to be taken seriously by his communist counterparts. More than fifty thousand Americans would die for that cause.

Unitas and Shula's theater of war was Baltimore, a place physically in the heart of America's eastern elite, but far from it. The nation looked at the old harbor town as a gritty, grimy, smelly place with little of redeeming value outside of incomparable seafood.

In fact, Baltimore was an industrial powerhouse in steep post–World War II decline. While Baltimore's smokestacks went cold, its citizens rhapsodized about their beloved city and abandoned it. The magnificent architecture and the charming old neighborhoods collapsed, while the ghettos that racism and real estate schemes created remained and grew.

Despite its masses of suburban refugees, Baltimore remained a relevant American city, and for several reasons. First, Johns Hopkins meant that Baltimore would always be the world's medical capital. Second, as the dividing line of North and South, Baltimore was on the cutting edge of the country's most crucial issue—racial justice. And finally, because of Unitas and Shula, Baltimore was the epicenter of the growing professional football juggernaut.

Pro football was just coming into its own during the '60s, propelled in large part by the on-field theatrics of Unitas alone. He made the game telegenic. He raised the standard of excellence and heightened the level of competition. More important, his heroics awakened an urgent need in other cities to get into the game. Lamar Hunt, scion of a rich Dallas oil family, also felt that need. After watching Unitas defeat the New York Giants for the championship in 1958, he went out and created the American Football League (AFL), doubling the size, scope, and interest of professional football virtually overnight.

Unitas's pairing with Shula seemed to fit Baltimore like a glove. The quarterback and coach with their Rust Belt roots and sensitivities appealed to their row-house dwelling fans. They were tough, manly, and indomitable, and their appeal traveled far beyond the provinces. They wore the Baltimore imprimatur, but they were American archetypes.

For a declining city in a deeply divided country, they provided a focal point of American goodness. They appeared to be hard workers and team players who were driven, tough, and, yes, even violent, but only in pursuit of the greater good.

That those two men were something far different from how they were processed and packaged said a great deal about their game and their world. Their brand was order, success, and teamwork.

Their reality was a whole other thing.

They vied with each other for control of the team and harbored competing visions for what the modern game should be. The rage they felt for each other propelled them and their sport to great heights, even while it broke their city's heart.

And in the end, everything for which they had worked so tirelessly—all of it came tumbling down.

# ONE

# A Legend Departs and an Ambitious
# Young Man Arrives

f anyone knew what Johnny Unitas was thinking, they certainly weren't saying so in print. The Colts, efficient and professional in all things, had just simultaneously made two blockbuster announcements. First, they had discharged their famous head coach, Weeb Ewbank, ending a nine-year reign in which he took the team from virtual bankruptcy to back-to-back world titles. Second, they were replacing him with a relatively unknown thirty-three-year-old Lions assistant who had no head-coaching experience whatsoever. That ambitious young bounder was named Don Shula.

Shula was one of the Colts himself, just a few years before. He spent four years toiling as a defensive back on some horrific teams, only to be released by Coach Ewbank just as the organization was on the threshold of greatness. He had been the teammate of eleven men, including Unitas, who were still active on the roster. Shula was younger than some of the men he was about to lead.

Team owner Carroll Rosenbloom, or "C.R." to his minions, disposed of Ewbank in a short, private meeting at the Colts' offices in January 1963. The news was delivered beneath a photograph of Weeb in full command of his champions. Afterward, the owner reported that the deposed coach "took it calmly, and like a man."

After releasing Ewbank, Rosenbloom, ever the paternalist, made the former head of his organization a rather insulting offer: the victorious coach in the Greatest Game and the man who made the franchise famous was offered an "unspecified job," in the front office. What would his duties be?

"Well, he couldn't get into actual coaching," Rosenbloom told reporters.

Ewbank turned him down. Nevertheless, the deposed coach gladly accepted a severance check for $60,000, enough money, in those days, to buy several well-appointed homes in the Baltimore area for cash.

Shula was having a far better day. Coroneted in grand style, he met the press on the marble floors and Oriental rugs of the Belvedere Hotel, a masterpiece of Gilded Age architecture and a standing relic of a once great city now in steep decline.

Reporters buzzed about the scene and looked for every angle they could find. They made much of the fact that Shula once played for the Colts, they described his physical features (especially his granite jaw), they commented about his almost cocky confidence, and, of course, they marveled at his youth.

They also interviewed the men with numbers on their shirts. Players like Carl Taseff, Bill Pellington, and Gino Marchetti were asked their opinions of the dramatic changes. Ostensibly, it seemed they were chosen for their long-standing knowledge of Shula, but, in fact, they may have been spoon-fed to the press. Behind the scenes these three had, for some time, urged Rosenbloom to make a change. And they all had lobbied for Shula. They were former teammates of the new young coach, they were all from the defensive side of the ball, and they were all Catholic.

Until the day he died the Protestant Ewbank believed that he was undone in Baltimore by a conspiracy of Catholic players.

John Constantine Unitas was Catholic, too, but he wasn't at Shula's press conference. The "Golden Arm's" opinion was neither noted nor even speculated upon by any member of the press. This was in character for Unitas, who could be blunt in personal conversations but was presented to the public as a kind of virtuous warrior who dutifully followed the chain of command. He was also famously unknowable, a laconic loner who seemed to live inside his own head. He certainly would never belong to any clique of players. He had an unusual personal and professional chemistry with Raymond Berry, who shared his passions for the game and unshakable work ethic. But if there was any one man in the organization to whom Unitas was most attached, it was Ewbank himself.

Weeb Ewbank was the only coach of any standing in either college or the professional ranks who had given Unitas a chance, signing him when he was a reject from the Steelers, the worst organization in professional football. As legend had it, the Colts received a postcard from someone who wrote to extol Unitas's virtues. Based on that they invited him to Baltimore for a special tryout. They were impressed enough by what they saw to keep him.

The truth was slightly different. In fact, the Colts often received communications of one sort or another about amateur players or physical specimens whom they should see. The player himself usually wrote those letters. Not the type of organization to let anything fall through the cracks, the Colts had a tryout for all these players every year. Usually, it was the same day as the Preakness, the famous horse race held at Baltimore's Pimlico racetrack. Unitas also came to the team's attention through a note, but he wasn't the same as the others. Ewbank was waiting for him.

"In the spring we would . . . bring in maybe fifty to sixty boys who had written to us for a tryout," Charley Winner, a former player of Ewbank's at Washington University, his son-in-law, and a scout for the Browns, remembered. "In college we had played Louisville [Unitas's school], and Frank Camp was the coach there for many, many years, very successful. He called Weeb, and he said, 'Weeb, don't overlook this boy Unitas. He was drafted by Pittsburgh, but they never gave him a chance.' So we invited Unitas for that tryout, and as soon as he threw the ball, I mean there was no question about it. He set up pretty quick, he recognized the receiver, and he was right on the money. Go passes he put it right on your fingertips. He could run, too. They called him Stilts 'cause he was kind of stiff at the hips, but he could avoid getting hit. So we signed him right away."

To an outsider it might have seemed that the coach brought in the young unknown quarterback to keep the bench from getting cold. The Colts already had George Shaw, who had only recently been the very first player chosen in the draft. But Shaw was a player Ewbank had never really wanted, and at practice Weeb paired Unitas with Berry, an unheralded receiver prospect whom the coach had maneuvered to bring to the Colts.

Eventually, Ewbank would pay Otto Graham, the great Cleveland quarterback who had recently retired, to come to Baltimore and tutor the developing Unitas. Graham had taken the Browns to ten championship games in a row and knew the intricacies of the Cleveland offense that Ewbank ran better than anyone else in the world.

In 1956, when Shaw went down with an injured knee in a typically brutal affair against the Bears, all of these machinations came together. Ewbank never hesitated before sending in the rookie Unitas to replace him. When the young quarterback's first pass was intercepted by the Bears' J. C. Caroline and run back for a touchdown, the Monsters of the Midway routed the Colts. But the very next week Ewbank penciled Unitas's name into the starting lineup again. By the end of the season the rookie had a stranglehold on the job. In 1957, just Unitas's second year, he was voted Most Valuable Player (MVP) of the league.

Ewbank didn't lead through fear or intimidation; he set an example of professionalism. Rather than drive the men, he saw himself as a teacher. He was highly meticulous about the tiniest details, such as stance, tackling technique, or even the slightest movement of a first step. Once, Royce Womble, a Colts receiver from West Texas, caught a 49-yard touchdown pass, yet Weeb pulled him aside when he came off the field to lecture him about some flaw in how he ran the pattern.

"Now Royce, next time you run it, do this," Weeb told him, and did a little demonstration.

Womble looked at his coach with a smile and said, "Hell, Weeb, you can't get any more than six points."

Ewbank was all business, but he had patience; he understood what it took for a player to develop. Unitas responded to this approach with unprecedented professional success but also with a depth of personal feeling. His own father had died when he was still a very young boy. His mother worked backbreaking jobs, day and night, just to keep the family afloat. So even though he was grown to full maturity and famous in every corner of the nation, even though he was a leader among diverse and tough men, many of whom had been to war, and even though he was already a father with his own family, Unitas may have still felt a painful void. Ewbank filled it with acceptance and gentle guidance. Though the two were of different religious affiliations, they sometimes worshipped together. Once, after Mass, as they walked home, Unitas abruptly turned to Ewbank and told him, "I love you." Charley Winner, the only other man present, knew exactly what Unitas meant: "Weeb was a father figure to many men," he said.

If only the relationship between Ewbank and Carroll Rosenbloom was that affectionate. In fact, theirs was a difficult marriage right from the start. Back in 1953 when he was looking for a coach, Rosenbloom's first choice was Blanton Collier, another Paul Brown acolyte. But Collier, loyal and perhaps even a little fearful of his autocratic boss, turned Rosenbloom down. An anonymous Browns board member had suggested to Rosenbloom that he should pursue Ewbank. But when the Colts asked for permission to speak with him, Coach Brown, a jealous man and notorious double-crosser where his assistants were concerned, told them that Ewbank wasn't interested.

And then fate stepped in.

Charley Winner happened to be on the same flight as Colts general manager (GM) Don Kellett. He was seated right next to the GM. First, he coaxed Kellett into discussing the Colts' coaching search with him, and then he told Kellett that Ewbank was, in fact, very interested in the job. He gave Kellett Weeb's home phone number, and the wheels were officially in motion.

Comically short and stocky, especially compared to the behemoths he ordered around, Weeb looked like a ten-pin ball in a brown suit and a crew cut. Despite his unlikely appearance, Ewbank knew as much about the business of winning football as anyone in the world. He not only coached the Cleveland tackles but was also a shrewd judge of talent who oversaw the Browns' annual influx of superb draft picks. His head was brimming with invaluable intellectual property.

Yet Rosenbloom *settled* for him. At the press conference announcing Ewbank's hiring, the owner wasted no time putting pressure on his new coach. Ewbank will either win or "take the consequences," the owner told the press, tempering the moment's joy. And then, just in case anyone missed the subtleties of that, Rosenbloom said with a big, warm grin, "I'd fire my own grandmother if I thought she couldn't do a winning job."

Despite the owner's misgivings, Ewbank instantly brought the organization credibility and a methodology. He and his staff poured through "movies" of all the team's games from the previous year and graded every Colt on every single play. This dedication created a kind of prescience about talent. For instance, he determined that one of the franchise's lone bright spots, Gino "the Giant" Marchetti, an offensive tackle under his predecessor, would be more effective disrupting quarterbacks than protecting them. So Ewbank moved the Giant to defensive end, where he quickly established himself as the best pass rusher in the game and an eventual first-ballot Hall of Famer.

In his very first draft with the Colts (1954), Ewbank was restricted from sitting at the team's table, a constraint that came as a small act of revenge from his fulminating former boss, Paul Brown. A master of gamesmanship, Brown successfully argued to the league that Ewbank was still in transition between the two franchises. Nevertheless, Weeb worked behind the scenes to aid his new team. He surreptitiously urged the Colts to select Southern Methodist University wide receiver Raymond Berry, in the twentieth round, the 232nd player chosen. The coach saw something in Berry, though the offensive and defensive end was still only a junior and appeared to others as slow afoot and a little odd. Berry had never produced much in college; he mostly played defense, and he was too small for that in the pros. On offense he'd caught only thirty-three passes his entire collegiate career to that point (he was a "future" pick with another year of school left). But for Weeb there was a lot to like in the lean, tall young man. Raymond was a coach's son who was meticulous in his preparation and approach to the game. Ewbank may have imagined a player in Berry who could understand and thrive in a complex professional offense. Whatever Weeb knew that others didn't, when he urged the fledgling Colts to select Berry, he had corralled a future Hall of Famer, one who would pioneer methods of preparation that fundamentally changed the way the game was played.

Ewbank's professional improvements to the Colts might've been obvious to him, but they weren't reflected in the bottom line. In his head-coaching debut his team lost to the Rams 48–0. The Colts limped through the rest of their schedule and eventually finished just 3-9. That was the very same record Keith Molesworth, Ewbank's supposedly inept predecessor, had mismanaged the year before. Worse even than that dismal record, Rosenbloom still didn't fully trust Ewbank's judgments a year into their relationship.

The night before selections commenced for the 1955 draft, dissension broke out in the Colts' hotel room. Ewbank told Rosenbloom he was prepared to select Georgia Tech linebacker Larry Morris. But one of his youngest assistant coaches, Joe Thomas, pushed his way into the conversation and impertinently spoke up to disagree with his boss. Thomas addressed the owner directly and argued that the team currently had enough defensive talent to compete. What the Colts needed, Thomas said, was an infusion of offense.

Thomas argued that the man to take was George Shaw, the highly regarded quarterback from Oregon. Rosenbloom sided with Thomas, then just a kid in his twenties, over his experienced head coach. The next morning, with the first and third overall picks in the draft, the Colts selected Shaw number one and, two picks later, collared Alan "the Horse" Ameche, the Heisman Trophy–winning fullback from Wisconsin.

With Shaw and Ameche somewhat thrust upon him, Ewbank never quite took to either. Shaw initially wore the mantle of first player chosen pretty well. He had a strong arm, and he was mobile, a fast runner who maneuvered well in the pocket. He quickly became the Colts' starter and generated a great deal of excitement among the fans. Yet Shaw never really amounted to much in Baltimore. After just a year or so at the helm he was injured and supplanted by a man who was his polar opposite, a scrap heaper who showed up not with fanfare but with a touch of bursitis in his throwing shoulder. That player was Unitas.

Ameche, of course, became a fabled name. He was permanently canonized in the lore of professional football as the man who plunged over the goal line and defeated sudden death in the Greatest Game Ever. Yet Ewbank saw him until the end as spoiled. They would accomplish great things together, the Horse and the keeper of the Colts, but they would simply never see eye-to-eye.

Larry Morris, the linebacker Ewbank had favored over Shaw with that first pick, went to the Rams. Eventually, he was traded to Chicago, where he led the pre-Butkus Monsters to the 1963 NFL

Championship. He was voted MVP of that title game and later named to the NFL's All-Decade Team for the 1960s.

The most interesting year of the rebuilding process was 1956, which also happened to be the first season NFL games were nationally televised by CBS. The Colts improved ever so slightly, going 5-7. To the rest of the world they still appeared to be a second-division team, but Ewbank, at least, could see some major progress. First, the Colts beat the Bears right out of the gate in the season opener. That was a significant victory. Chicago would finish the year as the Western Division champs. Weeks later, in the rematch, the Colts were soundly defeated but enjoyed what may have been the single most important in-season improvement a football team ever made when Shaw injured his knee and young Johnny Unitas tentatively shuffled in to replace him.

Things were changing as Weeb's plans were accelerating. Like the Israelites fated to wander the desert until the slave generations had passed, Colts players who made up the early losing teams faded away, while the great players of the nascent dynasty stepped to the fore. Though the transition was dramatic, it wasn't always easy to determine the has-beens from the genuine Colts.

Don Shula was a strong case in point. A defensive halfback, as cornerbacks were then called, Shula started in the NFL as an unlikely prospect. The Colts picked him up in the famous five-for-ten trade with the Browns. Cleveland, the most advanced organization in professional football at that time, had discovered him almost by accident. Paul Brown and his entire staff alighted for Cleveland Stadium one fine fall day in 1950 to see the players for Syracuse, a national powerhouse in town to play the tiny Ohio school John Carroll University. John Carroll didn't produce many NFL prospects, and Shula, then a not-too-swift running back, wasn't on anyone's radar. But Shula from nearby Grand River, Ohio, had a big day, rushing for more than 100 yards in the upset victory over the Orangemen. One of the Browns' coaches, acting as a scout, suggested that the team draft Shula and his teammate Carl Taseff.

That scout was Weeb Ewbank.

In the pros Shula projected as a defensive back. At five feet eleven he had decent size but lacked the speed typically required to cover NFL receivers. Nevertheless, Cleveland selected him in the ninth round of the 1951 draft, and Shula, having grown up in Ohio idolizing Otto Graham, was delighted to be with the Browns.

In his first year in Cleveland Shula proved that he belonged in the NFL. He played in twelve games, the regular-season total in those days, and raked in four interceptions. But in his second year, splitting time between the Browns and the army, he got into just five games and didn't pick off a single pass. Despite the promise Shula had shown as a rookie, Cleveland's interest in him waned, and he was packaged in the huge deal with Baltimore.

Shula and Taseff both went to the Colts, two of ten Browns sent to the talent-starved franchise. Though the Colts got double the players, they were also somewhat fleeced, since Cleveland picked up Mike McCormick from Baltimore, a future Hall of Fame tackle.

When Ewbank was named Colts coach a year after that deal, it reunited Shula and his old benefactor. Shula responded to Ewbank and his staff and became an integral cog of the early Colts. He would enjoy his salad days as a player in Baltimore, intercepting five passes per season for two straight years and picking off fourteen passes altogether in his four-year Baltimore career. Nevertheless, the Colts were an atrocious team during Shula's four seasons with the club, winning only sixteen games in that time and never finishing above fourth place.

Shula's successes belied the fact that his coaches didn't think much of his ability. "He wasn't talented," defensive coach Charley Winner confirmed.

But he was smart.

Shula was the "quarterback" of the defense, the man who called all the plays in the huddle. Even though "he didn't have speed," as Charley Winner said, he knew how to compensate for his shortcomings. "He used his head; he used his head to try to get position.

"Corner is a tough job," Charley Winner said. "You're out there all by yourself. The formations haven't changed that much [today, from back then]. We had flood formations and everything else they have today. They found a way to isolate somebody. Shula called the coverages out there, so he would always put himself in an advantageous position."

Shula's precocious intelligence didn't necessarily make him the most coachable player. Winner remembered that Shula "would recognize a receiver's talents, but he wouldn't always listen [to his coach's advice].

"I always watched the opposing team warm up," Winner remembered. "We were playing the 49ers one year, and Gordie Soltau, a receiver, was running a 15-yard out on Shula's side of the field. Shula was playing right cornerback. I hadn't seen [Soltau] do that before. So I went over to Shula, and I said, 'Don, I have a suspicion that they are going to open up the game with a deep out on you.' 'Aw, no, they won't do that,' Shula said. They opened up the game with a deep gain on him."

In the early '50s Charley Winner was an ambitious young man on the cusp of building one of the greatest defenses in league history. He had his eyes on his future and was already thinking of the day when he might be a head coach. Like his mentor, Ewbank, Winner was adept at evaluating talent. He could distinguish between a winning player and a pretender like Shula, and he could spot coaching talent, too.

"Don studied the game," Winner said. "I always had it in the back of my mind that if I ever got a head-coaching job, I'm going to hire that guy Shula, because he was a smart player and he was a worker."

In fact, Shula unselfishly mentored many young Colts on the finer points of professional football. He generously tutored inexperienced defensive teammates on the intricacies of the Colts' system, though one of them, one day, might very well take his job. He also provided invaluable instruction to someone who could really do him some damage.

"I was a struggling young player who didn't know his butt from first base about being a professional wide receiver," Raymond Berry remembered. "I came out of a college where I basically played defense, and running pass routes was totally outside of my whole realm of experience. [Shula] was just supportive and helpful to a guy who was struggling not to get cut. He tried to teach me little things that could help me as a receiver. He was a critical factor in me, I think, staying around my rookie year."

Whatever Shula was teaching, it was working. Berry developed into an extraordinarily intelligent and meticulous pass catcher. He spent many extra hours every day working on the moves and techniques that would soon revolutionize the game. His dawn-till-dusk workmate was the team's unknown backup quarterback, Unitas. The two quickly developed an extraordinary personal and professional chemistry.

On the surface Unitas, Berry, and Shula were similar players. None was particularly imposing athletically, but all three rose high above what others thought they were capable of accomplishing. And they all did it with great intelligence and dedication to the craft.

Unitas and Shula, especially, were extraordinarily similar men. Both were devout Catholics and no-nonsense Rust Belt characters. Their families were barely removed from Eastern Europe. Shula's people were Hungarian. Unitas was a second-generation Lithuanian. Shula was from Ohio. Unitas was born and raised a couple hours east, in Pittsburgh. Shula's father worked a variety of jobs for incredibly low wages. He jumped from a hothouse, where he was paid $9 a week to tend roses, to a fishing boat, where the quality of the air plummeted but the pay jumped all the way up to $15 per week. Shula, who often accompanied his dad to work, would maintain an aversion to boats and fish for the rest of his life.

Unitas's father, Francis, exhibited many of the same qualities, both admirable and disappointing, that would later arise in his son. He was an enterprising man who had his own business delivering and shoveling coal for his neighbors, most of whom labored in and around the great blast furnaces that wrought America's steel. He performed backbreaking work to provide for his family, yet he was also not above taking departures from his loyalty to them. He was an unfaithful husband, and in the most unimaginable way. One of his affairs was conducted with his wife's sister. That dalliance with his sister-in-law produced a daughter, Dorothy, who was raised as a cousin rather than as a sibling to the children Francis had with his wife, Helen.

Francis died young. Curiously, it wasn't his excessive sexual behavior that did him in; it was his sterling work ethic. One cold, damp September night, he labored around the clock, shoveling coal until morning. No doubt, through the many hours of darkness that he worked, he thought of the rest he would get in the morning. But instead of sleep he got pneumonia. Like John Henry of the folk story, he had literally worked himself to death in one grand exertion. The only differences were that he did it with a shovel instead of a hammer and that he had a real-life wife and children depending on him. At the time of his death Francis Unitas was thirty-eight years old. The future greatest quarterback who ever lived, John Constantine Unitas, was only five.

In pro football Unitas and Shula found a potential path out of their fathers' traps. The NFL offered them a better paycheck, and a lot more than that. In football there was a standing to be gained. The similarities between a hard hat and a helmet were easy enough to see. They were both plastic shells, protection from dangerous work. But they represented dramatically different lives. The hard hat epitomized mere subsistence and guaranteed lifelong anonymity; the helmet had the allure of a fame that might last many generations beyond a lifetime. Theirs was a society turning from culture to popular culture, right before their eyes. Their world was exploding with the images and icons that motion pictures, periodicals, newspapers, radio, and especially television created. Football could be their vehicle to the American table and take them far beyond any other work for which their backgrounds and educations might have prepared them.

In 1956 Unitas and Shula were both fighting like hell to keep the helmet and toss the hard hat. With the one a cornerback and the other a quarterback, they were squaring off against each other every day in practice. Competition was endemic to their careers; all the men around them competed every single day. Yet there must have been a great deal going on under the skin when these two particular men, so similar, battled each other. One was an established veteran with notable successes over the years covering some of the best receivers in the game. The other was just a dubious rookie whose only other brief experience in pro football was a rank embarrassment.

They "were both off-the-board competitors," Raymond Berry said, "as much as any players or coaches I've been around in all my years in the game."

Those confrontations, on the surface, were like thousands of others on practice fields across the nation, but they also weren't. Unitas and Berry versus Shula for a few yards of real estate would have huge implications for all three men, the game of professional football, and even the culture at large.

For one thing, Unitas's and Berry's tangles with Shula convinced Ewbank and the other coaches that the two long shots belonged; they could line up against an established player like Shula and come out on top. And so the quarterback and the receiver gained the toehold in professional football that had so painfully eluded Unitas in Pittsburgh. Soon, boosted by television, they would be a lot more than just football players. They would be icons of a manly code and creators of a billion-dollar industry.

On the other hand, Shula's practice-field tangles with Unitas and Berry left him on the ledge of missing everything. When the coaches noticed that he could not successfully cover the new players, he was let go. The very coach who had discovered him at a second-rate school and who had forcefully advocated for his entry into the league had just told him, at the prime age of only twenty-six, that he wasn't good enough anymore.

Years later Shula described the feeling of being cut as an almost rage. "I was so damned mad I didn't know what to do," he told John Underwood, a *Sports Illustrated* writer. "I had sunglasses on and I was glad of that because the players were going out to practice and I had to pass by. I got in my car, and I went out on the Beltway and just drove. Somebody said I threatened to go back and poke Weeb in the nose but that's not true."

Whatever the truth of it was, Shula would never again play for Baltimore. Just down I-95 a piece, the Washington Redskins were looking for a veteran defensive back, and they quickly snatched him up for the 1957 season. Washington was Shula's third professional team in his brief career, so he was officially a journeyman.

Getting cut from Baltimore may have been a trauma to Shula, but to Ewbank it was nothing more than a necessary step in the development of the great team he wanted to build. As marginal men like Shula left Baltimore's defensive backfield, superb players came to take their places. One of them was Andy Nelson, a quarterback and defensive back from Memphis State. Nelson impressed his Colts teammates so much with his aggressive play that they nicknamed him "Hard Nose."

"Andy was a heck of a football player," Coach Charley Winner remembered. "They sent me down to sign him when I was with the Colts. And Kellett said, 'Okay, Charley, start at $7,000 and go to $7,500 [if necessary].' So I had Andy up in a hotel room, and boy, I'm talking him blue in the face, and he's just sitting back there, looking at me. Finally, he says to me, 'Hell, Charley, you don't have to give me all that bullshit. I'm going to sign with you.' So I gave him the full $7,500, I liked him so much."

Despite stockpiling a cache of talent, the Colts' coaches had their problems. By 1957 Ewbank was entering his fourth season at the helm, and under his tutelage the team had never won more than five games in a season. He continually stressed organization and team building, but Rosenbloom, highly impatient, was dubious.

As the season started, however, everything was calm. Unitas led the attack. And the defense with Marchetti, Arthur Donovan, and many future Pro Bowlers was quickly developing into one of the best in league history.

## TWO

## Rise and Fall of the Colts

The Colts careened out of the gate in 1957. They won their first three games, including impressive victories against league powerhouses Detroit and Chicago. That created the impression that Baltimore had finally turned the corner. But in a rematch with the Lions at home, the Colts met with heartbreak.

The day started beautifully. Before the fourth quarter, Unitas had already thrown four touchdown passes, including a 72-yard bomb to Lenny Moore and a 66-yarder to Jim Mutscheller. But the Lions had Bobby Layne, a pretty decent quarterback in his own right.

Layne was the kind of guy who wouldn't quit on the field—or at the bar. His players would give him their full attention in the huddle because if they didn't, Bobby might deliver an uppercut, right out in the middle of the field.

The Colts' Art Donovan once ended up in the same pile with Layne and got a pretty strong sense of what Bobby's social life was like. "His breath reeked of whiskey," Donovan remembered. "I said, 'Dammit, Bobby, we're gonna get drunk smelling your breath. You must've had a hell of a night last night.' Layne said, 'Last night? I had a few at halftime.'"

Even on the sauce, Layne knew what he was doing. He led the Lions to three fourth-quarter touchdowns against the Colts that day, throwing for two of them. He even kicked all of the extra points, as Detroit came back and beat Baltimore, 31–27. It was a stinging defeat for Ewbank's team.

The following week would be even worse.

Playing Green Bay, the Colts were handling the atrocious pre-Lombardi Packers in Baltimore, 14–0, at the end of three quarters.

But the Pack's Golden Boy, Paul Hornung, the young Heisman-winning halfback from Notre Dame, ran for two big scores in the fourth, and Green Bay stunned the Colts, too, 24–21.

But the cherry on Baltimore's crumbling cake wouldn't come until the next week. The Colts came home to play the Steelers, traditionally one of the worst franchises in football. Continuing the trend of the last few weeks, the Steelers outscored the Colts 12–7 in the second half. No future Hall of Famer would undo Baltimore this time. It was second-year quarterback Earl Morrall, a young but already well-traveled man, who did the honors. He threw for two touchdowns in the Steelers' victory.

Ewbank was on thin ice. After three straight losses, his team floundering at 3-3, rumor had it that Rosenbloom might fire him at any time. The owner had supposedly asked the Washington Redskins for permission to talk to their coach, Joe Kuharich, who just happened to be Gino Marchetti's old college coach.

With three straight embarrassing losses in the Colts' rearview mirror, the Washington Redskins—Kuharich's Redskins—lay in wait. Washington was just 2-4 when the Colts traveled the thirty-five miles down to DC's Griffith Stadium for the early November game. It might not have been a big story line with the press or fans, but the game would revive the old, intense practice-field rivalry of Unitas and Berry versus Shula.

As it turned out, it wasn't much of a contest.

Lining up directly against Shula, Berry had a huge day. He abused his old mentor so badly, the *Washington Post* beat reporter called it a "murder." There was something to that.

Berry had an expert's knowledge of Shula's abilities and tendencies from practicing against him so often. More than that, he understood, like no one else, Shula's weaknesses. "[He] was limited in his speed," Berry said.

"They were used to running against Shula every day in practice," Charley Winner said. "It was hard for Shula coming in and playing Baltimore. [Unitas and Berry] knew what they could do to him. If you find a weakness, no matter who it is, or who you're playing, you're going to come back to it. You're going to come back to it until they do something to stop it. [Unitas and Berry] knew [Shula's] weakness before we went into the game."

RISE AND FALL OF THE COLTS

Berry demonstrated the mismatch on his first scoring reception of the day, a 67-yard touchdown. His second trip to the end zone was a mere 11 yards, but he used his size and toughness to haul it in with "'Skins all over him like a second skin," as the *Washington Post* wrote.

By the end of the game, Washington's defenders were so paranoid about Berry, Unitas easily outfoxed them. He sent Raymond deep into the end zone, where all the Redskins followed him; meanwhile, Johnny U's intended target, "Long Gone" Dupre, was wide open underneath. He snatched the perfectly thrown pass and easily scampered into the end zone for the winning tally as the Colts won, 21–17.

"I knew how great [Unitas and Berry] were," Shula said. "My whole thought in the game was that they weren't going to get behind me; I wasn't going to give up the cheap touchdown."

Then he stopped and smiled for a second. "But they caught a lot in front of me," he said. "I was making a lot of tackles on those 15- and 18-yard passes."

Undoubtedly, the biggest star of the day was Berry, who caught twelve Unitas passes for two touchdowns and a whopping 224 yards. Most of that magnificent haul was at Don Shula's expense. After the game the young, still unmolded Berry told the press two things, one of them astonishing. First, he stated the obvious: "It's the greatest day I've ever had," he said. And then, weirdly, in the afterglow of his triumphal moment, Berry said that he actually preferred to play defense. That revelation would have astounded anyone who had just watched his brilliant and dominating performance catching the ball, but no one more than Don Shula himself who, after the day he just had, must have taken no pleasure at all in playing defense.

The Redskins game was the start of better times for the Colts. After Washington they reeled off four victories in a row, before two losses to the Rams and the 49ers on a grueling West Coast trip dropped them out of contention. But for the first time Ewbank and his team finished the season as winners (7-5), and they had stayed in the thick of the race until the very end.

The telling series for the season was with Detroit. The Colts beat the Lions once and, save for Layne's miracle, narrowly missed nailing them a second time, too. That was significant because Detroit ended up as the league champs, crushing Cleveland in the title game, 59–14. The young Colts were holding their own against the very best teams in the league now.

After their long journey in the wilderness, the Colts were finally and clearly upper echelon.

Shula's humiliating day against Unitas and Berry was the end of the road for him as a player. He had already been traded by one team and cut by another. He could clearly see, via the Raymond Berry show that had just unfolded right in front of him, that the game had quite literally passed him by. Invoking Paul Brown's old, worn phrase for washed-up ballplayers, Shula said he knew "it was time to find my life's work."

In a sense Unitas and Berry had pushed Shula out of his job in Baltimore, and now they were playing a pivotal role in ending his playing career. Is it possible that permanent hard feelings had been created, especially between Shula and the quarterback who was so intense and irritating, that man who was so much like him?

"It was never in my mind, and I never heard that expressed, that there were hard feelings," Charley Winner said.

"No, I don't think so at all," Raymond Berry said. "When a game starts you kind of go into a zone anyway. I don't think you are all that aware of personalities or whatever. I wasn't even aware that [Shula] was out there. You go into the huddle, you hear the play, and then you do your assignment. That's about what it amounts to."

So everyone agreed that there was nothing personal in the one-sided practice and game rivalry Unitas and Berry established with Shula. But there was also no denying that Shula had paid a terrible price for coming out on the short end of it. Losing an encounter like that, unlike in high school or college, meant far more than a mere ego blow. Shula had lost his standing and his livelihood and found only bitter disappointment. The career, into which he had invested so much of himself, was slipping away.

Perhaps Shula really did take it all in stride. And maybe he truly maintained the bearing of a professional and carried no lingering bitterness whatsoever for his rivals. But that wouldn't have been in character for Shula—or anyone else who wasn't canonized. Shula was a man everyone knew as proud, hypercompetitive, and extraordinarily intense. Had he taken that beating well, it would have been utterly contrary to his nature.

Nevertheless, that November day in Washington was a turning point for all of the parties involved. Ewbank kept his job. Unitas and Berry discovered their mystique. And Rosenbloom, sated by success, backed off his constant threats.

The next few years brought everlasting fame to the Colts, whose excellence and on-field charisma catapulted the enterprise of professional football to the forefront of sports leagues and American entertainment. And at the center of it all was Unitas, whose indomitability and coolness under fire were almost cinematic.

It wasn't that he refused to lose so much as he prepared to win. If the game was tight and he had a chance, he knew how to work the sidelines and preserve the clock. He and his receivers used an entire game to set up defenders just so that they might unleash something totally unexpected at the game's most climactic moments. And Unitas theater could be seen in living rooms all across the United States, as the 1958 championship game was the first one ever broadcast on national television.

Shula, his playing days over, was living a striking contrast to his old mates. While they ascended, he seemed to disappear. He went from one to another in a string of low-paying, low-profile jobs. First, he coached the defensive backs at the University of Virginia. Then he went to Kentucky to work under the former Paul Brown assistant Blanton Collier. And in 1960 Shula returned to pro football, on the defensive staff of Coach George Wilson's Detroit Lions.

Motown was where Shula's precocious brilliance began to show. The Lions were formidable winners in those years, though they no longer had offensive superstars like Bobby Layne and Doak Walker to lead them. The Lions' attack was put in the hands of a string of lesser lights such as Jim Ninowski, Milt Plum, and Earl Morrall, who all took their turns under center for Detroit.

With Layne gone, defense became the Lions' bread and butter. Shula built a juggernaut on that side of the ball with genuine heroes like "Night Train" Lane, Alex Karras, and Dick Lebeau. During Shula's tenure the Lions more than held their own against their Western Division rivals.

In 1962 the Packers could manage only three field goals against Shula's defense, but those nine points were all the Pack needed to squeak out a 9–7 victory over the Lions in their first game of the season against each other. In the rematch the Packers did much better and actually crossed the goal line twice. But Green Bay suffered its only defeat of the season, losing to the Lions 26–14.

Shula's defenses were even more effective against the Colts. The young coach must have taken great pleasure as his unit often frustrated and contained Johnny U and Berry and whipped Ewbank's Colts five of the six times he faced them.

The living-color Kennedy years weren't nearly as kind to Ewbank's Colts as the black-and-white Eisenhower era had been. After winning two straight titles, Baltimore was wilting under a variety of factors, including the weight of expectation, the aging of their workforce, and the inability to sign draft picks. But nothing hurt the Colts more than the loss of one key man, cut down in the prime of his career.

Baltimore was rolling along to a third straight title in 1960 when the Colts met the Lions at Memorial Stadium on December 4. Shula's defensive squad frustrated Unitas and Berry in a way that Shula the player never could. Through three quarters the Lions held Baltimore to just six points and had already intercepted Johnny U three times. But in the fourth quarter, when Unitas hit Lenny Moore for a diving 38-yard touchdown right in front of Night Train Lane, the game appeared to be over. There were just fourteen ticks left on the clock, and the Colts held a 15–10 lead.

Then, in an instant, the unthinkable happened. Detroit's backup quarterback, Earl Morrall, hit Jim Gibbons with a 65-yard touchdown pass just as time ran out. Shula's defense had neutralized the NFL's vanguard offense, and Morrall's lightning strike traumatized and beat the champs. And it all presaged some very rough days to come for the Colts.

More painful than the defeat was an injury suffered by Alan Ameche. His powerful 220-pound frame was rendered inert and useless, not by a break to one of his massive femurs but by a tear to the delicate tendon that connected his ankle to his leg. It was a torn Achilles that felled the mighty Horse, and he would never play again.

The other Colts, of course, had no choice but to ride on without Ameche. Nevertheless, his loss would have a profound, long-lasting effect on Baltimore's vaunted attack and overall success.

From 1960 through 1962 the Colts would achieve little more than an average team, winning just twenty-one games and losing nineteen as they fell from the top back to the fringes of contention.

To the fans and the owner, all of this must have seemed unfathomable. When the Colts destroyed the Giants to end the '59 season with a second straight title, Weeb Ewbank, the little genius who had patiently orchestrated their success by recognizing great players and painstakingly developing them, still had a long career ahead of him. Unitas and Berry were both just twenty-six. Marchetti and Pellington were getting along in age, but were still maulers. And many more championships appeared to be easily within Baltimore's grasp. The fact that the Colts instead slipped back into the lassitude of a .500 ball club made Ewbank an easy scapegoat to the fans and, of course, the ever-aggressive Rosenbloom.

But deep under the surface a complex array of forces was eroding the team.

"The downfall of the Baltimore Colts from our great championship years began with Alan Ameche's Achilles tendon," Raymond Berry remembered. "It totally changed our offense, and I don't know that any of us were all that aware at the time. I know it took me a while to grasp the significance of it. But we lost our balance when we lost Alan Ameche."

In 1959, with Ameche lining up behind him, Unitas had the best year of his storied career, throwing for thirty-two touchdowns and just fourteen interceptions. But without his star fullback, his interceptions outpaced his touchdowns; from 1960 through 1962 he coughed it up seventy-one times and put it in the end zone only sixty-four times. The ratio wasn't very good for any quarterback, let alone the fabled Golden Arm.

But who was to blame?

Berry understood what the owner and the fans could not see. "The pass rush began to reach a tempo that we had never experienced before," he said. "And it was because they did not respect our running game, and they started teeing off on the snap of the ball. We had lost Alan Ameche. . . We started throwing the ball more and more. The defense wouldn't worry about our run. The pass rush started coming. And we did not have much time to throw the football. We were throwing too much without enough time, and our interception rate started going up."

Ewbank, of course, understood the problems *and* the solutions, better than anyone. He took immediate corrective measures. For Weeb, the builder, that always began with the annual player selection.

In 1960 the Colts experienced a brilliant yet enigmatic draft. With their first pick they selected a future Hall of Famer, Ron Mix, an offensive tackle from the University of Southern California. Jewish and highly intelligent, Mix fitted the Ewbank mold: he was unconventional and smart. He was nicknamed "the Intellectual Assassin," a moniker that spoke to his teammates' respect for his cleverness and physical play. After his playing days he became a successful lawyer.

The Colts envisioned Mix pairing with Jim Parker to provide Unitas an impenetrable shield; they saw in him another mauler to open gaping holes for the franchise's next great rusher. But Mix never played a down in Baltimore. He got a better offer from the AFL, the new league just formed by Lamar Hunt, the Texas oilman who said he had been motivated to enter professional football by his admiration for the Colts' dramatic victory in the '58 championship game.

Mix signed with the Chargers instead of Baltimore. It was a huge loss, but worse than that it was the start of a trend. All told, four of the Colts' first five 1960 draft picks signed with AFL clubs. The other defections included Don Floyd (a defensive end and two-time AFL champion and All-Star for the Houston Oilers), Marvin Terrell (offensive guard who went with the Dallas Texans and became an All-Star), and Gerhard Schwedes (a running back signed by the New York Titans).

This was an unusual situation for the Colts under Carroll Rosenbloom's demanding ownership. They were a ball club that traditionally did whatever it took to win. But that was under the old rules. The business of pro football was changing, thanks to the AFL, and the Colts were learning all about it the hard way.

When Rosenbloom reluctantly entered the football business, he did so with the full knowledge that it was a risky financial endeavor. The first Baltimore professional football franchise known as the Colts was a mess on the field and a financial loser, too. Its owner ultimately surrendered it to the league. But even that operation looked like U S Steel compared to the Dallas Texans, the bankrupt group the NFL sent limping back into Baltimore as a replacement.

Rosenbloom had no intention of running a faulty, failing franchise. He adopted a similar business model to the most successful professional sports team in the world, baseball's New York Yankees. Yankees general manager George Weiss was compensated with a bonus that would go higher based on how low the sum of all Yankees player salaries were. As a result Weiss was a cold man who dampened much of the joy of working for the world's premier professional sports organization. No expense was too small to carp about. He harangued his scouts for lying about bridge tolls and charging the team a dollar per trip instead of the fifty cents it actually cost. Rosenbloom's GM, Kellett, was similarly expected to play a key role in the team's financial viability. In fact, his compensation included a percentage of the team's *profits*. With this arrangement in place, Kellett, too, was a skinflint.

"We had a hard time buying a pencil or supplies because [Kellett] checked everything," Charley Winner said.

An executive who kept a keen eye on the paper clips to make sure his own pockets were full certainly wasn't going to overspend for players. In the spring of 1960, after two straight championships, perhaps Kellett was lulled into the belief that great players were abundant commodities, at lease for his invincible Colts. And so the stars of the future, the ones Ewbank was counting on to extend his great dynasty, were all lost, squandered, in a futile attempt to pinch pennies for the benefit of just one man.

Eventually, Rosenbloom called everyone, his coaches and executives, to his home in Miami to sort it out. With Ewbank and Kellett in the same room, eye-to-eye, the owner changed Kellett's contract to remove the profit incentives. But the damage had already been done.

Perhaps Baltimore's biggest personnel loss of all wasn't to the new league, but to another NFL team. In the ninth round the Colts selected Don Perkins, a 204-pound fullback from New Mexico.

Perkins clearly and immediately could have filled Ameche's horse-shoes and restored the Colts' running game. But in an odd arrange-ment, and with the league's blessing, Perkins had already signed a "personal-services" contract with the Dallas Cowboys *before* the draft. Dallas did the same thing with quarterback Don Meredith. The league permitted this unusual practice because Dallas, an NFL expansion team in 1960, had been hastily organized in order to fight Lamar Hunt's AFL franchise, the Dallas Texans, head-to-head. With everything moving so quickly, the Cowboys franchise wasn't prepared to participate in the NFL draft. The "personal-services" contracts signed with two college football heroes from the Southwest were the league's way of ensuring Dallas could build a credible and compelling roster for its fans. Dallas was going to be a key battleground city in the coming war against the AFL, and the last thing the NFL wanted was for its product to look inferior either on the field or at the gate.

The Colts' "make good" from the league for losing Perkins was an additional ninth-round selection in the 1962 draft, but that meant little. Perkins was a hard-to-find late-round gem, not to mention the rusher they needed. Although he was injured and couldn't play in his first season with the Cowboys, he proved his worth the following year by rushing for 851 yards. When he retired, in 1968, he did so as the fifth-leading rusher in NFL history.

Had the Colts merely been able to sign the players they selected in the 1960 draft, Ewbank almost certainly would have kept his job, and there's no telling how many titles Baltimore might've won. Instead, in that one moment, on that one draft day, they saw everything flutter away.

And so the loss of "the Horse" was just the beginning of a stampede of lost talent that would haunt the Colts for many years.

In 1961 Ewbank took bold but vain measures to ameliorate his team's reversals. He traded the massive defensive lineman "Big Daddy" Lipscomb to the Steelers and received in return a brilliant young receiver named Jimmy Orr. Orr enjoyed playing with Bobby Layne, one of the greatest quarterbacks in league history, and his performance showed it. In his rookie season Jimmy caught seven touchdown passes, six from Layne. Jimmy was short and slow but smart. Using, as he put it, "skullduggery," he fooled defenders for huge gains. In his rookie season his yards per reception, 27.6, was the highest in league history. Unfortunately, Layne and Jimmy hit it off a little too well. They became running companions off the field, where Layne was already a hall-of-fame drinker. And anyway, despite his fondness for Layne, Orr didn't think much of the Steeler organization as a whole. After the 1960 season he made the decision that he would rather quit the game than go back to the losing Pittsburgh franchise. So while his teammates were assembled for training camp in Pennsylvania, he was still home in Georgia, playing golf. And then he got an unexpected call.

"Will you play for Baltimore?" Don Kellett asked him.

Orr said, "Yes."

"Well, how long will it take you to get here?"

"I don't know," Orr said. "About a week."

"This ain't Pittsburgh," the GM shot back. "Have your ass here tonight."

After much phone wrangling with airlines, a plane from Georgia landed in Baltimore around ten o'clock, and Orr's ass was on it.

For Ewbank, Jimmy offered a corrective. With this talented new flanker in the receiving corps Lenny Moore would be able to move to halfback, where he could resuscitate the Colts' broken running game. But removing Moore with his speed, hands, and moves from the aerial attack was a risk. The "Reading Rocket" was one of the fastest men in the league, and with Unitas heaving him the ball he was a threat to score from anywhere on the field at any time. But Moore's diverse skill set also made him the most likely candidate to fix the team's running woes. In years past, playing out of the backfield, he had averaged more than 7 yards per attempt, an incredible figure.

Ewbank's moves offered an extraordinary and innovative solution to the Colts' problems. Yet many fans were enraged with him for removing Moore from the passing game. They believed, and not unreasonably, that it was a terrible waste of talent.

The results on the field only fueled fan displeasure. The 1961 Colts, though they had their moments, were ultimately an unsatisfying team. That was especially true in a city that harbored championship expectations every season. In '61 Baltimore narrowly lost to Detroit, by a single point, in the first matchup between the teams. The Colts beat the Lions in their second game. In Green Bay the Packers humiliated the Colts, 45–7. But just a few weeks later the Colts crushed the Pack, 45–21, in Baltimore. The Colts finished 8-6, good enough only for a tie with the Bears (a team that had beaten them twice) for third in the Western Division.

In 1962 the Colts teetered back and forth all year before going on a three-game losing streak to their Western Division rivals. First, they lost to the Packers in a close game. Then, the following week, the Bears took the Colts apart at the seams, 57–0. Finally, Detroit beat Baltimore, too. Two Baltimore victories at the end of the year could salvage only a mediocre 7-7 record for the season.

It was increasingly clear that no matter what Ewbank did, he couldn't win. He saw himself engaging in a necessary rebuilding process to overcome the many problems that were out of his control. But owner Carroll Rosenbloom chose to see a team that was floundering.

The players saw it both ways.

"Comes a time," said Dan Sullivan, an excellent young Colts guard from Boston College, "when your system wears thin with the players. It gets monotonous after a while. Weeb was a great coach, but it was probably time [for him] to move on."

Wide receiver Jimmy Orr, who had been acquired by Ewbank, agreed. "Weeb had been there quite a while. He had a lot of success there and won two championships. He knew he had a lot of good players, and he just figured they were going to play. I believe in the theory that you're not going to get more than you demand. It was a complacency deal. They weren't as great as they were in '58 and '59. It didn't seem like the same fire was there. They weren't demanded enough of, probably."

But Raymond Berry, who went back almost to the beginning with Ewbank, saw it differently. "Carroll Rosenbloom made a big mistake [when he fired Ewbank]. He was looking at won-lost record and not the injury factor, which cost us our balance. We didn't have the personnel to run the ball. [Rosenbloom] got a quick trigger finger and fired the best coach in the business; Weeb wasn't the problem."

Nevertheless, when the 1962 campaign concluded, Rosenbloom's patience for the man he never quite took to was exhausted.

With a smile on his face the owner saw Ewbank and his wife off on a well-deserved vacation, paid for by the team. It seemed like a typically generous Rosenbloom touch, but it had a sinister purpose. No sooner had the Ewbanks left town than Rosenbloom spirited Don Shula into Baltimore for a secret interview for Weeb's job.

Behind the scenes Rosenbloom had consorted with Gino Marchetti for some time. He asked his great defensive end whom he should hire in the event that Ewbank was fired.

"There's only one guy," Marchetti responded. "Shula."

Rosenbloom was nonplussed with the suggestion. "You mean that guy that used to play here who wasn't very good?" he asked Marchetti.

Eventually, "the Giant" convinced the owner that Shula might not have been a great player but that he had the makings of an exceptional head coach, and an interview was arranged.

Fifty years later Shula could still recall his meeting with the owner. Rosenbloom asked him if he was ready for the job. That, of course, was the key question. Shula was only thirty-three years old, younger than some of the players, and he had never been a head coach before at any level.

But combining forthrightness with cleverness, Shula had an answer that couldn't be refuted.

"'The only way you'll find out,'" Shula said to Rosenbloom, "'is if you hire me.' [Rosenbloom] liked that answer," Shula said.

Considering how much Ewbank had meant to the franchise, the depths from which he had raised it and the heights to which he had taken it, the ax fell callously. It came swooping down upon Weeb's neck amid a great deal of speculation, intrigue, and deception.

After a third straight disappointing season the assistant coaches were understandably fearful for their jobs and looking for reassurance. And they got it, for what it was worth.

"In those days Weeb coached the Senior Bowl every year," Charley Winner said, "and you could take two assistants with you. So every year he took two, and the other two assistants went to the NCAA [National Collegiate Athletic Association] meeting to talk to the coaches about players and so forth. Well, that year was my year to go to the NCAA meeting. So I called Weeb . . . and I said, 'Weeb, should I be out there doing Colt business, or should I be looking for a job?' He said, 'Oh, no, I just talked to Carroll, and everything is okay.'"

That sense of well-being didn't last long. Moments later Charley's wife, Nancy, who also happened to be Weeb's daughter, received a call from Cameron Snyder, the *Baltimore Sun*'s Colts beat writer. Cameron delivered contradictory intelligence.

"Nancy," Snyder told her, "you're going to be fired."

"They just told Dad he wasn't [getting fired]," Nancy replied.

"I know he is going to be fired," Snyder said.

"We got fired the next day," Winner recalled, laughing.

So Ewbank was terminated. If Shula felt any pangs of remorse about deposing his old mentor—the man who had discovered him, believed in him, brought him into the league, and coached him on two different teams—it was all pushed aside by his more pragmatic desires to achieve and provide for his family.

"It was an opportunity," Shula said flatly.

But it was also far more than that. The coaching transition that fateful January day was maybe the most extraordinary that had ever taken place in professional sports. Ewbank, the deposed coach, had used his knowledge and intelligence to quickly and methodically build a dynasty from a bankrupt franchise. Many believed his champion Colts of the late '50s represented professional football's highest achievement. Ewbank also had another, less obvious, accomplishment. He left the NFL as the only coach who ever had Vince Lombardi's number. He bested Lombardi's offense in the '58 championship game. In head-to-head competition as head coaches, Ewbank and Lombardi split their lifetime series, and Weeb would become the only coach in NFL history without a losing record to Lombardi. Because of Ewbank's excellence the horseshoes affixed on the Colts' helmets during his tenure became as iconic in professional sports as the NY on the Yankees' caps.

Though the Colts' on-field performance had regressed under Ewbank's watch, he handed to Shula a franchise that was still extraordinarily well stocked. Unitas, a man widely acclaimed to be the best player in the game, six future Hall of Famers, and many future All-Pros were all still on hand. He also left behind a superb coaching staff that included Don McCafferty, the offensive coordinator, and Charley Winner, architect of some of the best defenses in NFL history. Both would one day be NFL head coaches themselves. So would Raymond Berry, still an active player. McCafferty and Berry would eventually coach their respective franchises to the Super Bowl. McCafferty would have the further distinction of winning the ultimate game in his rookie season as coach.

So the cupboard left to Shula was far from bare.

Ewbank may have met an ignominious end in Baltimore, but he would soon sit atop another franchise and make that one famous, too. He would discover and develop another of the game's greatest quarterbacks. And he would again coach and win one of the most historic championship games in league history.

But that would all be far off into the future. For the moment Ewbank was humiliated. He was forced to hand over the reins of his team to a former protégé, a man he had personally discovered and brought into professional football, a player he coached and nurtured, a man whose heart he had once broken when he cruelly let him go.

And now Don Shula, a young man without a single day of head-coaching experience at any level, was the head coach of professional football's glamour franchise. Though he was a big question mark on the day he was hired, he was in fact beginning a run of more than thirty years at the top. He would eventually accrue more coaching victories than anyone in professional football history, including Lombardi, George Halas, Tom Landry, Chuck Noll, and Ewbank. Shula would win his own richly historic games and suffer his own humiliating defeats, but he would one day be defined as the only NFL head coach who would preside over an unbeaten and untied championship season.

Standing above this theater, pulling the strings on all of these extraordinary actors, was Carroll Rosenbloom. He was a man bold enough to fire one future Hall of Fame coach and visionary enough to land another. That transaction would take all of them, and the business of professional football, headlong into the future.

# THREE

# Complicated Men

When Don Shula was named Colts coach in January 1963, he inherited a dream situation. At least on the surface. Though it had been three years since Baltimore had last won a title, the Colts' history of success and roster of stars made them one of the most revered professional sports organizations in the world.

To outsiders Baltimore may have been a smokestack city, a provincial town of small-timers, but it was the Colts who had lit the fuse for the pro football boom that was then just beginning. The team's theatrical victory in the '58 championship game, on national television, quickly catapulted professional football to the top of the sports entertainment industry. That particular contest created a longing in tens of millions of Americans to get in the game with a hometown rooting interest of their own.

One of them was Lamar Hunt. He watched Unitas choreograph the profound victory on a television in a Houston hotel room. The son of a Texas billionaire oilman, he wanted to own his own professional sports franchise and was trying to decide between baseball and football. You could say that the Colts and Giants and especially Unitas had persuaded him that football was his game. After two years of trying to get into the NFL through either a purchase or an expansion, he started his own competing league. When his American Football League started play for the 1960 season, the number of teams, players, and cities in professional football almost doubled. Even with all the new teams and cities, the Colts and their brand dominated wide swaths of the country, especially in the American South. Colts hegemony spread from Baltimore to the city-states of the

South and the Southwest, stretching all the way to the shores of the Pacific.

As 1963 dawned many of the most important Colts responsible for the back-to-back championships of the late '50s were still on hand. Johnny Unitas and Gino Marchetti were yet leading the franchise, though Marchetti was past his prime and Unitas had struggled since Alan Ameche's torn Achilles tendon and subsequent retirement. Despite age or issues, Johnny U and Gino were considered the premier offensive and defensive players in the league.

The cast around them was excellent, too, owing to the fact that before his termination, Weeb had traded deftly and drafted wisely. In fact, he had left the team stocked with a great depth of young talent to complement Baltimore's steel core of veteran stars.

Despite losing drafted players to the AFL, the crew Ewbank assembled would figure prominently in professional football for most of the coming decade. Included among them were premium young talents such as Bob Vogel, Tom Matte, Bobby Boyd, Dan Sullivan, and, of course, John Mackey.

One of Ewbank's last draft picks at the helm, Mackey was a Syracuse fullback in the tradition of Jim Brown and Ernie Davis. Nevertheless, Ewbank's prescient coaching staff saw a tight end in him. Dick Bielski, himself a converted college fullback playing tight end in the NFL, was brought in to tutor Mackey on the finer points of the profession. Mackey learned the lessons well and took the position much further than anyone else ever had before him. He teamed with Unitas and redefined the tight-end position.

When Mackey came into the league, tight ends, with the exception of the Bears' Mike Ditka, were primarily extra blockers. But Unitas utilized Mackey's speed to exploit defensive seams. Together they proved that the tight end could be a potent deep threat as effective as, or more so than, any wideout.

"We were the only team in football where the tight end was faster than both of the receivers," Jimmy Orr said, praising Mackey while laughing at both Raymond Berry and himself.

Shula was blessed with a lot of talent, but he came to summer camp eager to show everyone that he was in charge of the team.

In his autobiography Lenny Moore remembered the young coach as "a guy who liked to holler and scream on the sidelines."

This surprised Lenny. He said that he and many of the other players were expecting someone much different.

"We felt that maybe since he played the game so recently [as a teammate of ours] that he would have an understanding of a player's point of view and our problems," Moore said. "I felt confident that we'd finally have a players' coach on our side, but that didn't last long."

Shula hired one recently retired player, Jim Mutscheller, to help coach the receivers at summer camp. Mutscheller and Shula went way back together. In addition to being teammates on the Colts for many years, they also lived across the street from each other as very young men. Mutscheller lived with his pretty wife, "Pert," while Shula lived with teammates. Needless to say, Shula and a few others spent a lot of time at Mutscheller's clean and comfortable place, where the food was good.

But after only one summer of coaching with Shula, Mutscheller was done. Jim's "idea or philosophy of what you're supposed to do as a coach and what Shula did differed," Pert said. "Shula hollered a lot, and Jim was a very quiet person."

Unitas did things that grated on Shula's volatile personality. That was apparent in their very first game as coach and quarterback, a preseason contest against the Philadelphia Eagles in Hershey, Pennsylvania.

The Colts beat the Eagles in the meaningless game, but it wasn't easy. Baltimore cruised to a 26–0 halftime lead, but Philadelphia scored all of the second-half points, including two late touchdowns. With just two minutes left to play, the Eagles had cut the lead to 26–21.

The Colts had possession, however, and after a first down there was only a minute left in the game. The offense merely had to hand the ball off for one or two perfunctory rushes into the line, and the game would be over.

But then something curious happened. Eagles cornerback Ben Scotti, a relatively small football player, began to taunt Unitas and challenged the quarterback to pass in his direction.

Johnny U took the bait. He sent Jimmy Orr in Scotti's direction and launched a long pass. Scotti backed up his loud boasts and picked off the great passer, just as he said he would. As time ticked off the clock, the cornerback raced downfield to the Colts' 10 and was headed for the goal line when, at the last second, the faithful and talented Orr, who had diligently pursued the play, grabbed Scotti's ankle, tripped him up, and saved the victory.

Preseason or not, Shula was steamed after the game. He didn't pull any punches when he called out the usually beyond-reproach Unitas and said that the quarterback had made "a bad call." So in a rare feat the new coach had shown up his star player *and* engaged in a gross understatement all in one fell swoop.

Despite the wealth of weapons that were left to him, Shula would soon find that the job also presented many hidden difficulties.

The public assumed his biggest headaches would come from two places. First, there was a widely held belief that Ewbank's loyal team of excellent assistants would disperse. That worry proved unfounded, however, as every coach Shula wanted to keep stayed. Initially, defensive coordinator Charley Winner was dismissed, a move everyone anticipated since Winner was Weeb's son-in-law. More than that, Shula wasn't sure how Winner would take to working for him since Shula had been a player under Winner's tutelage only a few short years before. But pragmatism soon stepped in when the new coach realized, after talking to his players, that Winner was the only one who really knew the Colts' highly successful defense. So Shula reconsidered and quickly brought Winner back.

Winner certainly didn't have to agree; he was a man with options. When Ewbank was hired to replace "Slingin'" Sammy Baugh as head coach of the AFL's New York Titans (soon to be renamed the Jets), he offered Winner a job with him. But eager to be viewed as his own man, Charley stuck with the Colts.

"Not that [Weeb] didn't treat me well," Winner said. "But everywhere I went people said, 'Oh, you're Weeb Ewbank's son-in-law.' I wanted to get away from that."

Shula's second concern, or so it seemed to the public, was how the Colts' on-field defensive leaders might react to a former teammate taking control. Shula himself conceded the difficulties inherent when a mediocre ballplayer is plucked from the ranks to control excellent ballplayers. But this concern was unfounded, since it was Marchetti and Pellington who had secretly recommended Shula to Rosenbloom in the first place.

Real heartburn was headed Shula's way, of course, but it would come from the most unexpected sources. First, Carroll Rosenbloom put immediate and enormous pressure on his new coach, as he did to Ewbank a generation earlier. He told the press, "If it were just a case of moving up to second place in our division, I never would have made the change. I think we will win the title, that's why I hired Shula."

The Colts had finished fourth in 1962 with a 7-7 record. Winning the title in '63 would mean climbing the rungs of the Western Division and leapfrogging the Bears, Lions, and, of course, Green Bay, the defending world champs.

In '62 the Packers had just completed their greatest season under Lombardi. They dominated the league on both sides of the ball and lost but one game all year. The Lions were the only team to slow down the Packers' juggernaut. And that was primarily due to Shula's work as defensive coach.

So Rosenbloom wasn't expecting much. He demanded only that his thirty-three-year-old coach best Vince Lombardi and take a .500 ball club to the title in his first year on the job.

This pressure wasn't all that Shula would contend with from his owner. Rosenbloom wore the uniform of white entitlement well. He had a conservative slicked-back haircut, he was attired in crisp suits accented with razor-sharp pocket squares, and he favored trim ties neatly knotted into starched collars. He looked every inch of what he was assumed to be—solid and conventional, an establishment figure. In fact, Rosenbloom was something quite different. He was a subversive of sorts who viewed laws, rules, and moral constraints with his middle finger high in the air.

The fawning press of the era presented him as a miraculous success story. According to their narrative, Rosenbloom had been an exceptional athlete who barely "got by" academically. Despite his supposed intellectual deficiencies, he was secretly the smartest man in the room.

In fact, Rosenbloom was accepted to the University of Pennsylvania, one of the nation's elite academies, primarily due to his exceptional talent on the football field. After graduation he turned down lucrative offers to join forces with his father, a brilliant textile manufacturer, fearing that they would not be able to get along.

As the legend had it, Rosenbloom changed his mind and joined his father, but quickly broke away from the old man's direct supervision anyway. He moved to West Virginia, where he commandeered one of his dad's subsidiaries, the Blue Ridge Overalls Company. The elder Rosenbloom had only recently acquired the organization for the sole purpose of liquidating it. But Carroll saw potential and asked to run the company instead of breaking it up. By saving Blue Ridge from destruction, he made an even-greater success than his father ever knew.

His labors delivered him to a life of ease. He retired to a farm on Maryland's Eastern Shore while he was still in his midthirties. He was dragged back into business only by his father's death and a request from an old friend. Bert Bell, who had been his coach at Penn, was now commissioner of the NFL. As it so happened Bell was searching for a solid man with deep pockets to take over the bankrupt Dallas Texans franchise, then relocating to Baltimore. He chose Rosenbloom, a native Baltimorean, for that opportunity.

Rosenbloom was a miracle businessman with incredible luck, timing, and understanding. But he also had an underside that went largely unreported. For one thing, his mercantile successes weren't all in textiles. One of his nephews believes that Carroll started his march to wealth during the Prohibition era, selling illegal liquor. However lucrative selling alcohol might have been, the work brought him something else that was valuable. It was during Prohibition Rosenbloom made a lifelong friendship with Joseph P. Kennedy, the father of the future president John F. Kennedy. Joe Kennedy was also flouting the law.

"In today's world where there is so much Internet and so much that's out there for anybody to find, Carroll probably would have been suspended by the league," Rick Rosenbloom, Carroll's nephew, said. "There's no question that he had friends in Las Vegas, friends in organized crime. He and Joe Kennedy had friends in organized crime. There's no question that they had business dealings that were not of the legal type back in the day. . . . The rumor is they bootlegged together."

The public also thought of Carroll as a devoted husband and family man. He had three children in Maryland with his wife, Velma (or Dolly, as she was called). In fact, Carroll enjoyed family life so much he actually had two families at the same time. In addition to his acknowledged wife and children, Rosenbloom had a secret second family with two kids. The mother of these illegitimate children was Georgia Wyler, a singer and actress twenty years Rosenbloom's junior. Georgia had already been married at least four other times before she met Carroll.

The same month that Shula was hired, Rosenbloom's secret life was leaching its way into the newspapers. The league announced it was investigating the Colts' owner for the most serious of professional sports crimes—gambling. Even worse, it was alleged that back in 1953 he had bet *against* the Colts. The case publicly tied Rosenbloom to a man named Michael J. McLaney, a casino operator in pre-Castro Cuba. McLaney, who reportedly had "Mob ties," and Rosenbloom were friends, golfing pals, and business partners. Together they had purchased a Batista-era Cuban casino from the notorious Jewish gangster Meyer Lansky. It wasn't a good deal for the partners, however, as they bought the operation just months before Fidel Castro and his troops descended from the mountains and seized control of both the country and its casinos.

Despite their social and business ties, by the early '6os Rosenbloom and McLaney were at odds with each other for a number of reasons. McLaney, in fact, was Carroll's chief accuser in the gambling probe.

As a result of its 1963 investigations, the NFL ultimately suspended two star players for gambling, Alex Karras of the Lions and Paul Hornung of the Packers. Hornung and Karras were both banned by the league for a year. Five other players were fined for the same offense. Rosenbloom, on the other hand, skated free of any trouble. Then commissioner Pete Rozelle, a former Rams public relations (PR) executive who had ascended to his lofty job at age thirty-three after Rosenbloom had suggested him for the position, explained it away for the public. In a scene reminiscent of *The Godfather*, Rozelle reported that Carroll's "three accusers later repudiated or withdrew their charges in new affidavits."

Even as the NFL let Rosenbloom off the hook, however, it was clear that his behavior was troublesome. Everyone, it seemed, took it for granted that he was a gambler, and a big one.

"He [Rosenbloom] . . . freely admitted that he has bet substantial sums on activities other than professional football, principally golf games," Rozelle's report stated. Despite the league's "findings," it was an open secret within the Colts organization that Carroll bet on league games.

Rosenbloom "was a gambler," Charley Winner said. "In those days I scouted the teams, and he would always call me when I would be on the road and would want to know my opinion on these games. I would say, 'Carroll, I can't really tell you. There's too many things involved,'" Winner recollected.

"So later on, a couple of years later when I was off of the scouting and I was traveling with the team, I sat with Carroll on the plane going someplace, and he says, 'You know, I've hired a full-time handicapper. You coaches can't pick 'em. You analyze too many things.' He'd get on the airplane every now and then and say, 'Weeb, I put a hundred bucks on such-and-such a game for you.'"

Winner wasn't the only member of the Colts organization who had encounters like that with Rosenbloom. Bert Bell Jr., the son of the previous and revered NFL commissioner, worked for the front office. He told Baltimore journalist John Eisenberg that he personally witnessed Rosenbloom placing a bet on the Colts.

"I walked into his room and he was on the phone and hollered to me, 'Bertie, do you like us today?'" Bell Jr. said. "Then he said into the receiver, 'Yeah, give me some of that.' I just sauntered away."

Bell Jr., once considered a candidate to be the Colts' general manager, eventually left the organization, disillusioned with Rosenbloom. "I could never have worked as a GM under Carroll," he told Eisenberg. "I knew there would come a day when he would have asked me to do something illegal."

When the Colts drafted the great tight end John Mackey, he took a walk around the locker room with Rosenbloom before signing his contract. "[Rosenbloom] introduced me to Unitas, who looked at me and said, 'Keep your eye on him [Rosenbloom] because he'll fuck you.' Rosenbloom replied, 'That's our John,' as if it were a joke. But it was no joke." Mackey recounted that story in his autobiography, *Blazing Trails*.

Prior to 1963 Rosenbloom had been painted only in heroic terms. His many virtues included his energy, intelligence, business acumen, civic-mindedness, and generosity as an employer. And, in fact, he was beloved by his employees.

"Carroll treated the players real well," Charley Winner said. "He had a bonus schedule, and at the end of the year we all got a bonus, players and coaches alike, if you won so many games. It was a total of $15,000 divided. That was one of his sources of motivation."

That bonus schedule was later deemed illegal by the league. Nevertheless, Winner said Rosenbloom enjoyed providing small kindnesses to his players and coaches and, especially, demonstrating that he wasn't above them.

"We were practicing at the Pikesville Armory," Winner said. "Carroll was late, and we waited about a half hour for him. He finally comes in and says, 'Okay, I apologize for being late.' And the late fine was 50 bucks for the players. He said, 'Well, the fine for being late is $50, and tomorrow you'll all have $50. And we all got 50 bucks the next day. That's the kind of guy he was."

The '60s are generally remembered as an era when team skinflints controlled tight purse strings on the players. Mike Ditka of the Bears once growled about his beloved but cheap boss, George Halas: "He throws nickels around like manhole covers." Halas, of course, was owner as well as coach. Vince Lombardi's title in Green Bay may as well have been czar. When Jim Ringo, one of his best players, brought an agent to Lombardi's office for contract negotiations, Lombardi supposedly stood up from his desk and departed the office. When he returned he announced to Ringo and his stunned agent that the All-Pro center had just been traded to Philadelphia.

In Baltimore Shula sought this same kind of dictatorial control over his players, and, eventually, his responsibilities were expanded to include player contracts. But thanks to Rosenbloom, it never carried quite the same cachet for Shula that it did for Lombardi. Colts players knew there was always a higher power to whom they could appeal.

Rosenbloom, if he liked a player, could be a benevolent presence at contract time.

"I had come up for a contract negotiation, and [Shula] wasn't willing to give me anything close to what I thought I should be getting," offensive guard Dan Sullivan said. "I played most of the . . . season without a contract. I was being paid on what I was making from the previous year. They could have gotten rid of me anytime they wanted, and I could have just walked away.

"In my personal opinion I thought Don Shula was too close [to the situation] to make a true evaluation of what I was worth in dollars and cents. I called [Detroit guard] John Gordy up from the . . . Lions and I called Jerry Kramer from the Packers that year, and when I told them what I was looking for from Baltimore they said, 'Shit, go for it. You're going to get it.'

"I knew Shula wasn't getting anyplace with me, and I would eventually get a sit-down with Mr. Rosenbloom. I sat down with him, and I know he had access to every contract in the National Football League because he is an owner and all he has to do is call Pete Rozelle up. 'What's Kramer make? What's Gordy make?' Those were the premium guards in that era. He knew what they made. Now he didn't know I knew what they made. So I said, 'Here's what I'm looking for.' He looked at me and said, 'Are you sure that will satisfy you?' I say, 'Yeah, that will satisfy me.' He said, 'Stand up.' We shook hands, and we had a deal. Now that pissed Shula off, because he couldn't do it."

Running back Tom Matte remembered Rosenbloom galloping to the rescue for him, too. "He measured you by what he felt, and if you were really helping the team," Matte said. "I remember . . . my contract was up, and I wanted to stay in Baltimore. They had made Harry Hulmes GM. Harry was a PR guy and didn't have the first fucking clue about what was going on. Nobody even talked to me about my contract. So we go to training camp, and in those days if you got hurt in training camp, you got a 10 percent reduction in your salary and that was it. I finally went up to Shula, with a preseason game coming up, and said, 'Don, I'm not going to play. I'm risking my life here, and I don't even have a contract and Harry won't even talk to me. What in the hell is going on here? I'm not going to play.' So [Shula] calls Rosenbloom, and Rosenbloom calls me and says, 'Now, Tom, I'm coming in on Monday. I want you to play in this game, and we'll get this resolved right away.' 'All right, Mr. Rosenbloom. I'll play.'

"[Rosenbloom] came in Monday and said, 'Now, what is it you are looking for?' I said, 'I'd like to stay here in Baltimore, and I would like to have a three-year, guaranteed, no-cut, no-trade contract. He said, 'It's never been done before.' I said, 'Is there any reason it can't be done?' He said, 'No, let me think about it.'

"So he calls me in after lunch and says, 'Here's what I'm going to do for you. I'm going to give you 65, 75, and 85 with some incentives. Guaranteed contract—you can go to the bank with it.' I said, 'Can I think about it?' He said, 'Don't walk out the door and think too long.' So I open the door, close the door, open it up again, and said, 'You've got a deal.'"

"I guess if you played for the Baltimore Colts, you loved Carroll Rosenbloom," Sullivan said. "He came into the locker room, and he knew everyone. He used to call me 'Boston.' And he knew the Kennedys. He used to say, 'Hey, Boston, how you doing? I saw some of your old friends, Jack Kennedy and Bobby Kennedy.' He knew them all. He was great with that type of thing. He always had the personal touch. Thanksgiving time you got a big, big basket with turkey and National Bohemian beer and all that stuff. It was really a nice touch. At the end of the season the wives and the players got gifts from Mr. Rosenbloom. So he was the type of guy that you looked up to and said, man, he's some . . . guy, what a class act this guy is, all the way."

He courted the favor of his players in many other ways. With Rosenbloom's encouragement and assistance, Marchetti, Ameche, and Colts linebacker Joe Campanella founded a chain of hamburger restaurants that were a clone of the burgeoning McDonald's business model. The Colts' owner, sagacious in all mercantile matters, suggested that the players utilize the power of their celebrity as a business asset. Initially, there were "Ameche's" and "Gino's" restaurants. Eventually, all were consolidated under the "Gino's" brand in order to leverage the ongoing popularity of Marchetti, the trio's biggest star (literally and figuratively). McDonald's largest sandwich was the "Big Mac." Gino's had the "Giant" and was the Baltimore distributor for Kentucky Fried Chicken, which was then also a new fast-food brand. The venture was highly successful and eventually netted the founder-players millions.

Rosenbloom's largesse, however, wasn't always so innocent.

His charm and generosity could also appeal to a player's darker side and affect team discipline.

"We were in Los Angeles to play the Rams," one of the old Colts remembered. "And the night before the game I'm out with some girl in a bar, and it's way past curfew. My wife was back home in Baltimore. I spot Carroll across the room; he's also out with a woman who's not his wife. I thought, 'Shit! If he sees me I'm going to get fined for sure and in all kinds of trouble.' So I snuck into the men's room and waited in there for a while. When I thought the coast was clear, I came back out, and he was gone. I went over to the bar to pay my bill, but the bartender wouldn't take my money. Instead, he handed me a room key. I said, 'What's this?' And he says, 'Mr. Rosenbloom paid your tab, and this is the key to his suite. He said he's staying somewhere else. It's all yours. Enjoy yourself.'"

Rosenbloom's kindness for his players marked a sharp contrast to how he treated at least one of his siblings. His sister Rose Constam believed he was cheating her out of hundreds of thousands of dollars in transactions related to their father's estate. She filed a breach-of-trust suit against Carroll and claimed misconduct by him.

When Rosenbloom's father, Solomon, died at the beginning of World War II, he designated Carroll executor of his estate. It was a job that carried many ongoing responsibilities, as it left Carroll to run his father's two large companies: S. Rosenbloom, Inc., and the Blue Ridge Overalls Company. In turn, Carroll was required to make distributions to his siblings/partners and their children.

Carroll's personal holdings in these two companies were unequal. He only owned 9.948 percent of S. Rosenbloom (an equal share with his siblings), but he owned 32.82 percent of Blue Ridge. His sister alleged that Carroll diverted money and other assets from S. Rosenbloom, Inc., to Blue Ridge so that he would reap disproportionately from the estate.

In her initial filings Rose claimed that Carroll had benefited $1.5 million more than he should have owing to his many manipulations. She also said that she was bilked out of $500,000 when Carroll sold S. Rosenbloom, Inc., and delayed distribution of shares to her. These numbers would go up a great deal before the suit was settled.

The case ended up in court more than twenty years after their father's death. Rose said she had to take that measure because she had asked Carroll to provide proper accounting of the estate assets, and he declined to comply. It took two years before the case was finally heard, but when it was it featured some sensational aspects. First, Rose claimed that Carroll had "fed a large volume of sales to multiply the profits and book value [of Blue Ridge]." In that way he was able to sell it to "the family trust at a capital gain of more than $700,000," according to testimony that was reported in the *Baltimore Sun*. Second, to sort all of this out required ledger books from the Blue Ridge Company that detailed the years Carroll was in charge. These ledgers, according to the firm's accountant, were mysteriously missing.

In the end the suit was settled out of court. Rosenbloom's sister walked away with an amount "in excess of $400,000," but after all was tabulated her lawyer claimed that Carroll had personally gained more than $5 million due to his many manipulations and shenanigans.

This problematic man was now Don Shula's to handle.

The most significant headache Shula would inherit in Baltimore came not from ownership, the front office, the coaching staff, or the fans. In fact, it came from the most unexpected source, the one man most were certain would be Shula's meal ticket.

That man was Unitas.

Johnny U was often, almost reflexively, portrayed as a "blue-collar guy in a blue-collar town." But the description was a gross oversimplification. Baltimore's row houses were filled with middle-class families, usually headed by a factory-worker father. The city's east side featured the Dundalk Marine Terminal, Baltimore's famous inland seaport with its nineteenth-century rail connections to the West. On a ribbon of concrete called Broening Highway, Baltimoreans made steel, automobiles, electric appliances, and aircraft components. Neighborhoods all over town had factories tucked into them, including those that made textiles, cans, tools, cigars, candy, underwear, beer, and much more.

But Baltimore, with Johns Hopkins University and Hospital within its midst, was also a city renowned for world leadership in the practice of medicine. For most of the twentieth century, until the '50s, Baltimore was one of the nation's intellectual centers. The *Sunpapers* of Baltimore had more foreign bureaus than any newspaper in the United States except for the *New York Times*. Baltimore housed Edgar Allan Poe's tomb and celebrated it as if it contained the bones of Joseph. The Enoch Pratt Free Library was one of the nation's oldest and best library systems. Baltimore's most famous resident for the first half of the twentieth century wasn't an athlete or businessman; it was H. L. Mencken, the celebrated Sage of Baltimore. Mencken was editor in chief of a major daily newspaper when he was still in his midtwenties. He moved on to become the nation's most influential humorist, political writer, and literary critic. At the Democratic National Convention he was almost nominated for vice president of the United States, even though he was too young for the job, wasn't a politician, and wasn't running. Mencken wrote more than twenty books and edited two highly influential magazines, the *Smart Set* and the *American Mercury*. His work required him to be in New York on a weekly basis, but it was always a point of pride with him that he returned at the end of every week to Baltimore, where he maintained his permanent residence. His prestigious and energetic presence attracted many other literary figures to the city. F. Scott Fitzgerald called Baltimore home for five years and wrote *Tender Is the Night* during that time. Gertrude Stein, Upton Sinclair, Dashiell Hammett, John Dos Passos, and Ogden Nash were also residents for important periods of their lives or careers. Baltimore wasn't just smokestacks; it was stacks of books.

Unitas appealed to every aspect of the complex and diverse town. He was the son of a coal-shoveling father and a mother who swabbed floors. Unitas worked construction after the Steelers cut him from their squad even though he had spent four years in college. After he entered professional football he was celebrated for his blue-collar qualities, including exhausting physical labor, enduring through pain, and performing while risking both his health and his life. All athletes worked out. Unitas outworked.

But on another level Unitas was an intellectual creature celebrated in Baltimore as a kind of Edison in cleats. The *Sunpapers* ran photos of him sitting at a school desk in shoulder pads and practice jersey, studying plays and opponents' tendencies. His

COMPLICATED MEN

long, grueling hours on the practice field led only to the classroom, where he studied for hours more. When he finally got home more work was waiting for him, as he descended to his basement and poured over film for the rest of his waking hours. His daughter Jan remembered sitting in his lap at night as a little girl while he clicked the projector back and forth, looking for every tiny edge or advantage. Journalists celebrated his cerebral approach to the game in their articles.

In fact, Unitas took preparation to levels that had never occurred to even the greatest of his predecessors. Defensive coach Charley Winner remembered the first time he saw the blending of work ethic and innovation in the young Unitas.

"After [his] first season Unitas called me and said, 'Charley, I would like to come over to your house in the evening and go over movies.' So I got the films home, and he'd come over to my house and he said, 'I want to learn defense.' That's the first quarterback I'd ever heard of who wanted to learn pass defense. He wanted to learn how to recognize certain things. He started it."

Unitas's plans were far from theories. He made them work in three dimensions. His talented flanker Jimmy Orr remembered that Unitas's intellectual approach gave him a kind of fearlessness about attacking any defender in the league, regardless of how good he was.

Night Train Lane, Detroit's spectacular cornerback, was the one player who gave Orr the most trouble.

"Night Train was six feet three and 215 pounds, and he could fly," Orr said. "And he was punishment. He gave you that clothesline. I caught two touchdowns against him my rookie year in Pittsburgh before I understood who he was."

No such luck on the Colts. In fact, Ewbank was so frustrated trying to attack Night Train, he told Orr and Unitas to avoid him altogether. In effect, the coach was giving up.

That didn't sit well with Unitas or his receiver. Instead of avoiding Lane, they used film to set him up like the sucker in a confidence scheme.

"We get ready to play Detroit, and Weeb says, 'We ain't throwing over there,'" Orr remembered. "I said to Unitas, 'No! We've got to throw over there.' Unitas says, 'We're throwing over there.

Don't worry.' So Unitas and I cooked this up. We had a pattern where you slant in and take off up the sideline 18 yards. For three weeks before we go to Detroit I slant in toward the sideline just like I'm running a regular out pattern. So we get up to Detroit, and I slant in, take off sideline."

That was the move Night Train had seen on film for three straight weeks, the one he was expecting. "But now," Orr said, "I'm going to the post. Well, as soon as I slanted in, Night Train just steps here, out where he thinks I'm supposed to be after watching three films. But I just stutter and [whistles] go. I catch the ball right in stride. He's facing this way when I head that way. And he still slaps me on the heel as I crossed the goal line! That's how fast he was. You had to work to beat him."

But Unitas and Orr proved it could be done.

If there was a kind of poetry, science, or theater to what Unitas did, the implications of his genius were all business. In the days before football helmets were used like cell phones to blast plays and profanity from the sidelines to the quarterback, Unitas was a true "signal caller."

In a very real sense this made Unitas chief executive officer (CEO) of the entire organization every Sunday. He held high-level strategy meetings in the huddle, drilling subordinates for the results of their field research. "Raymond, whattaya got?" he would ask again and again. "Dan, can you handle that guy, or do I need to call a trap and slow him down a little for you?" "Jimmy, have you set him up yet? Can you beat him to the corner?" In these huddle "meetings" no one spoke; no one was permitted to speak, unless Johnny U spoke to him first.

Right there on the field he literally charted the course of success or failure for the entire organization. If Unitas made intelligent calls on Sunday, the owner and the executives were enriched. If he made poor decisions, the fans stayed home and the advertisers took their dollars elsewhere. If Unitas threw more touchdowns than interceptions, the scouts were admired all over the league, the assistant coaches were stolen away to lead other teams, and the head coach could add immortality to his worldly rewards.

If Johnny U did his job well, it was all backslaps and picked-up bar tabs and fat paychecks for all the Colts. But if he was slinging it to the wrong shirts, everyone got fired in a thunderstorm of acrimony and derision. That was the pressure and those were the stakes.

In 1963 Johnny U was the biggest star in the game. Players all over the league admired, respected, and feared him. He was revered in Baltimore and by sports fans in all corners of the nation. But he was no longer quite the same player or person whom Weeb Ewbank had discovered and developed.

Weeb's Unitas was young, raw, and hungry for opportunity. Don Shula's quarterback had already won two championships and was a two-time MVP of the league and the championship game. He had established himself as the unquestioned leader of the team's offense. Shula, only a few years prior, was Unitas's teammate and practice-field competitor. At least he was until Unitas's superior talent had chased him out of town. In their only meeting in an actual game, Unitas had one of the biggest days of his career, exploiting Shula's porous coverage of Raymond Berry. Shula the player had been run off into oblivion, while Unitas quickly became the biggest star in football.

And now, incredibly, Shula was Johnny U's boss.

# FOUR

## Shula Encounters Unexpected Problems

One of the trickiest situations Don Shula would have to navigate in his first season as a head coach was the status of Lenny Moore. Weeb had run into trouble with his owner and especially the fans when he made the bold stroke of trading Big Daddy Lipscomb for flanker Jimmy Orr.

Ewbank's plan was to fix the team's broken running game by moving the multitalented Lenny from flanker to halfback, even though Lenny was then the most potent deep threat in the game. Ewbank viewed these manipulations as a necessity, since the Colts' fortunes had plummeted after the injury and subsequent retirement of Alan "the Horse" Ameche, their great fullback.

One of the first decisions Shula made after being named coach was to follow Weeb's path. He would also start Orr on the outside and allow Lenny's running to grind out the yards and take the heat off Johnny U. It was a solid plan, but no matter how creative and well conceived it was, it never quite worked out for Ewbank, and, in 1963, it wouldn't work well for Shula, either.

On Friday the thirteenth, just two nights before the season opener against the New York Giants, Moore came down with a "red-hot appendix." At least that was the team doctor's diagnosis. Less learned men might have referred to it as acute appendicitis. Either way, Moore was expected to be out of action three to four weeks.

In fact, Lenny Moore would play very little football during Shula's entire first season as Colts coach. Later in the year, after the appendix had healed, Moore was kicked in the head and suffered a severe concussion. His symptoms included dizziness, vertigo, and nausea. All told, he would miss seven weeks.

There were no concussion protocols in 1963, only concussions. The long-term implications of head injuries were simply not understood then, and the doctor's advice was treated as secondary to the wants and needs of the football coaches. The Colts claimed that there was "nothing physically wrong" with Moore, and the coaches didn't bother to conceal their disappointment at his inability to get on the field and play. The newsmen, taking their cue from team management, described Lenny as "controversial." Eventually, they would call him trade bait.

For Lenny all this was beyond the pale. He saw something sinister in it and believed the team was trying to portray him as a shiftless Negro. His bitterness was understandable. He was clearly one of the most unique and productive players in the history of football. His career rushing yards per attempt was 4.8, higher than Walter Payton (4.0 yards), one of the most celebrated running backs to ever play the game. As a receiver Moore averaged 16.6 yards per reception. That number eclipses Calvin Johnson, the best receiver in football in the 2000s, who averaged *only* 15.9 yards per reception.

Moore wasn't only about gaudy statistics; he was money in the bank. He had a streak of scoring at least one touchdown in eighteen straight games. It was a record that stood unequaled for forty years until Ladanian Tomlinson finally *tied* him in 2005. Their shared record was still unsurpassed in 2016.

Statistically speaking, if Moore were playing today, he would be among the best running backs *and* finest wideouts in the game. There is no comparable contemporary player to Lenny Moore. For that matter, no player in history compares to him.

Moore's accomplishments could not have come from a lazy player looking for excuses to avoid games. They could have come only from a man who was extraordinarily impassioned and highly motivated for success, a man who worked hard and worked well with his bosses and teammates.

Yet somehow when Moore suffered his catastrophic injury, it seemed that no one was willing to give him the benefit of the doubt. When Shula, the Baltimore fans, the press, and some of Moore's own teammates looked at him, they saw a shirker. Was he merely unlucky, or was there some larger force at work that explained how they viewed him?

Lenny was sure he knew the answer. In 1958 the Colts played San Francisco in a crucial late-season game with the opportunity to clinch their first-ever division title. But they weren't playing well, and at halftime they were losing 27–7. A huge part of the Colts' legend, the brand that endures to this day, was built in the furious second-half comeback they made that day against the 49ers.

Engineered by Johnny U's deft play calling, the turnaround featured Lenny galloping to the end zone for a 73-yard touchdown. Moore was so hot that at one point, Unitas called his number six times in a row. After the last carry Lenny came huffing back into the huddle and told his quarterback that he was simply too winded to carry the ball again, for a seventh straight time.

That episode of heroic play followed by the plea for *no mas* became an anecdote in the mouth of Art Donovan, the team's huge and wry defensive lineman. Moore claimed that Donovan's story had Johnny U responding to his request for relief by replying, "Don't tell me to cool it! I'll run your ass until you die." Moore said the story was not only untrue but racially motivated, an attempt at portraying him as "a lazy nigger."

Was Moore correct in his interpretation? It didn't really matter. How he saw it, rightly or wrongly, pointed to a larger truth. NFL players in the 1950s and '60s, though rising stars achieving a celebrity status in a somewhat integrated work environment, felt the same racial divide experienced by other Americans. For the black players especially, that chasm brought frustration, humiliation, and paranoia. It was highly destructive and contributed to a great deal of unhappiness and even tragedy.

On the field the Colts' players appeared to be a band of merry brothers, working together to elevate football to higher levels of excellence than the game had ever known. Behind the scenes, however, many of the black players mistrusted their teammates.

"Leonard Lyles was one cornerback for me, and Bobby Boyd was another cornerback, a white and a black," coach Charley Winner remembered. "Well, Leonard Lyles made a mistake in coverage, and I got him on that telephone and I said, 'Leonard if that happens again, I'm going to get your ass out of there.' You know, just like that. So after the game Leonard came over to me and said, 'Coach, if that had been Bobby Boyd, would you have said the same thing to him?' I said, 'Absolutely.'

"I didn't see what he was getting at, at the time," Winner said. "But I told him, 'I'm going to correct whoever is making a mistake and get him out of there if he isn't doing the job.'"

Later, Winner would better understand where Lyles was coming from.

"One of my best friends [on the Colts] was Milt Davis, a black player from UCLA [the University of California at Los Angeles]," Winner said. "Milt and I stayed in touch, and he told me one time [many years later] how bad it was between the blacks and the whites. They would never socialize. [The black players] were never invited to anything. At training camp they would never mingle."

One exception to this voluntary social segregation between the players was Johnny Unitas. Perhaps looking to avoid the expectations or cliques of the white players, the quarterback would often seek out the black ones, at least at work.

"Johnny Unitas would go over and eat with the black players most of the time," Charley Winner said, though he was at a loss to know what made the quarterback more progressive than his contemporaries. Charley assumed that Unitas was simply less spoiled and more grounded than many of his teammates.

"I guess John came from a working background," Winner said. "He was just an open person. He seemed to get along with everybody. He didn't bitch or moan. John was always right there. He could get the biggest honor there was or lose everything he had, and his disposition was always the same."

When the Colts drafted Lenny Moore in 1956, he reported to Western Maryland College in Westminster, Maryland, for training camp like the other players. He quickly found, however, that his ethnicity made his experience there quite different from the one the white players had. While the Caucasian Colts would remember their time in Westminster with great fondness and recall how easily and enjoyably they mingled with the fans and residents, Moore said the experience for black players was different and dispiriting.

It "was a blatantly racist town where, outside of going to practice once or twice a day, there was nothing for a black person to do," the running back wrote years later in his autobiography. "We couldn't go to the movies or the restaurants. The only thing we could do was walk the streets. Thinking back it was dehumanizing and we hated it."

He said the worst part was accommodating fans with souvenirs after practice: "All of us would be besieged by autograph seekers of all ages, which we would gladly accommodate," Moore wrote, "but see one of these townies on the street later that night and the white players would be invited into the local tavern for a beer on the house while the rest of us received scowls."

In Baltimore things weren't much better. Moore found that the chemistry between the races on the field did not translate into camaraderie after hours. When practice and games were over, the black players went in one direction and the white ones in another. They never were invited guests in each other's homes; they didn't drink together or chase women together. They did those things, of course, but white players did them with white and black players did them with black. Colts blue and white had its limits. Off the field there was only black and white.

This wasn't merely a case of people finding a comfort level with "their own." Moore told Michael Olesker, one of Baltimore's most important print and television journalists for more than thirty years, how frustrating it was just to go out and see a movie with his wife.

"When he reached the box office," Olesker wrote, "the woman inside said, 'You can't go in.'

"'What?' Moore said.

"'Sir, you can't go in.' Then she pointed to Moore's wife, who was light-skinned. 'She can go in, but you can't.'"

In the context of 1963 Baltimore that incident might have been humiliating but understandable. It could be written off as simply the way things were in an old racist town. Far worse than that were the outrages the Reading Rocket encountered all over the league. In fact, the wider world of the NFL wasn't much more enlightened than Baltimore. Moore and other black players believed that all the teams kept them in short supply by adhering to an informal, hidden quota system that limited each franchise to only seven black players. Those players, he said, were further confined to the positions they were allowed to play. Moore said blacks had to play as far away from the football as possible. Every new black player who came to the team was signed at the expense of another black player's roster spot. The one losing his job might be released late at night and hustled away before daylight to make the racial machinations less obvious.

Though integration was generally viewed as a positive development in progressive circles, it came with complications for both the league and the black players. One particularly dramatic example occurred in August 1959. The Colts were slated for an exhibition match against the Giants, whom they had just defeated the previous December in "the Greatest Game Ever Played," the '58 championship game. The preseason rematch was being played in Dallas.

Earlier in the decade Dallas had its own NFL franchise, the Texans, but that team was a spectacular failure on the field and in the ledger books and folded in January 1953 (when it was moved to Baltimore and renamed the Colts). But as the decade came to a close the city was growing in size and importance, and oil money was transforming the old town of western legend into a major American metropolis. Professional football had its eye on Dallas again, and in 1960 it would have not one but two professional football franchises, the NFL's Cowboys and the Texans of the start-up American Football League. The Colts and Giants were flown in to prime the pump.

But in 1959 Dallas was still a virulently racist town with its own segregation customs that were about to surprise the black players on both teams. When the Colts landed they were met at the plane by two buses. The white players were shepherded onto those vehicles, while the black players (Lenny Moore, Big Daddy Lipscomb, Sherman Plunkett, Jim Parker, Milt Davis, Johnny Sample, and Luke Owens) were left behind.

"That was the first time we knew," Moore told Michael Olesker about being separated from the white players. While the white players were quickly and comfortably motored to the Sheraton in Dallas, the travel-weary black players stood at the front of the airport and watched five empty taxicabs pass them by. Don Kellett, the Colts' general manager, eventually hailed them a cab and squared them away at the Peter Lane Motel, a run-down hotel in one of Dallas's black sections. The accommodations were so basic, they didn't even include a TV or a radio. The room was good for little more than a flop. Kellett stayed just long enough to make sure there would be no trouble and then quickly joined the rest of the "white" team at the Sheraton.

Meanwhile, the black players on both the Colts and the Giants (also duped by their employer) found each other by phone and set up a meeting at a diner to discuss how they might respond to the outrage. The players' first reaction was to boycott the game.

But Emlen Tunnell, the veteran Giants safety, disagreed. He cited the courage of Marion Motley, the dignified Cleveland fullback who had preceded them in the league, and other black players who came before them and endured worse. He reminded everyone that some of those players had to deal with much more than a lousy motel; they heard regular death threats. Moore chimed in and told the others that he was thinking about Jackie Robinson. He mentioned that Jackie was the only black in his sport and had no one else to talk to, but he still went out and did his job every day.

In the end, they all agreed to play.

The next day, in a "meaningless" game, the Colts bullied the Giants 28–3. Unitas played only two quarters but threw three touchdown passes. Lenny Moore, outraged though he was, shook off the distractions and gave the fans a show with a 44-yard touchdown run. The people of Dallas didn't want to see him wandering their streets or sleeping in their sheets, and the NFL disregarded his dignity. But when the turnstiles clicked and the lights went on and the greatest football players in the world took the field, Lenny Moore was a star attraction.

At least, you might think, the football owners would be grateful for the graceful, athletic men like Moore whose rare blend of talents was creating the demand and enthusiasm for their enterprise. But it wasn't so.

John Steadman, the legendary sports editor of the Hearst-owned *Baltimore News-American*, later told Olesker about a sports banquet in Baltimore in the 1960s attended by Redskins owner George Preston Marshall. Marshall, a West Virginia native, had long been known around the league as a bigot's bigot. His team was the last one in professional football to integrate. One of the evening's featured speakers was black, a fact that enraged Marshall, who sought out Steadman to vent his displeasure.

Olesker quoted the Redskins' owner: "'I'm never coming back here [to Baltimore],' Marshall thundered. 'Never, ever again. To have a nigger speaking. You don't bring those kinds of people up here to speak to an audience. Those are the kind of people you use to clean out the toilet in your bathroom.'

"'It was Lenny Moore he objected to,' Steadman said."

By 1963 attitudes such as those demonstrated by the unreconstructed Marshall were starting to change. Harper Lee's seminal novel, *To Kill a Mockingbird*, was published in 1960 to great critical acclaim. Lee borrowed a literary device from Mark Twain's *Huckleberry Finn*, when she showed the corruption of racism through the innocent eyes of a young child.

Harper Lee's message and technique were a triumph. Lee and her fictional ideal man, Atticus Finch, emerged as heroes to "enlightened" Americans, and tens of millions of copies of her book were sold. Decades after it was written, *To Kill a Mockingbird* remained one of the most frequently taught pieces of literature in the country.

Television in the early 1960s also presented southern characters, especially lawmen. Southern cops appeared nightly on the national news programs, where they were seen aiming high-pressure fire hoses or turning snapping dogs on peacefully gathered black citizens. The cops shouted at black Americans through bullhorns and blocked them from entering public schools. Some of these southern lawmen were uncovered as members of the Ku Klux Klan terrorist organization, and a few of them were even implicated in conspiracies to murder civil rights workers.

On commercial television, where everything was as processed as white bread, *The Andy Griffith Show* presented a totally different kind of southern lawman. In the fictional Thomas Wolfe–inspired town of Mayberry, North Carolina, the streets were loosely patrolled by sheriff Andy Taylor and his best-friend, deputy Barney Fife. Andy was a sagacious hillbilly who handled problems with a smile. He and Deputy Fife did no wrong, as they maintained clean, crime-free streets without the aid of weapons. (Barney had a firearm, but due to his many self-inflicted accidents, he was allowed to carry only one bullet, which he was required to keep in his shirt pocket.)

All the show's charm and humor might have been lost had the producers merely depicted an ordinary black man sitting down at the counter of the town diner and ordering a cup of coffee. Would Andy and Barney have handled it with a smile, or would they have acted as many police in their region did and delivered a beating to that coffee drinker's black skull?

The country simply wasn't ready to know.

Baltimore's attitudes and customs regarding race went all the way back to the Civil War. Maryland, a slave state, remained in the Union. Even so, Baltimore had enough Southern sympathizers to credibly threaten Lincoln's life as he passed through on his way to Washington. Southern sympathizers also attacked Union troops passing through the state, provoking the first bloody confrontation of the war. Lincoln coerced Maryland's loyalty by aiming cannons at the city and threatening to fire them in the event of a secession vote. Nevertheless, he prevented the possibility of such a poll when he threw the Baltimore mayor, a Maryland U.S. congressman, Baltimore's police commissioners, and the entire city council into jail.

Lincoln also suspended habeas corpus in Maryland, a citizen's most basic defense against unlawful detention, before locking up private citizens who were outspoken in their support of the South. One of the facilities used to imprison these offenders was Fort McHenry. Ironically, one of the inmates rounded up by Lincoln and imprisoned at the old fort was Frank Key Howard. Fifty years earlier Howard's grandfather, a lawyer, had been at Fort McHenry, too, arguing for the freedom of prisoners held by the British. While he was there he wrote a poem. That verse was "The Star-Spangled Banner," and Howard's grandfather was Francis Scott Key.

Many ex-Confederates, despite their powerlessness during the war, were a vital part of Baltimore's business and political leadership in the late nineteenth century. They and their descendants played a huge role in shaping the city and its racial attitudes for the next one hundred years. Baltimore was home to three monuments to the Confederate cause, but only one erected to the Union. All of the Confederate statues were commissioned and constructed in the twentieth century. In 1917 the city also named one of its many handsome parks "Robert E. Lee," in honor of the Confederate general.

Baltimore schools were completely segregated by law for the first half of the twentieth century. Real estate investors conspired to create segregated neighborhoods, first through laws and then through protective covenants that buyers were forced to sign. These tactics not only kept the races apart but also kept Gentiles separate from Jews, since the Chosen People were also considered detrimental to home values. Some Baltimore-area swim clubs infamously hung signs at their entrances that read, "No blacks, Jews, or dogs."

Journalism, that supposed watchdog for the people, offered no salvation for the oppressed races. Publisher and majority owner of the *Baltimore Sun* Charles Henry Grasty was also a residential real estate investor, and he played a key role in the development of the protective covenants. The *Sun*'s most famous writer, H. L. Mencken, had a national following and was considered one of the most important editors, authors, and critics of his era. Mencken was an outspoken opponent of the lynching phenomenon, and he also advocated for the right of black citizens to attend public universities, in some instances, and to be able to utilize public facilities, such as parks and tennis courts. But Mencken was a German American who wrote negatively of the Jews. He also wrote a positive literary review of *Mein Kampf,* Adolf Hitler's demented and blatantly anti-Semitic manifesto, in the early 1930s.

These were the cultural influences that shaped Johnny Unitas and Don Shula's Baltimore in the 1960s. Two separate-but-equal societies, as the town fathers promoted, never existed. The city was a single coarse community that was an embarrassment to both black and white, Jew and Gentile. Although these groups lived near each other and interacted in most public places, white Gentiles held a position of privilege that wasn't exactly earned, while blacks languished in an underclass that was all but impossible to escape.

The year 1963 was a particularly hard time for race relations in Baltimore. That was evident in the tragic deaths of three black

Baltimoreans, the causes of which ran the gamut from overt to covert racism.

The first one happened exactly one month, to the day, after Shula was hired and feted in luxury at the swanky Belvedere Hotel. Just a few blocks away from there, at the Emerson Hotel, a barmaid named Hattie Carroll lost her life and helped accelerate the civil rights movement.

The night started off happily, with the Emerson hosting the annual "Spinsters' Ball." A tradition for the city's "postdebutantes," it was meant to offer a genteel forum for young society ladies to invite gentlemen out for a formal evening. In 1963 the theme, portentously, was "Old Plantation." By the end of the night one of the guests, William Zantzinger, would prove he was no gentleman.

A farmer from southern Maryland, Zantzinger arrived at the ball rip-roaring drunk and twirling a toy cane he'd bought at a carnival for about a quarter. He spent the entire evening annoying just about everyone with whom he had come into contact by running his roaring mouth and lashing out with the stick. All night long he delivered racial epithets and an occasional whack with the cane to wait staff. At some point he actually pushed his own wife to the ground.

This sad evening's nadir came only when Zantzinger ordered yet another drink, this time from a "matron" named Hattie Carroll. Carroll was apparently too slow to please Zantzinger, so he struck her on the neck and shoulder with the cane and called her "a black bitch." Soon after that attack she sat down and suffered a massive stroke. She was taken to nearby Mercy Hospital, where she died the next morning.

Zantzinger was arrested and led out of the ball in handcuffs. Still intoxicated, he left the scene barefooted and screaming for both justice and his shoes.

Mrs. Carroll cut a highly sympathetic figure. She was fifty-one years old, and, despite the hue of her skin, she possessed an abundance of American virtues. She was a churchgoer, a hard worker, and a mother. When she died, she left eleven children behind.

The next Sunday the Reverend Theodore C. Jackson was at Gillis Memorial Church, Hattie Carroll's place of worship, seething in the pulpit.

"There is something wrong with this city," Jackson thundered. "There is something wrong when a white man can beat a colored woman to death and no one raises a hand to stop him."

White Baltimoreans might've been ashamed of the simple truth of Jackson's spare, elegant statement, but the *Sun* did not send a single reporter to cover Carroll's funeral, and it published no obituary for her.

Hattie's life and death escaped the notice of the journalists in her hometown, but one aspiring young writer in New York took notice. Sitting in some all-night greasy spoon, reading the details in the *New York Times*, twenty-two-year-old Bob Dylan instinctively understood that a human being had died, and, black or white, she had a highly poignant story.

Dylan penned "The Lonesome Death of Hattie Carroll" that night, a factually inaccurate and clumsy ballad, though it demonstrated his storytelling ability and righteous passion. Curiously, the song never even mentioned Carroll's race, as though it were incidental to the larger tragedy of the powerful abusing the weak.

Back in Maryland lawyers, judges, and medical examiners discussed whether there was a cause-and-effect relationship between a strapping young man striking a middle-aged woman with a weapon and her death just a few moments later. The white power structure moved the trial from Baltimore ninety minutes west to Hagerstown. They put the case in the hands of three judges instead of a jury. Those wise men ultimately determined that Zantzinger's crime was manslaughter, not murder. His penalty for forcefully taking the black woman's life was only six months in jail and a paltry $500 fine. For Dylan the matter was far simpler than all of that. When he noticed that *Zantzinger* rhymed with *murder*, the civil rights movement had one of its earliest anthems.

The death of another black Baltimorean that year hit even closer to home for the Colts. Big Daddy Lipscomb, a famous member of their championship teams in '58 and '59, died in a way that was becoming all too common for young men in the ghetto.

Lipscomb took well to the streets of Baltimore, probably because they were so similar to the ones in Detroit where he grew up— and grew and grew and grew. Nevertheless, the streets were never good to him.

He was gargantuan, six feet six and almost 285 perfectly propor-tional pounds. He could run like a gazelle and tackle ferociously. He became a three-time All-Pro defensive lineman, though he had never played a single down of college football. Pete Rozelle, the future commissioner of the league, was the general manager of the Los Angeles Rams when he discovered Lipscomb. At the time Big Daddy was playing his ball in the U.S. Marines. He gave himself his unique nickname by constantly referring to everyone smaller than himself as "Little Daddy." Naturally, they called him "Big Daddy" in return.

In those early days his talents were crude but undeniable.

"I remember one game at Green Bay," Charley Winner said. "Lipscomb dropped out of the line to cover [Packers running back] Tom Moore on a close flare-pass situation. He chased Moore for 40 yards and then knocked down the pass in the end zone. It was one of the best efforts I've ever seen by a big man against an offen-sive situation which is almost impossible to stop."

Lipscomb's Superman appearance and abilities were highly effective camouflage for the complex and highly vulnerable man beneath the surface. Eventually, though, signs of his inner pain rose to the surface. He suffered from relentless insomnia, and instead of sleeping he paced the halls all night long. When he got into bed it was usually with a gun under his pillow and his bed frame jammed up against the locked door.

Both of Big Daddy's parents died when he was still a little boy. His father passed away before he was even old enough to know him. When he was just eleven his mother was murdered. She was killed by her own boyfriend, stabbed to death right out on the street, the blade plunged into her forty-seven times.

Lipscomb came under the care of his mother's parents, but that, too, was a troubling experience. He worked several jobs because his grandfather demanded rent and board. Once he pilfered a bottle of whiskey from the old man and drank the whole thing. When his grandfather discovered the theft, he tied his grandson to the bedpost and whipped him.

Lipscomb survived this desolate upbringing and even man-aged to grow into an ebullient manhood. He had a great sense of humor and was highly popular with his teammates, both black and white. He traversed the town in a flamboyant yellow Cadillac convertible. In the off-season he put his magnificent physique on display and worked as a professional wrestler. He was also generous to a fault, with a soft spot for children. His teammates saw him pick up more than one poverty-stricken kid off the street to buy the child shoes and clothes.

But Big Daddy could also wander in gloom. When friends had a drink, he demanded a bottle. His thirst for women was equally insatiable. He married three times, and two of his wives overlapped. That was hardly enough to satisfy him, as he was also known for his trysts with hookers and hotel chambermaids.

Other encounters with women were less loving. In November 1960 a Baltimore waitress brought suit against him, alleging he slapped her. She asked for $15,000 in damages.

All of this took a heavy toll on him. His close friend Lenny Moore remembered that Big Daddy could suddenly and utterly lose his composure.

"We'd be in a cab," Moore told Michael Olesker, "and he'd start crying. I'd say, 'Hey, man, what's wrong with you?' He'd say, 'The Daddy don't feel too cool, man. . . .' These episodes would happen all of a sudden. He'd just break down and cry."

There were many sources of that sadness, but an anecdote that Art Donovan, Big Daddy's Colts teammate and friend, used to tell was unintentionally revealing. It was less dramatic than most Lipscomb stories but also a little sad in its own right.

One day Big Daddy asked Donovan about his ancestry.

"Irish, of course," Donovan replied.

Happy to play the straight man, Donovan replied, "What descent are you, Big Daddy?"

Without a trace of a smile Lipscomb replied, "I like you Artie, so I'm Irish, too."

This story, reported by the *Sun*'s Colts reporter Cameron Snyder back in the '50s, derives its comedy, such as it is, from the ludicrous idea that a giant black man could be Irish. Of course, the humor ignored how a man might feel who had no ancestral language, culture, religion, or food to tie him to his forebears.

In July 1961 the Colts traded Big Daddy to Pittsburgh in a multiple-player deal that also included the outstanding young receiver Jimmy Orr. Big Daddy became a Steeler, but he never really left Baltimore. He continued to make his permanent home there. That didn't turn out to be a wise decision.

Baltimore was the place of his biggest achievements and best friends. But not all of those friends were good for him.

One of them, Timothy Black, a young construction laborer who had known Lipscomb for about a year, had a long history of arrests and a bad habit that he soon passed on to Big Daddy. That habit was heroin.

Black bought Lipscomb his first taste of the drug, and it wasn't long before Big Daddy was a regular user. According to Black, his football player friend was "shooting up" three times per week.

One night in May 1963 Lipscomb spent the evening hanging out at Black's apartment. Around midnight the two left in Big Daddy's Cadillac to pick up beer and prostitutes. They left again around three in the morning to take the girls home and came back an hour later with about $12 worth of heroin. Lipscomb had a bad reaction to the drug and lost consciousness.

Black and an unidentified man he called for help tried to revive Lipscomb. They slapped him and applied ice packs to awaken his senses, and then they injected him with saline, which, at the time, was believed to be an antidote for a narcotics overdose. None of it helped.

All told, Big Daddy was unconscious for about two hours before an ambulance was even called. He died in the back of that emergency vehicle wearing a polo shirt and slacks. He had $73 still jammed into his pockets, though he had started the night with $700.

The cops found a homemade syringe and other drug paraphernalia in Black's apartment, and he was eventually charged with the possession of those items. Those charges were dropped, however, when it was discovered that the Maryland General Assembly, which had recently revised its drug laws, had somehow forgotten to include a penalty for possession of narcotics paraphernalia. Nevertheless, Black was in jail by that October, sentenced to eighteen months on a burglary charge, unrelated to the Lipscomb case.

More than twenty thousand people filed through the Baltimore funeral home where Lipscomb's body had been taken. Eventually,

Big Daddy's remains were released back to his grandfather, the same man who had brutally whipped him as a child.

Friends were shocked by Lipscomb's death and professed disbelief. Unitas, like many of the Colts, thought that Big Daddy had been murdered. Charley Winner wasn't sure what had happened.

"Every year, for the physical, we would get some shots," Winner said. "Big Daddy hated the needle. Somebody had to get him addicted. Buddy Young [a Colts front-office official and former player] came back from [Big Daddy's funeral] and said that his arm was like a pin cushion."

The chief medical examiner, Dr. Russell S. Fischer, felt that Lipscomb's overdose was "possibly administered by accident."

Nothing was ever proven, nor ever would be.

Whatever the truth, in the eyes of the majority culture the circumstances of Big Daddy's death would strip away his life accomplishments. In the eyes of whites the man who was once one of the greatest defensive linemen in the history of the league was, in death, just another pathetic ghetto junkie.

White attitudes were summed up a decade later in the movie *The Godfather* when powerful Mafia don Zaluchi spoke up, not only for the solid business advantages of selling heroine but also for the exact marketplace. "In my city," Zaluchi said, "we would keep the traffic in the dark people—the colored. They're animals anyway, so let them lose their souls."

There would be yet one more prominent and telling death in Baltimore's black community in 1963 when prizefighter Ernie Knox was killed in the ring.

Knox was a rising star in Baltimore's boxing scene, though sometimes it was hard to understand why. In his five-year professional career he was only 10-5-3, and he had never earned a purse larger than $300. Despite these lackluster numbers, he quit his job as a hod carrier hauling bricks on construction sites to concentrate full-time on his boxing career.

Knox had once been a promising amateur good enough to tally a 31-3 record. One of those three amateur defeats was a disputed loss to Puerto Rican Jose Torres, a future Boxing Hall of Famer. But Knox would never know the same success as a professional. One reason for his professional struggles may have been that he was a natural light heavyweight who fought as a heavyweight (175 pounds or more), probably a financially motivated decision. He often weighed in at 178 pounds, but it was unclear if he was truly that size or cheating his way through his weigh-ins to qualify for heavyweight bouts. If cheating, he was facing off against men who were significantly heavier and stronger than he was.

Not surprisingly, he gained the reputation of a defensive fighter.

"He was the best 'taker' I've ever handled," his trainer, Mac Lewis, said. But that "achievement" only gave rise to the belief that he wasn't aggressive enough, something that didn't bode well for a boxer aching to contend.

"I've told him that no one is going to come out to watch him block punches," Lewis said. "He's got to be aggressive and sell himself to the fight crowd."

In October 1963, when he signed to meet a savvy and experienced fighter from New York named Wayne Bethea, Knox hoped to find his moment.

Bethea, thirty-one, was a tomato-can packer by trade and a little past his prime, but he had once been a bona fide contender who had beaten the former heavyweight champion Ezzard Charles. In fact, Bethea had taken on a host of formidable fighters and had a solid reputation. In 1958 he unfortunately ran into the rock-hard fists of Sonny Liston, who knocked him to the canvas in little more than a minute, just enough time for Bethea's knees and his whole career to buckle.

Bethea would never quite bounce back from his embarrassing loss to Liston, but his career in the ring was far from over. He enjoyed a 1960 victory over Ernie Terrell, a top contender. In '63 Bethea broke out the American Express travelers' checks and toured Europe. He outdistanced an Englishman, lost two decisions to the same German fighter, and then abused a bevy of Italians.

By the time he came to Baltimore to meet Knox, Bethea was a little long in the tooth but experienced and dangerous. Lewis emphasized the importance of the Bethea bout for Knox with prophetic words.

"Ernie realizes this is the fight that will make or break him," Lewis said.

The fight was scheduled for the Baltimore Coliseum, a grandly named dump. In fact, it was a facility with all the trappings of a Depression-era high school gym. Sitting on the corner of Monroe Street and Windsor Avenue, it was on the edge of the ghetto. Knox and Bethea's Monday-night tussle drew a measly crowd of little more than eight hundred souls, this despite regular and well-written newspaper coverage that created a strong narrative and hyped the possibilities.

What that sparse crowd saw was something less than sport. They witnessed a grueling and brutal affair in a sweltering kiln, the stifling air made even more unbearable by the bright lights trained on the ring.

According to Alan Goldstein, the magnificent boxing writer for the *Baltimore Sun*, the ninth round was the fateful one. Knox "was bullied against the ropes," Goldstein wrote, "where Bethea scored heavily with right uppercuts to the body and short left hooks to the head." Knox was "in a state of near exhaustion" when "Bethea floored him with a looping right."

Knox, so desperate for success, wouldn't stay down. He composed himself and gamely resumed the fight after a standing eight count. But the damage had been done.

"Bethea was quick to follow up his advantage and decked Knox again with a volley of blows," Goldstein wrote.

This time Knox did not get up, not for a long time. He was on the canvas, semiconscious, for about ten minutes. Meanwhile, Knox's friend Joe Sheppard, an artist with an interest in boxing who sometimes sparred with him, was a ringside spectator for the bout. Sheppard watched on in horror as the inept staff fumbled to help Knox. He saw them vainly and inadvisably try to improve the fighter's condition, while others frantically attempted to locate a stretcher, a piece of emergency equipment that should have been easily at hand.

Through all of this chaos Sheppard had the presence of mind to sketch the scene. His hastily scribbled figures tell a pathetic story of three men working at cross-purposes. They don't seem to know whether the inert athlete should be carried away or merely put back on his feet. The simple but heartbreaking sketches reveal a grotesquerie in progress, a man so destroyed he looks like a limp marionette.

Knox was eventually taken by ambulance to Provident Hospital. At one in the morning he asked a nurse to get him a glass of water, and those were the last words he ever uttered. Soon after that he fell into a coma.

On Wednesday morning a neurosurgeon made a last-ditch effort to save Knox's life. He drilled two holes into the boxer's skull to relieve pressure, but the fighter showed no improvement. He died soon after the operation; the official cause of death was subdural hematoma, a hemorrhage of the brain.

But Knox's end was only the beginning of the controversy.

Dr. Charles S. Petty, Baltimore's assistant medical examiner, unleashed a bombshell when he announced that the fighter's autopsy weight was just 153 pounds. Two days earlier the fighter weighed in for the bout at 178. It would have been illegal for him to be in the ring at anything less than 175.

The huge discrepancy prompted an investigation by the state's attorney and the Baltimore grand jury. Sheppard, who was in the gym the Thursday before the fight, said he saw Knox on the scales unofficially weighing himself. The artist confirmed that his friend weighed 178 pounds.

But something didn't add up.

At the official weigh-in both fighters wore trousers. This was highly unusual; the athletes would typically strip down for the scales. Bethea's manager, Bobby Gleason, one of the people present at the weigh-in, later told *Sports Illustrated*, "With those clothes on Knox weighed 184 pounds. They credited his clothes with weighing six pounds and made his weight 178."

Had Knox been hiding lead weights in his pockets?

"No one bothered to check," *Sports Illustrated* reported.

Dr. Petty didn't need to speculate; a man of science, he did the math. He said that Knox might have reasonably lost a pound every round in the sweltering heat of the arena. But that would have only brought his weight down to 169 pounds. He also said that a man deprived of all food and fluids would lose anywhere from one and a half to four pounds. That would have brought Knox down to about 163, still ten pounds more than his weight at autopsy. Of course, the young fighter was not deprived of fluids; in fact, he was receiving them intravenously at the hospital.

Dr. Petty also accounted for the weight that might have been lost due to Knox's emergency operation, but he said such a procedure would have reduced the fighter's weight by only a few ounces. So there was simply no reasonable explanation as to how Knox could have lost 25 pounds between his official weigh-in and his autopsy just a few days later.

Unless, perhaps, there was a deception at the scales.

The more investigators and journalists looked into Baltimore's night of boxing, the more plausible that seemed.

The Knox fight wasn't even the worst fiasco of the evening. The undercard featured a feared and experienced local welterweight named "Irish" Johnny Gilden. His scheduled opponent was a Washingtonian named Hal Bristol. But just prior to fight time Bristol disappeared without explanation.

When the bell rang a substitute fighter named Kenny Joseph timidly walked into the ring to a chorus of boos. Joseph was a slight man who *Sports Illustrated* said "did not appear to weigh more than 125 pounds." That would have been too light to meet a welterweight, as Gilden supposedly was. Joseph's "official" weight, at weigh-in, was 146.5 pounds.

The point was moot anyway. Gilden's official weight was 147.5 pounds, half a pound more than the welterweight limit. No matter how you looked at it, by rule, the two should have never entered the same ring.

To make matters even worse, Joseph didn't even appear to be a legitimate prizefighter. Goldstein wrote that he was "obviously a complete novice." Accordingly, Joseph attempted to keep Gilden at bay like a school-yard coward might. He raised a knee. Even that embarrassing tactic was in vain, however, as Gilden bashed the unskilled fighter until the referee stopped the action just sixty-two seconds into the bout.

Two such fishy matches naturally brought scrutiny on the event's organizers. And the more it was looked into, the more it looked like the underside of a lifted rock. There were plenty of disgusting creatures scurrying in the light. Many on the Maryland Athletic Commission appeared not to know anything about boxing or even their own responsibilities. In fact, the commission chairman, D. Chester O'Sullivan, created that impression himself when he said, upon his appointment, "I'll do the best I can do on this job as soon as I find out what I'm supposed to do."

O'Sullivan was primarily a political creature who delivered Irish Catholic votes for the type of civic hacks who hired him Appointments to the commission weren't made on knowledge or merit, but rather doled out as a kind of patronage distributed in return for political favors. At least O'Sullivan showed up for work. One of the commission members said he had never seen his other two colleagues.

Even that sorry crowd looked like the architects of the Manhattan Project compared to the promoter, Civic Sports. Benny Trotta, an eminently disreputable man, headed up that organization. Trotta's other business interests included ownership of a strip club on the Block, the city's sleazy red-light district. A nefarious character, Trotta was reportedly also a draft dodger and a thug. He had been stripped of his promoter's license back in the 1950s due to his connection to the notorious New York gangster Frankie Carbo. Carbo's outfit had an iron grip on boxing and had been accused of "fixing" bouts in a number of states.

Despite all this, the Maryland Athletic Commission restored Trotta's license in the summer of 1960, but it didn't take him long to land right back in hot water. Just a few months before the Knox fight, Trotta's license was once more in question as federal tax agents arrested him for bookmaking.

All in all, the various forces that led to Ernie Knox's death painted a grim mosaic that even his artist friend Joseph Sheppard would have had a hard time fathoming. Many triumphs lay ahead for Sheppard's career. He would win important commissions for public art all over the world. His sculptures would adorn cities, and his paintings would hang in prestigious private collections and in major museums. Yet one of his most enduring works would be *The Death of Ernie Knox*, a huge, extraordinarily dramatic piece depicting the gloriously muscled form of the fallen fighter descending from the ring, his lifeless arms lifted by others. In Sheppard's eyes the fighter was a bronze-hued Christ descending from the cross at Calvary.

But Ernie Knox couldn't absolve any of the many sinners around him, nor would he ever spend a penny of the measly purse from his exhaustive night's work, just $250. It wasn't much by any measure, of course, except what he gave up to earn it.

Lenny Moore wouldn't die in 1963, like these other black Baltimoreans, but at times it felt like his career might expire. Lenny would have to endure both his physical problems and the taunts he believed were directed at him from the team, but he would have to do so largely alone. The 1963 season would go on mostly without him.

In Shula's first game as Colts coach, Baltimore fell to the Giants. A few weeks later, after a 31–20 loss to the Packers, the team was struggling at just 1-2. Next up was a date with the Bears at Wrigley Field, and more frustration. Unitas threw an interception, and the Colts failed to score a touchdown all day as they lost 10–3.

The Bears game was noteworthy for the fact that Unitas and Bears quarterback Billy Wade seemed to make the same gaffe: they both fumbled while attempting to pass. Early in the game Wade's misstep turned out to be harmless; the officials ruled it was an incomplete pass. But in the fourth quarter, with the Colts desperately trying to rally the steam to win, Bears defensive end Doug Atkins tapped Unitas's arm as he attempted to pass, and the ball popped out. This time the referees decided it was a fumble, and the Bears recovered the ball.

On the Colts' last offensive play of the game, with desperation setting in, Unitas passed to tight end John Mackey. The play gained only 2 yards instead of the 4 that were needed for the first down. Shula admitted that the play call had come from the bench. That was a curious development, since Unitas was long considered the best play caller in football and the most clutch. The fact that Shula and the coaches disregarded him with the game on the line and made the call themselves was smoke signaling fire. But while the young coach took credit for choosing the play, the blame for its failure was left a little more ambiguous.

"John had two receivers," Shula told the *Sun* after the game. "The longer one got into a jam and Unitas threw to the short man hoping he could get in the needed yardage."

Whether the play was inadvisable or the execution was poor, the fact was thirty-three-year-old Don Shula took the ball, metaphorically at least, out of the hands of the most outstanding field general in the game. Was this a point of contention between the two men? At the very least it seemed to be an inefficacy. Incredibly, nobody in the press raised the pertinent questions to the principal players.

The Colts regained their footing a little, won the next two games, and were 3-3 when the Packers came to Memorial Stadium for a late October rematch. The Pack had already defeated the Colts in Wisconsin back in September. Still, nothing prepared Baltimore for the miserable first half they were about to play. Unitas completed just three of eight passes to his receivers. He was almost as accurate in connecting with the Packers, throwing two interceptions to them, in addition to fumbling the ball. Despite a vast improvement by Unitas and the offense in the second half, the Colts lost 34–20. They had turned the ball over six times, literally handing the game away.

Worst yet, Baltimore's record under its new coach was now a miserable 3-4. After the contest Shula sat on a table and met the press with a clenched jaw and an uncomfortable truth on his lips. When Cameron Snyder, the *Sun*'s longtime Colts reporter, asked Shula if he "had entertained any notions about replacing Unitas," the young coach bluntly replied.

"Yes," Shula said, "if things had continued to go bad in the third period, I would have taken him out. He had a bad first half. There's no use denying it."

It was a stunning admission. Worse than that, it was a show of disunity even as the Colts' most bitter rivals sat just a few feet away in the visitors' locker room. Nothing seemed to sum it all up like the wry observation of the Colts' reserve halfback Alex Hawkins.

"When we win, we win as a team," Hawkins said. "But when we lose, it's Unitas' fault."

And life wasn't about to get any easier for Unitas and Shula. Next up was a rematch with the Chicago Bears. Halas's men had marched their way to a 6-1 record, and they were in first place in the West, tied with the Packers. Chicago was as tough and hard-nosed as their coach's cranky old visage. The Colts lost to them, too, and Unitas was again in the crosshairs. He personally gave the Bears the ball three times, fumbling twice and throwing an interception. When the miserable day was over

Green Bay and Chicago both stood at 7-1, and the Colts were all but done at 3-5.

The Colts finally found their footing after the second Bears game. Even without Moore Shula developed an effective running attack that finally opened the passing lanes for his great quarterback and talented trio of primary receivers. Baltimore went 5-1 in its last six games.

That hot finish proved that the Colts had responded to Shula's methods. They didn't win the title, as Rosenbloom had all but demanded, but at 8-6 there were a game better than they had been with Ewbank the year before. The Colts scored more points and gave up fewer points than they did under the old coach's direction in 1962. And they jumped from fourth place to third in the Western Division.

Shula achieved all this while, to a certain extent, putting Johnny U in his place. The coach had been unsparing in his approach to the star player, yelling at him, usurping his play-calling ability, and even publicly admitting that he had considered benching him. By season's end, however, the vicissitudes of Unitas had been reversed. Johnny U had his best year since 1959, leading the league in both completions and yards. His interceptions plummeted, from twenty-three to merely twelve.

Shula's prospects brightened right along with Unitas's. By finishing strong the young coach took on the appearance of a prodigy. At just thirty-three years of age he had replaced Ewbank, a bona fide legend, and improved upon him. Rosenbloom didn't get his third title, but he saw what he had wanted to see. He had confirmation that in callously firing Ewbank, a man who had won two world championships for him, he had made a plausible decision. Despite the Colts' progress, or perhaps because of it, 1963 was looked upon as a mulligan.

But in the long term no one in Baltimore would settle for third place. Not the fans, not the coaching staff, and, most assuredly, not Carroll Rosenbloom.

# FIVE

# The Colts' Greatest Season Yet

On September 20, 1964, the Colts traveled to Wisconsin for the second game of the season. The Packers were waiting for them in Green Bay. Under Vince Lombardi's stern leadership the Pack had gone to three championship games in a row from 1960 to '62, winning the last two. But in 1963, with Paul Hornung suspended for gambling and quarterback Bart Starr fighting through injuries, they weren't quite the same team, and they missed the postseason. The commissioner reinstated the Golden Boy for '64, and with Starr fully convalesced the Pack came roaring back into everyone's expectations. They were once again heavy favorites to win the West and regain the title.

In the season's debut, one week before, the Colts lost by ten to the Vikings, who had won just five games in 1963. Meanwhile, Green Bay handily defeated the Bears, the defending champions, 23–12.

By this time the Packers and Colts were bitter rivals. The roots of their feud stretched beyond Green Bay all the way back to New York. It all started with the '58 championship game, where Unitas, Berry, Moore, and Ameche outplayed and overshadowed Lombardi's archaic but effective Giants offense.

When Vince moved on to become Green Bay head coach the next year, the rivalry traveled with him. Unitas and Ewbank continued to have his number for quite a while, beating him in four of the first six games they met his Packers. Now the task of trying to beat Green Bay's great man had fallen to Shula. He also knew Lombardi well. As a young assistant with the Lions, Shula's Detroit defenses befuddled the Packers. In Shula's short tenure the Lions played Green Bay as competitively as anyone in the league could. Without much offense Detroit beat Lombardi's resurgent Packers three out of six games.

Besides standing up to Vince on the field, Shula had the pleasure of playing golf with him.

"I knew him when I was an assistant at Detroit and George Wilson was the head coach," Shula said. "In the off-season we would have a golf tournament. One year it would be in Green Bay. One year it would be in Cleveland. And one year we would have it in Detroit. From that two or three days of golf and having a few drinks and stuff, we got to know each other a little bit."

That familiarity didn't breed much affection. While many found the gregarious Lombardi charming, the young Shula found him overbearing. "[Lombardi] was bombastic," Shula remembered. "His way was the only way."

There can be but little debate about Lombardi's place in history. There is no doubt that he was one of the greatest coaches in the game. He arrived on the scene as a head coach when he was already in his forties and only after being passed over for job after job after job. Many journalists and biographers have noted that a strong anti-Italian bias had kept him out of more than a few top positions. Nevertheless, his skills were tempered as an assistant under Red Blaik at Army, then one of the nation's premier college football programs. Blaik had a powerful impact on Lombardi, and he was the only man who could rightly be called Lombardi's mentor. In 1954 Vince left West Point to join Coach Jim Lee Howell's New York Giants staff. Howell, a huge man and a former marine, managed an odd combination. He was somehow both highly successful and lightly regarded by his peers, players, and the press. His two top assistants, Lombardi on offense and Tom Landry on defense, enjoyed the lion's share of credit for Howell's excellent teams and big victories. Not surprisingly, there were deep tensions and rivalries among the three coaches, though they worked together well enough to guide the Giants to the 1956 championship. In 1958 they might've won it again had not Ewbank, Unitas, and Berry elevated the level of play briefly beyond even the brilliant comprehension of the Giants triumvirate.

Lombardi came to Green Bay when very few fans were clicking

the turnstiles. The team was drawing little more than ten thousand spectators per game. In 1958, the year before Lombardi's arrival, Green Bay was the worst team in the league, with just a single victory. In 1959, his first season, the new coach famously told his charges, "Gentlemen, I don't associate with losers." True to his word, he directed a dramatic improvement, and the Packers finished as winners at 7-5. In 1960 he took it a step further. The Packers won the Western Division, and Green Bay went all the way to the championship game, only to lose to the Eagles. In 1961 the Packers won their first title under his leadership. By 1967 they had won five championships, including three in a row. Among the Packers' huge victories were the famous Ice Bowl game, played in subzero temperatures, and the first two Super Bowls.

When Lombardi got to Green Bay the city was in danger of losing its team. By the time he resigned just nine years later, that frozen hamlet was famous throughout the States, enviously known as Title Town.

As great as these accomplishments were, however, they have also been mythologized to the point where legend and fact have intersected. It is hard to tell where the flesh-and-blood coach Lombardi has receded and the supernatural Saint Vincent has emerged.

The myth tells us that Lombardi freed the enslaved Packer tribes by parting football's Red Sea. His miracles seemed to emerge from the hands of God. In fact, there were sound and logical reasons for his success. Unlike Ewbank, who came to the Colts when the team was more or less in a financial and talent bankruptcy, Lombardi walked into a franchise that was oddly primed for success. His first squad, filled almost entirely with inherited players, was overflowing with future All-Pros and Hall of Famers. This spectacular roster wasn't assembled by Lombardi but was hand chosen for Lombardi's use by a brilliant young man named Jack Vainisi.

Vainisi was a potbellied, balding, and ordinary-looking man who was conceived in the womb of the enemy. He grew up in Chicago, closely connected to the Halas family. Jack was a boyhood friend and schoolmate of Papa Bear's own cub, Mugsy Halas. Vainisi played high school football well enough to earn a scholarship to Notre Dame. But he lasted only one season in South Bend before enlisting in the U.S. Army for World War II. He contracted rheumatic fever in the service and permanently damaged his otherwise ample heart.

Gene Ronzani, an associate from Chicago, brought Vainisi to the Packers in 1950. Ronzani had only recently been hired by the Packers himself when he was brought in to succeed Curly Lambeau as the second head coach in Packers history.

In the 1930s and '40s Lambeau's Packers were among the premier teams in football. But the '50s were a lost decade for Green Bay. During the entirety of the era the team was a spectacular failure on the field, rarely finishing above fifth in the standings. In the nine dismal autumns before Lombardi, from 1950 to 1958, the Packers won three games or fewer five times.

Ronzani was only the first in a string of Packer coaches who were rank failures. Yet he would have as much to do with the Packers' dynasty as anyone, if for no other reason than that he secured the services of Vainisi, which was one of the single greatest hires in league history.

Young Vainisi was initially listed as a Packer scout, but it didn't take him long to rise to the "position" of de facto general manager. He seized the opportunity and shrewdly assembled the players who would dominate professional football for the next decade.

Peter M. Platten III, a future Packers president, grew up in Green Bay right next door to Vainisi, but reported nothing unusual about him. He said that Vainisi was an ordinary man.

"He was one of the nicest guys you would ever meet in your life," Platten said. "He was a normal guy; he just knew talent better than anybody I have ever seen."

That was high praise coming from Platten, who led the Packers organization during Ron Wolf's successful reign. Platten said Vainisi's secret was his vast football network.

"[Jack] knew everybody," Platten said. "People really respected him. He was able to dig down into the ranks of the players and pick out excellent ones. That's what everybody in personnel is supposed to do, but he did it all the time."

Vainisi's "network," such as it was, wasn't even constructed of personal contacts. To a large extent it was built of men he had never even met in person. Pat Peppler, an assistant coach at North Carolina State in the 1950s, told the *Milwaukee Journal Sentinel* that he didn't even really know Vainisi. Yet he provided the Packers' GM detailed information anyway in exchange for tiny bits of money.

"I'd give Jack scouting reports at the end of the season for $100," Peppler said.

In an era when many team's draft-room decisions were still driven by magazine articles, Vainisi kept detailed files of more than four thousand players. Each folder was filled with reliable information. He created his own system for ranking the worth of every single prospect. It obviously worked. Vainisi accumulated talent at an unprecedented level. Even as the team crumbled on the field, his deft drafts yielded Paul Hornung, Bart Starr, Forrest Gregg, Jim Ringo, Jerry Kramer, and Willie Wood. His 1958 draft is still considered the greatest of all time, as he selected linebacker Dan Currie, a future All-Pro; Jim Taylor and Ray Nitschke, future Hall of Famers; and Jerry Kramer, the fundamentally sound guard who delivered the most famous block in league history to end the bitter Ice Bowl.

Vainisi even unearthed Lombardi. Though Vince had been a well-respected NFL assistant for years, he hadn't yet received a single head-coaching offer in the major college ranks or the pros.

Lombardi and others felt that he was overlooked solely on the basis of his olive skin, inky hair, and exuberant personal manner. Many NFL executives felt that Lombardi simply did not present the right image for their team or program. Prejudice against Italians simply wasn't an issue for Vainisi; his name also ended with a vowel. Anyway, he wasn't constrained by nonproductive baggage. In searching to end the Packers' woes, he only wanted a man who could properly manage the talent he had assembled for the Packers.

George Halas and Paul Brown both recommended Lombardi to Vainisi. Brown, in particular, felt invested in Vince's success and generously made a list of promising Browns players he'd trade to the Packers. That's how Lombardi acquired Henry Jordan and Bill Quinlan as well as Willie Davis. Paul may have been far more generous than he intended. His gift to Lombardi included three-quarters of Green Bay's defensive line for their first two championship seasons under Vince. Those players were also selected to multiple Pro Bowl All-Pro teams. Willie Davis was a future Hall of Famer.

Lombardi was also greatly aided by something that no other coach or organization in the league enjoyed. The Packers were a publicly owned organization, and the people of Green Bay were its stockholders. Unlike the other teams scrimping to make a profit, the Packers were mandated to spend profits to make a successful team. So while Ewbank lost his job and the Colts' dynasty in Baltimore because he couldn't sign the very fine players he drafted, the Packers were signing their picks at the highest rate in the NFL.

So Lombardi's unprecedented success did not come out of the blue. It was in the making for years. In Green Bay his ability to teach and motivate intersected with the hard work of a brilliant personnel man and the star players he unearthed, not to mention the best situation in the league for signing them.

Interestingly, despite his success, Lombardi had an incredibly limited legacy. None of his assistants went on to notable head-coaching careers. Phil Bengston, his handpicked successor in Green Bay, lasted only three seasons and finished with a 20-21-1 record.

Though Lombardi's offenses and defenses were highly ranked every year of his tenure, and though contemporary league players were unanimous in their belief in the excellence of those Green Bay units, no one followed in the footsteps of his system. His playbook was considered too basic and conservative by other coaches. So while Vince had many admirers, he had but few imitators.

Lombardi himself seemed to hold just one team in high esteem, and that was the Baltimore Colts under Ewbank. Despite some painful losses to Baltimore, he was generous in his praise of Unitas. After a 1959 Colts victory over the Packers, Vince told reporters that Johnny U was "the best quarterback I've ever seen." In 1960, when Lombardi finally beat the Colts for the first time as a head coach, he called it "my greatest day in football." In 1961, in the midst of his first championship season, he told reporters that Unitas was "the greatest football player in the world."

Unitas was unimpressed with all the praise. "That and a dime will get you a cup of coffee," he said.

Despite Lombardi's ardor, the Packers bid adieu to Weeb by beating Baltimore twice in '62. In 1963 they rudely welcomed Shula and swept him, too.

In 1964 everything seemed to point to more of the same between Green Bay and Baltimore. But when the Colts' plane touched down in Wisconsin for an early-season matchup, nothing went as others thought. And in the tiny statistics a fascinating story was told.

Shula's team was finding the winning balance. Unitas threw the ball just twelve times against the Packers, while Colts runners carried thirty-seven times and gained 123 yards. All of a sudden Green Bay's swarming pass rushers couldn't pin their ears back for Johnny U and disrupt his rhythms anymore. They had to hesitate and consider that there was something else that might afflict them. With that tiny advantage Unitas was sacked only once on the day, for 9 yards. Meanwhile, he slung it downfield for 154. He connected with his old target Lenny Moore in the first half for a 52-yard touchdown. According to the *Baltimore Sun*, Moore was "yards and yards behind the defender," who was necessarily drawn in to protect against the effective running game. While the suddenly balanced offense was making its mayhem, those old marauders—Marchetti, Pellington, and their henchmen—swallowed Starr whole. The Colts sacked him six times, good for 47 yards of lost ground. Meanwhile, when he could actually stay upright long enough to pass, the results were no better. The Colts' defenders intercepted Starr three times.

Despite it all, though, Green Bay was in their usual position to win the game at the end. The Pack needed only two points to pull it off when they found themselves in easy field goal range with time ticking off the clock. But Starr inexplicably attempted to pass, and the ball ended up in the hands of Baltimore's Don Shinnick. That, and a missed extra point by Hornung earlier in the game, ensured the Colts' 21–20 victory.

The breaks that typically went Green Bay's way were, for once, in Baltimore's favor. More than that, the Colts had their old balance back. It seemed that Baltimore could run and pass as well as play incredibly rough defense.

In week three those indicators would all prove true beyond everyone's imagination when they met another old rival with a legendary coach.

The defending-champion Bears and George Halas came to Baltimore.

The Colts had a long, stormy history with Halas and his Chicago grizzlies. Every game against Papa Bear was a brutal struggle. A Colts victory at Wrigley Field in 1960 bolstered the Unitas legend even while it dashed all hopes for a third straight title under Ewbank. The Colts left Chicago that day leading the West by two games with just four to go. But with seventeen seconds left on the clock, the Bears held a 20–17 lead. Unitas had already been sacked five times on the day. The last of them was a vicious hit by Doug Atkins that split the bridge of Unitas's nose. Blood was spurting out of the wound and both nostrils. The referee, surveying the gruesome scene, told the quarterback to leave the field. As the legend has it, Johnny U instead ejected the official from his huddle and cauterized the bleeding with mud scooped from the Wrigley turf and shoved into his two nostrils by his teammate Alex Sandusky. Jim Parker later recalled that the sight of the wound and its filthy remedy almost set him to vomiting right on the field. But the patient himself played on as if nothing had happened. Unitas dialed Lenny's number, and with the mud and the blood streaming down his face he hit the Reading Rocket with a perfectly thrown 37-yard pass in the corner of the end zone. Lenny hauled in the missile, and the referee threw his arms in the air in two parallel lines just as time expired. When asked to explain how it was possible, Unitas missed the point of the question entirely. "I thought Lenny could beat [the cornerback] on that pattern," he obtusely said.

Unitas bore the scar from that Bear wound on the bridge of his nose for the rest of his life.

Dramatic as that conquest of Halas may have been, it was nothing more than a pyrrhic victory. The game was so brutal, and extracted such an awful physical toll on the Colts, the team lost all four of its remaining games. After the season ended (with a loss to San Francisco), Weeb's thoughts were still in Chicago. "We won the game but lost the title there," he said in pity for himself and his hapless and drained men.

Now, in 1964, facing off against the Bears would be unlike any of the previous brutal Chicago experiences. This time the Colts embarrassed and humiliated the Bears, 52–0. It was the worst whipping in the entire history of the old and venerable Chicago franchise. Just as they had against the Packers, the Colts' runners really poured it on. They lugged the ball forty-one times and scampered for 213 yards against the Monsters of the Midway. Unitas threw only thirteen passes, but those were good enough for 247 yards and three touchdowns.

The rest of the season went much the same way. The running attack enabled the passing attack, and the passing attack featured only the toughest, smartest, and most feared man in football.

The Colts finished 1964 with a 12-2 mark, better than any season under Ewbank and also the NFL's best record. Shula, in only his second year on the job, found vindication. Regardless of who opposed Shula, or why, everyone had to admit that his fiery leadership and ability to repair the run game had brought the Colts back to their glory days and even restored a little luster to Unitas. The brilliant young coach and his team did it the hard way: They beat Lombardi twice and they beat Halas twice. They scored the most points in the league and gave up the fewest. Shula was named Coach of the Year, and, of course, Johnny U was exactly what his teammates thought he was, the Most Valuable Player.

The Colts were off to the championship game on the road in Cleveland; that they would win it was a foregone conclusion.

## SIX

## Black, White, and the Browns

U nderstandably, much of the chatter in the newspapers leading up to the big game centered around Jim Brown and Johnny Unitas. It was as though Superman and Batman were about to go into a dark alley and settle a score. Both players were recognized, even in their own time, as among the best in the game's history. Certainly, both engendered enormous respect from fans, teammates, and players all over the league. Their fame reached far beyond the provincial towns where they played to every city and hamlet in the country.

In addition to their superlative skills, Unitas and Brown brought the title game an engrossing contrast of styles and abilities. Unitas was all finesse and cunning. Jim Brown was a mighty hammer with the power to run through even the biggest and toughest players and the speed to leave anyone behind. Unitas represented America idealized: virtuous, pious, masculine, indomitable, deadly, and, of course, white. As a player who had been dumped and reclaimed, a man who rose from the ravines of failure to the high summits of professional success, he was a breathing demonstration of American meritocracy.

Jim Brown, on the other hand, was an aching tooth, a constant reminder of how *unfair* America was. In 1956 he led Syracuse University to a 7-1 record, rushing for 986 yards and fourteen touchdowns. Nevertheless, Heisman Trophy voters scorned him. Brown didn't win the award, and he didn't finish second or even third. Somehow, when all the votes were tallied, he was way back in fifth place. The man who actually won the trophy was Paul Hornung, the snow-white Notre Dame quarterback whose qualifications for the high honor were three touchdown passes and thirteen interceptions. The only thing that distinguished Hornung, and in a bad way, was the fact that he presided over a 2-8 season, a rare torturous autumn in South Bend, Indiana, where the victories typically blew in like the inevitable cold midwestern winds.

The feeling by many was that Jim Brown was snubbed for only one reason, his black skin. The great sportswriter Dick Schaap, a Heisman voter, was so disgusted by the outcome of the award, and the implicit racism, he vowed never to participate in the Heisman again. In the NFL draft five teams passed Jim Brown by before Cleveland finally stepped up and selected him. But it was no sign of racial progressiveness by either the organization or its boss.

"I was baffled as a rookie," Gary Collins, one of the Browns players remembered. "On road trips the coaches, rookies, and the black guys rode in the first bus at the airport. And the veterans rode on the second bus. [That policy] was changed in 1963 only when Blanton [Collier] took over." It said something that Collins was shocked by the policy. By his own admission he grew up in working-class Pennsylvania among "prejudiced Protestants and Catholics." Collins never played with or against a black player in his entire life until he was chosen for the same college all-star team with Syracuse's famous running back Ernie Davis.

The irony in all of this is that the Cleveland organization was considered among the most racially liberal in professional sports. The Browns integrated before the Brooklyn Dodgers did. When Marion Motley joined Cleveland in 1946, he beat Jackie Robinson to the Majors by a year. The Browns reaped the rewards on the field for that decision. Motley spent seven years in Cleveland, averaging 5.7 yards per carry, the highest total for a running back in the history of professional football. Yet they weren't convinced that a black man would be the equal of a white when it came to the intellectual aspects of the business. After Motley's stellar playing career was over, he sought a position as a coach. The first place he turned, of course, was the Browns, but despite his many accomplishments for their organization, Cleveland turned him down flat. So did every other team in the league. Motley felt that racial discrimination played a part in his failure to land work in a game he once dominated. And Motley wasn't even considered a "race man," then a euphemism for an "uppity" black who insisted on talking about the obvious inequities of society. He was viewed by the white power structure as quiet and accepting of the status quo.

Jim Brown was a whole other story. "Paul [Brown] was afraid of Jim," Collins remembered. "He didn't know how to deal with a black man."

Jim Brown wasn't old-timey. He didn't accept slights and indignities with a good nature. And he didn't view mistreatment as an inevitability, as Motley did.

Just the opposite, in fact.

Jim Brown radiated and asserted power. He not only proved a black man could have leverage against a white but also showed that a workingman could prevail over a manager. To the surprise of no one he had a stormy relationship with Paul Brown, and he ultimately led a player revolt against his coach. It all resulted in the termination of the star coach, something that was once unthinkable.

Not everyone saw Coach Brown as the problem. In fact, some white players in the league considered Jim hostile, and they tagged him with the "racist" label. Nevertheless, Jim Brown made it clear that he didn't care. The running back intertwined his game and his rage so effectively that even some of his many detractors viewed him as the greatest football player in the world, the same title Vince Lombardi admiringly bestowed upon Unitas.

So each team had their man, but each man did not have an equal team. Baltimore had finished 12-2, while the Browns were only 10-3-1. The Colts were fearsome on both sides of the ball. The Browns were second in offense, but their defense was the worst in league and the Achilles' heel of that disrespected unit was its backfield. The maligned cornerbacks and safeties were the very men who were expected to be the team's shield against the nuclear threat of Unitas. It didn't bode well.

Yet Cleveland had its strengths. Number one was Coach Blanton Collier. Like so many other great coaches and players, Collier came into football under Paul Brown's tutelage. The two met during World War II at Naval Station Great Lakes, the only boot camp in the U.S. Navy. Brown, who left his job leading Ohio State's football program to join the service, was named head coach for the installation team. As always he ran an efficient operation, and Great Lakes played and prevailed against some of the top collegiate teams in the country. Great Lakes was an important part of Brown's career because it was there where he first met and worked with many of the coaches and players who would later help him elevate the Browns from a start-up club, in a start-up league, to the very best team in professional football. Among the people he met there, in addition to Collier, were Marion Motley and Bud Grant. Collier later became a trusted and important member of Brown's machinelike Cleveland operation. The organization won seven professional championships, the first four in the All-America Football Conference (AAFC), an early NFL rival league.

After the franchise's initial owner, Arthur McBride, sold the team to New York advertising man Arthur Modell, Brown's standing slowly began to erode. First, it was obvious that the rest of the league had caught up to him. By 1962 he hadn't won a division title or league championship in five years. But success, or the lack of it, wasn't his only problem. He was didactic and grated on his players, none more than the quarterbacks. Brown still insisted on calling all the plays from the sidelines, sending his instructions to the huddle with rotating "messenger" guards. His play calls were considered sacrosanct (at least by him), and the quarterback, either in the huddle or at the line of scrimmage, could not change them. But where Brown was once the unassailable and eponymous czar of the franchise, his moves were now openly questioned. That was especially true of a trade he had made with Washington that sent the spectacular halfback Bobby Mitchell to the Redskins. Mitchell, shifty and fast, was the counterpunch to Jim Brown's power. He once rushed for 232 yards in a single game. The fans found the trade ludicrous, though it netted the Browns the rights to the sensational Syracuse running back Ernie Davis.

Davis broke many of Jim Brown's records at Syracuse, and he achieved the signature honor that had once been denied Brown when he became the first-ever African American to win the Heisman Trophy. But unknown to all, Davis was tragically suffering from leukemia even as the Browns selected him in 1962. He died before starting his pro career. So for the Browns, in addition to the horrible personal tragedy was the fact that they had just given away Mitchell, a future Hall of Famer, for literally nothing.

The mere attempt to acquire Ernie Davis, however, helped Coach Brown make a point: anyone could be replaced, even Jim Brown.

Tensions between Jim Brown and Paul Brown eventually led to rumors that the great fullback was on the verge of being traded to Baltimore, in return for Unitas. Paul Brown denied the veracity of that rumor, and in fact it seems unlikely that Ewbank would have traded Unitas for any player. Nevertheless, Browns owner Arthur Modell felt alienated by Paul Brown's personnel machinations. The threat that Jim Brown might be moved without the owner's knowledge or consent was the last straw. He quickly wrested control of his team. One day after Ewbank was terminated in Baltimore Modell fired Paul Brown, the man who gave his very name to the franchise. When the press asked for an explanation as to how it was possible, all Modell could manage to do was shrug his shoulders and say, "When I bought this club, I idolized Paul Brown."

Now Modell had canned his idol. In replacing him he wanted someone who knew what Paul Brown knew, someone who understood Brown's theories of personnel and strategy, but who didn't come with the unfortunate quality of actually being Paul Brown.

Blanton Collier fulfilled all of those requirements.

Collier accepted Modell's offer but only after a week of hand-wringing and only after receiving Paul Brown's own reluctant blessing. Though Collier spent most of his career as a self-effacing assistant, he had replaced a fiery legend before when he filled the head-coaching position vacated by Bear Bryant at Kentucky.

When the Bear left Kentucky for Texas A&M and his famous rendezvous with the Junction Boys, Collier stepped in and proved to be a mostly mediocre college head coach with a reputation as a poor recruiter. His teams never approached the upper echelons of the Southeastern Conference except for his very first season when, coaching Bryant's leftover talent, he finished third. Sixth place was Collier's high-water mark for his remaining seven years at the school, and he never took the Wildcats to a big-time bowl. He did, however, exhibit the one skill endemic to almost all great head coaches: he found and mentored coaching talent. Over the years his staff included sensational future coaches such as Chuck Knox, Howard Schnellenberger, and Bill Arnsparger. All would make their own indelible marks on the profession in both the NFL and college. But Collier's star pupil was Don Shula. The two spent only one season together, in 1959, before Shula bolted Kentucky to reenter the NFL as defensive coordinator in Detroit.

Though Collier had never really been a successful head coach, let alone on the professional level, he had one thing going for him when he replaced Paul Brown: he had the universal respect of both the Browns players and their ownership. His bespectacled and professorial approach appealed to everyone. He was seen as a tonic bottle for a variety of Brown-borne ills, everything from pomposity to racial disharmony.

Collier, of course, inherited an enviable operation from Brown that included a wealth of playing talent and excellent assistant coaches. But Collier accomplished one thing on his own that hadn't really been done in Cleveland in many years, and that was to develop a fine quarterback.

In 1955 Johnny Unitas, freshly released from the Steelers, approached Brown and asked him for a tryout. The famous coach knew all about Unitas's professional potential. He was encouraging and told the young quarterback that Cleveland was interested in him but couldn't give him a look until the following year, when Otto Graham was expected to retire. In the interim Unitas was "discovered" by Ewbank, who signed him to the Colts. So while the single greatest quarterbacking talent of the next two generations went to Baltimore, the Browns began an era of mostly mediocre play behind center.

None thrived under Brown, and, in fact, some were outspoken in their complaints against him. Less than immortal passers like George Ratterman, Milt Plum, and Jim Ninowski all shuffled through Cleveland. Len Dawson was there, too, but Brown didn't see much in him. Len eventually left the team to seek opportunity in the AFL with his old college coach, Hank Stram.

Although Stram had his own impressions of Dawson, he hadn't seen the quarterback in years. He picked up the phone and called Paul Brown to get his impressions of Dawson. Brown responded negatively and tried to warn Stram off.

"Leonard Dawson will cost you your job," Brown told him.

Stram signed Dawson in spite of that dismal evaluation from one of the most respected men in the profession. Ignoring Paul Brown turned out to be a wise decision, since Stram and Dawson would eventually win three AFL Championships and the Super Bowl together. In essence, they assisted each other to the Hall of Fame. Far from costing Stram his job, as Brown predicted, Dawson ensured his coach a place in history.

Paul Brown, meanwhile, may have lost out on Unitas and Dawson, but he hadn't completely lost his touch for spotting and developing quarterback talent. He eventually acquired a quirky castoff from the Rams named Frank Ryan.

Ryan held a PhD in mathematics, but his intellectualism wasn't considered an asset by anyone. In fact, it was something of a liability. Sportswriters groping for adjectives to describe him latched on to the word *genius*. Ryan bristled at that meaningless label, but the writers never let it go. Instead, they conjured images of him calculating distances and angles in his head as the game swirled around him. Ryan rejected those descriptions as silly, but he was so self-effacing about his own athleticism, he may have encouraged the view that his elevated mental faculties were the only explanation for his presence in the world of professional athletes.

To hear Ryan tell it, he was physically the furthest thing in the world from a starting quarterback in the National Football League. "I was never very fast or well coordinated," he told *Sports Illustrated*. "I never played any sport well. I couldn't hit in baseball. I couldn't dribble in basketball or play tennis or golf."

His NFL coaches before Brown might have agreed with that assessment. Before Cleveland, Ryan had spent four hapless seasons with the Los Angeles Rams, where he played under two men with huge quarterback reputations. The first was Sid Gilman, often hailed as the father of the modern passing game. Ryan admired and respected Gilman but developed little under his tutelage. His second coach, Bob Waterfield, was himself a former NFL quarterback, and a great one. A huge star in his day, Waterfield led the Cleveland Rams to the NFL title. When the franchise relocated to Los Angeles, he was the star attraction. He led Los Angeles to three straight title games, though he split time there with tough-talking Norm Van Brocklin. When the newly minted

LA Rams won it all in 1951, it was the only title they would ever win in Southern California. Waterfield was the first rookie to ever win the MVP Award, and he was the lucky groom of Jane Russell, a bosomy beauty who looked like the brunette Marilyn Monroe.

None of this had any effect on the math whiz under center. Ryan thought Waterfield was a "terrible coach," and Waterfield thought little of Ryan's potential. With just the slightest mistake the coach would pull Ryan from the game and stick him on the bench. After four years in Los Angeles the mathematician had started only eleven games for his franchise.

The Rams' leadership, believing they had seen everything there was to see in Ryan, traded him to Cleveland. The move afforded the quarterback an opportunity for a new beginning, but many of his new teammates didn't quite take to him, either.

"He was not a good athlete, smarter than hell, though," Gary Collins remembered. "But I don't know if he had the football smarts, like, say, a Joe Namath. He had a powerful arm, but it wasn't that accurate."

Collins echoed a common sentiment when he said, "[Ryan] was too smart for the game of football. He didn't fit. He tried to be one of the guys, but for Frank to be one of the guys he had to step down to these prehistoric monsters 'cause his IQ is Einstein. He had gray hair when he was twenty-seven. You only have gray hair when you're young if you're smart."

Paul Brown also respected Ryan's intelligence. The coach saw how effective his young quarterback could be when the Browns' starter, Jim Ninowski, was injured midway through the 1962 season. Brown summoned Ryan and handed him the reins for Cleveland's remaining seven games.

Given the first real chance he ever got in the league, Ryan proved that he was a player. He connected on almost 58 percent of his throws and hit the end zone ten times, numbers that projected out to a sensational full season—good enough, anyway, to establish his worthiness as the Browns' starter. From then on he would lead Cleveland, and Ninowski would be *his* backup.

Although Ryan had learned a lot under Brown's tutelage, he felt, much like the other Cleveland quarterbacks had, that the coach's run-first offense was confining. He also had to live with Brown calling plays from the bench that he couldn't change. But Brown was fired at the end of the year, and when Collier took over Ryan's career took off in earnest. In fact, Collier and Ryan seemed to enjoy a couple of things that even Unitas and Shula did not. One was a personal chemistry, and the other was an understanding.

"Blanton Collier gave me the opportunity to call any play I wanted," Ryan said. "I didn't even have to run the plays that he sent in if, in my judgment, I thought I should do something else. We really got along pretty well that way."

With Ryan coming of age and calling the plays, the Browns' offense fulfilled a vast potential. Theirs was an incredibly diverse and balanced attack, rich in talent. Obviously, many focused on Jim Brown and the superb running game he created. But a couple of young players teamed with Ryan to give Cleveland an enviable passing game, too.

On one side of the line was the future Hall of Famer Paul Warfield. The rookie split end was a sprinter with great hands. On the other side was Gary Collins, a player of subtler talents. Collins, an emerging star from the University of Maryland, wasn't fast in the conventional sense, but he had something called "burst," the ability to pull away from a defender at the key moment. Colts ends Raymond Berry and Jimmy Orr both had the same quality. Like them, Collins had terrific moves and reliable hands, but he brought something to the field that they never could. At six feet four he had a huge, muscular body that towered above most defensive backs. At 215 rock-solid pounds Collins also had the strength to hold his own against even the roughest linebacker.

In 1963, Gary's first full year as a starter, he led the league in touchdown catches. In '64, in a more balanced attack, with the sensational rookie Warfield also in the lineup, his touchdowns and yards receiving were both down, but the team was rising.

Collins was a rugged individualist who spoke a kind of profane truth. He was unheralded and overshadowed by the other great stars on his own offense. Nevertheless, he lacked nothing in confidence. When Frank Ryan said he felt good about his chances against the Colts because "I had better receivers than Johnny Unitas," Gary Collins was quick to agree. "[Ryan was] right," Gary Collins said. "He had Gary Collins."

Bravado aside, outside of the die-hard Browns fans, very few people thought Cleveland had much of a chance. The Colts had five players on the All-Pro first team: Johnny Unitas, Jim Parker, Gino Marchetti, Lenny Moore, and Bobby Boyd. Unitas, of course, was the league MVP. Shula beat out Collier as Coach of the Year. And Lenny Moore was the Comeback Player of the Year and, in at least one poll, Most Valuable Player of the league.

In predicting the outcome of the game *Sports Illustrated* saw Baltimore's many virtues. Specifically, the magazine cited two factors in Baltimore's favor, the Colts' crushing defense and Unitas. "There is no great difference between the teams," SI wrote, "but in the two most important areas of the game Baltimore has a clear edge: quarterback and overall defense."

As it turned out, the writers couldn't have been more wrong. The so-called football experts typically disdain fans and their reliance on hype, emotion, and mythology in predicting victory. Like scientists peering down their noses at religionists, the experts strain to uncover demonstrable facts as the basis for their superior opinions. They break down film, plays, and tendencies in their quest to bring concrete reasons for why games will resolve the way they do.

The fans, on the other hand, are true believers. They are fascinated by the intangibles that make every underdog a potential David. Scientists see empirical evidence. Religionists propound God. Football experts stick to the numbers and "facts"; the fans are intrigued by stories.

Somehow overlooked in the rush to read the tea leaves, however, was the fact that the game would be played in Cleveland. The Browns' Municipal Stadium held more spectators than almost any other venue in pro football. More than eighty thousand rabid Clevelanders were expected to jam through the turnstiles for the game. In addition to that, the field and weather conditions promised to be challenging, especially for the visiting team.

In Baltimore NFL football was played in a brick-and-concrete fortress. Memorial Stadium was like an ugly cousin to Yankee Stadium. It had a similar shape and dimensions to the Bronx venue, but none of the fine architectural details that made Yankee Stadium so iconic, historic, and memorable. Yankee Stadium's magisterial frieze draped from the upper deck and lent a solemn importance to the events on the field. Its monument park thickened the atmosphere with history and deep meaning, much as the battlefield statues did at Gettysburg.

Memorial Stadium's best features were all on its exterior. The entrance behind home plate was a huge war memorial that featured distinctive, handcrafted aluminum lettering expertly shaped into an Art Deco font by skilled artisans. This facade poetically declared that the sacrifices of American soldiers were ageless and never to be forgotten. "Time will not dim the glory of their deeds," it said, a quotation from General John J. "Black Jack" Pershing, a genuine American hero. The stadium bowels protected an impressive urn that contained sacred soil from every American military graveyard in the world.

Memorial Stadium was charmingly tucked into a working-class neighborhood. Picturesque houses were visible from its open end. The stadium's boundaries were rimmed with two stately high school edifices. One of them, City College, was a magnificent stone castle, a medieval temple of learning such as the type where Merlin might have taught the young Arthur metaphysics. City College produced some of the finest men in the state, including multiple Baltimore mayors and Maryland governors, respected journalists, and glorious athletes. Weather impacted Memorial Stadium, of course, as it did all outdoor venues. It could be ice cold for football. Blinding fogs might roll in and enshroud the action, making ghosts of the players, like the Angel of Death did to the Egyptians in *The Ten Commandments*. A late-season contest in Baltimore could also feature a light dusting or even a heavy snowfall. But overall Memorial Stadium was like Baltimore Harbor: it was deep inland, cozy, and safe from the extremes.

Cleveland's Municipal Stadium, by contrast, was huge and cavernous. Built on the shores of Lake Erie, it was often victim to an angry nature, especially the cruel winds and crippling lake-effect snows that descended on the town as if from a great, god-like machine. The experts were as sanguine about Baltimore's ability to adapt and thrive in those conditions as Napoléon and his troops ever were storming across the Russian border.

# SEVEN

# Story Lines

As the championship game approached, the writers followed many story lines. One narrative was about Blanton Collier, the old mentor squaring off against Don Shula, his former protégé. When Collier was a Browns assistant in the '50s, Shula was one of his players. And, of course, Shula had only recently been one of Collier's assistant coaches at the University of Kentucky.

The way the writers saw it, though, Shula might've taught Collier everything. To them Shula was a star, self-possessed, with a youthful charm and a kind of cranky charisma. He was still young and handsome and had the sheen of a John F. Kennedy with a whistle. Like the martyred former president, Shula had wrested control of a sacred institution, one usually entrusted only to an older and wiser head, yet delivered masterful results.

Collier, on the other hand, was flat and unexciting. To a large extent he still lived in the cold, dark shadow of his dour and exiled predecessor. No one, it seemed, had noticed that in Collier's two years in Cleveland, the Browns had won more games than anyone in football, including Shula's Colts and Vince Lombardi's Packers.

There was one crucial story line that bizarrely received little notice or analysis. On Christmas Day, the Friday before the championship game, the *Washington Post* reported that Unitas had been suffering from a sore throwing arm. Shula scoffed at the very idea. "You saw him pass against the Redskins, didn't you?" the coach rhetorically scolded an inquiring reporter. "His arm looked all right, didn't it?"

But even as Shula energetically insisted there was no problem, Unitas bluntly confirmed that there was one.

"I hurt my arm about five games ago," the quarterback admitted. "It gets sore but treatments take care of it and I have no trouble whatever with it when I pass."

Interestingly, the revelation provoked no panic in Baltimore and no elation in Cleveland. Such was the faith that friends and foes alike had in the indestructibility of Johnny U. Like so much else about Unitas, this aspect of his legend was born in 1958. That's when, in midseason, the Packers broke two of his ribs and punctured one of his lungs. The very serious injury forced him out of the lineup for two, crucial, midseason games. But it couldn't keep him down for long. As soon as his lung reinflated he returned to action with the help of a crude aluminum cast. Despite his frightening injury, Unitas never missed a beat. He quickly regained his superb form and led the team to its first title.

That incredible display of toughness convinced the Colts of Unitas's immortality. After the season they traded their well-regarded backup, George Shaw, still in his prime, to the New York Giants, and they never even bothered to replace him. In case of emergency defensive back Andy Nelson was expected to step in behind center. That meant Unitas was the only full-time quarterback listed on the Colts' roster for 1959. If he felt any pressure from that fact, it didn't show in his performance. He enjoyed one of the greatest seasons a quarterback ever had, throwing thirty-two touchdown passes for the year. No one else in the history of the game had ever thrown thirty before. Meanwhile, he coughed up the ball only fourteen times. Unitas won the MVP Award and led the Colts to their second straight title. But that sensational performance only obscured the fact that Johnny U played the entire year with broken vertebrae, cracked in the preseason. In both 1961 and 1963 he suffered jammed and swollen fingers but played admirably through that pain, too. To the extent that the public was aware of these insults to his body and health, they looked at his magnificent performances and concluded that he simply wasn't vulnerable to the same dangers, fears, and threats as other men.

Unitas's peers in the NFL might have been even more impressed with his ruggedness than the fans were. His greatest admirers, it seemed, were the very best defensive linemen.

Bill Curry, the Colts' starting center in the late 1960s, recalled a game against the Rams in which Hall of Fame tackle Merlin Olsen broke free for a direct shot on the Colts' quarterback.

"I hit him with all my might," Olsen told Curry. "I drove my shoulder pad into his sternum, picked him up, and drove him into the dirt."

After such a hit Olsen liked to look into a quarterback's eyes to see the pain and especially the fear. Unitas not only disappointed Olsen but turned the spell of foreboding back on the lineman. "I got nothing," Olsen said. "Just those cold eyes glaring into mine. It was unnerving. I knew—we knew—he was going to get us sooner or later."

Detroit's Alex Karras, another one of the era's best defensive linemen, didn't even bother trying to intimidate Unitas. Dan Sullivan, a mainstay on the Colts' line throughout the decade, noticed something unusual about the way the usually violent Karras let up on Johnny U.

"Karras would come free a lot of times, you know, and when he could've really creamed Unitas, he just kind of put his arms around him," Sullivan said. "So I said to Karras one day after the game, 'How come you don't try and put Unitas out of the game?' Karras said, 'Because he's as tough as any guy playing up front, and I admire him for that.' Unitas had the admiration of all the opponents that we played against," Sullivan said. "He was one tough SOB."

A little more than a decade later, acknowledging the marquee value of the quarterback, as well as the damage inflicted on the position by the game, the league changed its rules both to protect quarterbacks and to increase their influence on the contest. Ironically, the mythology and allure of the quarterback would only decrease, as he was transformed from the most fearless and feared man on the field to the most privileged. His courage had once been defined by his vulnerability. He was, after all, willing to stand almost still while acts of savagery played out all around him. On most passing plays he was ferociously hit in the legs, back, chest, or knees, though it wasn't unusual for him to also take direct blows to the head and face. Many of the most painful clouts were delivered well after the ball had already been flung toward its target. Even in those brutish days that kind of play was technically illegal but an accepted custom of the game. If a team played an exceptionally good quarterback, it wasn't unusual for the opposing defense to take a collection before the game and give the proceeds to any player who could knock the signal caller out. The successful quarterbacks were cerebral in the face of these dangers. They seemed to ignore the very real threats to their own well-being while simultaneously outthinking their attackers. It was as though they were asked to play chess on an exploding board. The quarterbacks who could do it well were revered even among their enemies.

Quarterback pain was detailed in monochrome photographs and reproduced in newsprint. It was also evident in television slow-motion replays, just then coming into vogue. The newspaper image of New York's Y. A. Tittle on his knees, blood streaming down his face from the crown of his bald head, elicited admiration and pathos in other men. Because of its raw emotion the photo became one of the twentieth century's most iconic sports images. It perfectly captured the peril and indomitability of the effective quarterback who had to display grace under fire, just as Ernest Hemingway explained a true man would. The quarterback had become a metaphor for the modern American male who also felt besieged by dangers—in his career, his military obligations, and even his marriage. It was an era of increasingly sinister city streets, domestic gunfire, drug lords, and political assassinations. Authors such as Truman Capote and Norman Mailer explored a new American literature that captured the drifting loners who would kill for no reason at all. Country singer Johnny Cash emerged from the "Bible Belt" but went far beyond its narrow limits to cultivate an outlaw image. His songs were about jailbirds and brawlers, pill poppers and cocaine shooters, wife beaters and murderers. Many of his protagonists were spinning their sad tales from behind bars. The most popular album he ever recorded was taped live at Folsom Prison, where inmates could be heard on the tracks cheering and shouting their felonious approval of Cash, a man who had done a little time himself. In that era even Uncle Sam was sometimes derided as a "murderer," responsible for blasting and bombing the indigenous peoples of both Korea and Vietnam, not to mention wasting the lives of American boys in uniform, who fought for what? Nobody knew.

The world offered the modern American man many choices, but obscured and endangered the winning one. Every Sunday the pro quarterback personified all of that.

After the rules changed, however, the old "field generals" became something different. Jack Lambert, the toothless and pitiless Steelers linebacker of the 1970s, summed it up best when he snarled, "Quarterbacks should be wearing dresses." His criticism was leveled through the atomic megaphone of Howard Cosell on *Monday Night Football*, where tens of millions of Americans were tuned in to Lambert and his taunts.

Ironically, Lambert attacked an admirable group of signal callers who were then still active in the league. These men included Lambert's own teammate Terry Bradshaw, as well as Oakland's Kenny "the Snake" Stabler, Roger Staubach of the Cowboys, Miami's Bob Griese, and also Unitas's worthy successors in Baltimore and San Diego, Bert Jones and Dan Fouts. Lambert may well have been wrong about this rugged generation, but with time, as the rules evolved to further separate quarterbacks from football players, his cranky observation would make him seem like a prophet.

By the 1980s sensational talents like John Elway and Dan Marino had entered the league and put up statistics that guys like Bobby Layne and Bart Starr could only imagine. Elway's and Marino's powerful throwing arms were assisted by rule changes that shifted football's paradigm. Offensive tackles, for instance, were finally free to work with their arms extended into a defensive end in order to hold him at bay. This was a stark contrast to the blockers of the '60s, who were required to face the Deacon Joneses of the world with their hands tight to their own chests. Meanwhile, Deacon was unencumbered by the rules and could deliver solid cracks to any opposing lineman's skull. Dubbed the "head slap" by Deacon, this tactic was meant to stun the tackle while Deacon galloped to the quarterback's ear hole. The new rules also afforded the next generation of quarterbacks another extravagant advantage: their receivers were allowed to run the field, unmolested, after the first 5 yards from scrimmage. Previously, linebackers and defensive backs could harass receivers all the way down the field.

By the mid-1970s the quarterback no longer enjoyed the status of bravest man on the turf. It was as if he were now part of an aristocracy, where his community was gated and his kids attended private schools. His health and interests, once most at risk on the field, were suddenly in a protective cocoon, closely guarded by the men who made the rules and collected the receipts. As a result, passing statistics rose across the board. Quarterbacks threw more often, for more yards, and for a higher completion percentage than ever before. Passing touchdowns were on the rise, and interceptions were down. The very best quarterbacks were topping the 4,000-yard marker, and the scoreboards were lighting up like pinball machines.

Almost fifty years after tough guys like Norm Van Brocklin and Y. A. Tittle had defined the position, the transformation from the tough to the entitled would reach its apex with Tom Brady of the New England Patriots. Brady entered professional football much as Unitas did, rising from the ignominy of a late-round draft pick. In a way Brady was as emblematic of his generation as Unitas was of his. The world had moved from the authentic to things that were touted as authentic. In Brady's America there were virtual reality and reality shows. In the world Unitas knew, there was only reality.

The quarterbacks of Unitas's era threw fewer times for fewer yards and less touchdowns. They threw far more interceptions. Their accomplishments appear much less impressive than their successors over the decades. But in the 1960s playing quarterback in the NFL was dangerous and difficult. It *really* was.

# EIGHT

## The 1964 Championship Game

If Johnny Unitas had a sore arm heading into the championship game, no one believed it would make any difference. A madman could have broken into his hotel room the night before the game and severed his right wing at the shoulder with a Black and Decker saw, and still everyone in Baltimore, everyone in the country, would have fervently believed three things: Johnny U would show, he would play, and he would find a way to win.

On Christmas Eve, just a couple of days before the game, another critical injury might have occurred. As the Colts practiced a fight broke out between two seemingly inconsequential players: defensive tackle John Diehl and fullback and punter Joe Don Looney.

"John and Joe rammed into each other and they grabbed hold of each other with both hands," Shula told the *Baltimore News American*. "Others jumped in to pull them apart. And that was the end of it. No punches were thrown so I guess it won't qualify as a fight at all."

Over the next few days Shula would point to that episode several times as evidence that the Colts' practices were "spirited" and engaged leading up to the championship contest. But fisticuffs were nothing new for Joe Don. As many teammates and coaches already knew, Looney wasn't only a name; it was a perfect description.

Before sojourning to Baltimore, the peripatetic Joe Don had brief stays with four colleges and the New York Giants. The son of former NFL player Don Looney, a Steeler and an Eagle in the 1940s, Joe Don seemed bred to football stardom the way others are to a throne. He had a tousle of black hair, a handsome if coarse face, and a body that was large but well proportioned and improbably built for speed.

Among his many contradictions, he managed to be both a magnificent football player yet quickly unwanted by virtually every coach and teammate with whom he had ever come into contact. The first program to fall victim to his siren was the University of Texas. He lasted only a single semester there, as his academic achievement was found somewhat lacking. He took five classes and received four Fs and a D. Naturally, that performance sent him packing. He landed at his father's alma mater, Texas Christian University, but things didn't go well for him there, either. That left him busted down to junior college, and in 1961 he enrolled at Cameron, where he led the Aggies to the Junior Rose Bowl title and the National Junior College Championship.

That success propelled Joe Don back to the big time. The next season he played for Oklahoma and was a weapon of mass destruction. With his speed and size he was a threat to score from anywhere on the field. He sprinted 60 yards for a touchdown against Syracuse. Against Kansas his touchdown came after a 61-yard run. He really pummeled Iowa State. The Cyclones were nothing more than a cool breeze to Joe Don. He raced into the end zone three times against them and passed for another touchdown. Joe Don also led the nation in punting.

Thanks in large part to Looney's performance, the Sooners won the Big Eight Championship and went to the Orange Bowl. But that was about the high point of Looney's entire football career.

In the spring Joe Don said he was quitting football to run track. The coaches on that squad clocked him at 9.5 in the 100-yard dash. It was a lightning time, especially for a 230-pounder.

In the fall he was back on the football team, but not for long. After just three games he had a dispute with an assistant coach in which he supposedly slugged a young graduate assistant in the face. Coach Bud Wilkinson, at the request of the Sooners players, dismissed him from the team.

Despite this checkered history and a lack of playing time in Looney's senior year, the New York Giants chose Joe Don with their very first pick in the 1964 draft, number twelve overall. They instantly regretted it.

Looney reported to training camp sullen and difficult. He created a minor furor and embarrassed the organization when he declined to speak to reporters. After that he frustrated and defied his coaches by refusing to have his ankles taped, a standard precaution taken by all players. After that he simply refused to attend team meetings.

Not knowing what else to do, the Giants asked their highly respected veteran quarterback Y. A. Tittle to talk some sense into Looney. They hoped that a benign father figure might persuade him to calm down. But even the great quarterback had no luck: "I've been in pro football for 16 years, and I've seen a lot of rookies come and go," Tittle said, "but I have never met one like him before."

After several more weeks of late arrivals and skipped practices, the Giants had had enough. They traded him to Baltimore, eager to acquire another part for its still rebuilding running game, while the Giants got two players who had seen better days. One was creaky, old R. C. Owens, a ballplayer with virtually nothing left in the tank. The other was the once magnificent defensive back Andy Nelson, who was also at the end of his career.

Meanwhile, Looney, the number-one draft pick, had been a Giant for all of twenty-eight days.

In Baltimore Shula gave Looney a clean slate, and two jobs. On offense he was a backup fullback, and on special teams he was the starting punter. The Colts seemed to succeed with Looney where the Giants had failed. Baltimore trainers protected his now infamous ankles by taping them outside of his socks. Generally, they babied him in that way, making meaningless concessions to which he seemed to respond. He came to practice and attended team meetings, and he was prompt to both. On special teams he was a true asset. He ranked among the league leaders in punting, with an average 42.4 yards per punt. He boomed one for 64 yards.

The Colts had the magic touch, it seemed. They were the Looney whisperers.

But then one night in November that all changed.

On this particular evening Looney and his roommate, Preston Ray Smith, an old high school friend, were drinking beer at their apartment. Smith later testified that they were "intoxicated." Like many young men in that state, they decided to go hunting for women, specifically three nurses who lived in their building. The only problem with their plan was they were too drunk to find the correct apartment. Instead, they happened on the residence of Robert Schu, a neighbor who was at home with his young wife, baby son, and their friends Mr. and Mrs. Richard Smith from Philadelphia.

Convinced that the nurses were inside Schu's apartment, Looney started banging on the door. Mr. Schu pleaded with Looney, through the locked doorway, telling him that the girls he sought were not in the apartment. That disappointing news only enraged Looney, who insisted that Schu was lying to him. Joe Don commenced to smashing at the door so violently that the wives retreated to a bedroom and locked that door while they screamed in horror.

Eventually, Looney knocked the front door completely down and entered the apartment. Preston desperately tried to keep Joe Don from attacking anyone, but to no avail. Looney continued to exchange words with Schu before finally striking and spitting on Richard Smith, Schu's out-of-town guest.

Meanwhile, as this violent and maniacal scene played out, the two wives and the baby slipped out of the bedroom window and ran to alert the police about the home invasion. Looney and his buddy Preston were both arrested.

In Baltimore Municipal Court the two malefactors faced Judge I. Sewell Lamdin. Their cases were heard separately. In the morning Preston Ray Smith told Judge Lamdin how he had tried in vain to calm Looney down and talk him out of harming the men in the apartment. Nevertheless, Smith was found guilty and given a suspended six-month jail sentence by the judge, thus ensuring a criminal record for the young man.

In the afternoon Looney was at the mercy of the very same judge but got a different brand of justice. At first, Judge Lamdin talked tough. "Had you broken down my door," the distinguished jurist told Looney, "I would have shot you."

Despite those mean and manly words, jurisprudence in Baltimore went only so far. Judge Lamdin was clearly unwilling to punish a Colt in the midst of the team's best season since '58. So

Looney—the culprit who bashed the door down, punched and spit on the victim, terrorized the women, and traumatized the child—received probation before verdict. No criminal record.

The man in the robes who had only moments ago said he would have summarily executed Looney for knocking his door down wasn't willing to incarcerate him for even a single minute. He meekly ordered the ball player to pay $150 in fines and make restitution for half the door (Preston Ray Smith would pay the other half).

It wasn't hard to tell which defendant played in the NFL. Later in the day, perhaps ashamed of his own flagrant hypocrisy, the judge softened Preston Ray Smith's verdict to match Looney's.

To add insult to the victims' injuries, Looney's lawyer praised the outrageous verdict. He told the *Baltimore Sun* it would keep his client from developing "a persecution complex" and further menacing the Schus and Smiths. Of course, sending Looney to jail would have provided the victims an even greater sense of security, but the lawyer failed to mention that.

To their discredit the Colts treated the assault as though it was a fraternity-house prank. They fined Joe Don an undisclosed amount and downplayed the seriousness of his crime.

"We do not condone such action, but the boy shouldn't be castigated where this has happened just once," general manager Don Kellett said. Cameron Snyder, the *Sun*'s Colts beat reporter, perhaps too close to the team and its interests, referred to Looney's crime as a "minor breach of conduct episode." Shula "joked" about it and said, "Maybe the Colts should be housed in a motel on Tuesday nights [the evening of the incident] instead of Saturday [as was the custom]."

The donnybrook at Colts practice on Christmas Eve clearly wasn't a sign of "spirit," as Shula had called it. It was the further acting out of a mollycoddled child with a demented mind. It seemed that Looney was intent on drinking, fighting, and screwing his way out of the league.

What was worse, it was very likely that Looney was injured in his fracas with his teammate Diehl, just two days before the game, and now his gaudy punting foot would not be available for the Colts' most important day in five years.

Rather than being chastened by Looney's antics, others on the team seemed to catch the bad-behavior bug from him. The night before the game the Browns had a chance encounter with the Colts in a movie theater. Going to a film on the eve of a game was an old Paul Brown tactic devised to keep the players calm (that is, sober) and occupied until curfew. Collier and Shula, both Brown disciples, had picked up that practice. The only problem was that the coaches, unbeknownst to each other, had selected the same theater, for the same feature. The Browns arrived second and ended up seated right in front of the Colts. While James Bond, secret agent 007, fought a Cold War terrorist named Goldfinger on the screen, in the seats the Colts behaved like punks.

"Our game plan was to go to the movies and then go back to the hotel and get a good night's sleep," Cleveland quarterback Frank Ryan remembered. "But there was spitting and things like this raining down on us. I got up and left early. I cleared out."

Baltimore fans overlapped bad manners with overconfidence, though they were more humorous than boorish. The celebrated Colts Marching Band encountered the Browns eating breakfast in the hotel lobby and serenaded them with an impromptu rendition of "Taps." The impudence of that funereal performance seemed to reflect the attitude of everyone in Maryland. The day *before* the game, state, city, and airport officials sent out the word that they were hoping for calm in the wake of the team's victory. Under the headline "Please, No Reception," the *Evening Sun* published a small blurb urging Baltimoreans toward "something resembling sanity . . . when the Colts return from Cleveland." The game was still two days away, but in Baltimore they were already quelling the rowdy victory riots.

In Cleveland a vastly different story was unfolding. Dawn rose over a cold and damp city on game day. By kickoff temperatures had dipped to thirty-three chilling degrees, and winds were gusting off the lake at twenty knots. Municipal Stadium was foreboding. After a full season its turf was heavily scarred, and the real estate between the hash marks was reduced to a foul quagmire. It all added up to less than ideal conditions for a precision passer, and Unitas, of course, was the prototype of that breed.

The first half was brutal and defense oriented, with both teams running right at each other. The offenses were so archaic and unimaginative, the *New York Times* described it as "antediluvian" football.

Neither team threw very much. When they tried they didn't enjoy much success. Ryan was intercepted early, and Unitas, stymied, took off with the ball more than he tossed it. In the first thirty inartistic minutes of the game, there were four turnovers and not a single point was scored.

The Colts had a chance to crack the scoreboard first early in the second quarter when they lined up to kick from the Cleveland 22. But when the ball was snapped back to the holder, Bobby Boyd, the hand of fate intervened. A gust of swirling stadium wind grabbed the ball and pushed it from Boyd's grasp. Lou Michaels, the Colts' kicker, never got a toe on it.

The first half might have been dull, but it told two interesting stories. Number one, Cleveland's defense wasn't the same terrible unit that had statistically been the worst in the league. During the regular season the Browns defenders, compensating for their deficiencies, played conservatively. The Cleveland defensive backs customarily put plenty of cushion between themselves and their opponents' receivers. But in the championship game they gave Unitas something different to see than what he had surely watched on film.

"We've been known as a team that plays pass receivers very loose, giving them short yardage," Browns cornerback Bernie Parrish said. "I felt the Colts expected us to back off. I thought we would do better by playing their receivers closer."

Browns safety Ross Fichtner agreed. "We moved up and forced their receivers to cut before they wanted to," he said.

The idea was to disrupt Unitas and force him to hold the ball longer than he would like. "We decided," Coach Collier told journalists after the game, "that we wanted to have everybody covered when Unitas took his first look at his primary receiver. That way, he'd have to look for a second receiver. And if he still didn't see anyone open, maybe he'd wait some more. By then our pass rush should be on him."

Six times in the game that strategy forced Johnny U to lower his arm and take off with the ball himself. That suited the Browns just fine. "I'd rather see him run than pass," Bill Glass, Cleveland's defensive end, said.

The Browns were delighted to see Unitas running, but the Colts were paranoid about Jim Brown doing the very same thing. Baltimore's mighty defense, number one in the league, was hyper-aggressive and focused on not allowing Brown to be the one to beat them.

"We weren't overly awed by their defense," Frank Ryan said about the Colts, who had allowed only about sixteen points per game for the season. Baltimore "leaned towards a man-to-man coverage. [That] brought the defensive secondary up a little closer, and they could participate in stopping the running game. And they were also very adventurous on blitzing."

The Colts' tendencies were only magnified for the championship. They were sure that the Browns' only hope resided in Jim Brown's legs, and Baltimore's coaches took that threat seriously. Knowing from long experience that no one man could stop Brown, they vowed to swarm him. If Ryan was forced to throw, the Colts would limit what they thought was his best option and double-team the speedy rookie Paul Warfield.

All of this left Gary Collins in single coverage on the outside. The Colts weren't overly concerned about that, since the man who would cover Collins, Bobby Boyd, was one of the most competent defenders in the business. The bald cornerback had picked off nine enemy passes in 1964. In his eight years in pro football he had twenty-eight interceptions. Boyd played a key role in fueling the Colts' success, since every pickoff of an inaccurate passer (as Frank Ryan supposedly was) put the ball in Unitas's incomparable hands. But Boyd had a tall order in front of him. Gary Collins was six feet five and Boyd only five feet eleven. Literally half a foot separated them. Collins was also a pretty tough customer.

Gary Collins was born in coal country, Williamstown, Pennsylvania, in 1940. The town was in decline, even then, with fewer than three thousand residents. In 2010, after decades of steady erosion, there were only about a thousand souls still left there to keep the lights on. The Collins family was poor, and in that they had a lot in common with their neighbors. Collins's father worked several jobs to make ends meet. He descended down into the dark world of the coal mines for twelve years. Later on he fixed the fuel tanks on airplanes. Eventually, he owned his own small bar, and that brought him the only taste of success he would ever know. When he died at age fifty-eight with lungs full of coal dust, gas fumes, and cigarette smoke, he was both old and young.

Gary Collins was becoming a ray of hope in his decrepit hometown, even while his unlucky father was fading away. In his junior year of high school, only two weeks before the start of football season, Williamstown's starting running back broke his ankle. With no viable option apparent, the coach pulled the team together, looked around, and asked his boys a key question.

"Does anyone know the runner's plays?"

Collins was the only one who raised his hand. So he won the position by default. In the season opener, with almost no time to prepare for a completely new position, all he did was score five touchdowns.

And that was just the beginning.

In nineteen games during the Collins era, Williamstown High went 18-1. Gary's athleticism seemed to know no bounds. In addition to his versatility on the football field, he could dunk a basketball. In baseball he was both a pitcher and a shortstop with a rocket arm and a booming bat. Collins was so adept on the diamond, he attracted offers from the Cincinnati Reds and the Baltimore Orioles, two shrewd organizations that were both gearing up to win multiple World Series championships.

Nevertheless, Collins had decided that football would be his ticket out of Williamstown. Though he was swimming in offers, he chose Maryland for reasons he could never quite remember. It certainly didn't hurt the Terps' chances that they sent veteran assistant John Idzik to recruit him. Idzik had also gone to Maryland and was just gaining his footing in a coaching career that would last from the early '50s to the 1980s. Idzik's odyssey through the game led him from the college ranks to the Canadian Football League to the NFL. Idzik told Collins's mother that Gary would be an All-American before his junior season. That lavish assessment must have created some sort of advantage for Maryland because Collins ultimately chose the Terps.

Gary excelled at College Park, but only after he got off to a slow, unhappy start.

"I had a separated shoulder, and I wasn't doing well," he said many years later. "My first wife was pregnant when I was eighteen or nineteen, and I had trouble with the books. It was awful."

For the first time in his life, even his athletic career wasn't going well. At two-a-day practices in July and August Collins was relegated to the fourth string. This could have been a result of his separated shoulder or, more likely, due to his poor relationship with his head coach.

Tom Nugent came to Maryland to follow in the footsteps of legends like Bear Bryant and Jim Tatum, but he had already made something of a name for himself at the Virginia Military Institute and Florida State. It was at VMI, his first job, that Nugent earned his lifelong reputation as an innovator who influenced coaches far more successful and famous than he was.

In his first season Nugent's "Keydets" lost in a humiliating defeat to in-state rival William and Mary. "Bill and the Bitch," as the school from Williamsburg was crudely called, dished out a beating to VMI, 54–6. That loss haunted Nugent, and in the off-season he struggled to find a way to counter W&M's strong defensive line and linebackers. The solution he eventually developed was the "I formation," a variation on the T, in which the fullback and halfback line up in a straight line directly behind the quarterback. The virtues of the formation were many: it offered power and deception, a platform to run inside the tackles with a fullback either carrying the ball in a quick burst or escorting the halfback through the hole as an additional blocker. The formation was also effective for running outside, especially sweeps. If the preference was to pass "the I's," running backs provided either extra pocket protection or low-risk "flare" receiver options for the quarterback.

The next season, with Nugent's innovation at the ready, VMI upset William and Mary in the rematch. They also knocked off Georgia Tech, which was favored by twenty-eight points. VMI racked up more than 400 yards of offense in both games. In the two years after Nugent developed and implemented the I, VMI went 13-7 overall and 10-1 in its own Southern Conference. In the highly imitative world of football, it didn't take long for Nugent's ideas to catch the eye of coaches at the country's most prestigious programs. Soon John McKay at Southern Cal and Frank Leahy at Notre Dame were both running the offense. They did so with such sensational results that the I formation came to be more highly associated with them than Nugent, the man who invented it.

In 1953 Nugent moved to Florida State, where he coached Lee Corso and Burt Reynolds, among other luminaries. He took over a Seminole program that was fewer than ten years old and had won only a single game in 1952. But in just two seasons Nugent's Seminole tribe had an eight-win season and was invited to the Sun Bowl.

Nugent moved on again in 1959, this time to Maryland, where his direct predecessor was Jim Tatum. Tatum's Terps had only recently gone undefeated and won the national championship. The year 1959 was also Collins's first full season at Maryland. Though the convergence of two such seminal men at the same school, at the same time, should have foretold great things, the coupling of Nugent and Collins was never easy. Collins's personal problems depressed him and compounded the physical pain he felt from his separated shoulder. Though he started summer practice on the fourth string, by the beginning of the season he was not only a starter but a virtual sixty-minute man. On offense he was the Terps' number-one receiver. On defense he played a hybrid of end and safety, a kind of stand-up linebacker who sacked quarterbacks and intercepted their passes, too. On special teams he both boomed and blocked punts.

Nugent called Collins "the finest player I ever coached," but Collins said, "Nugent was just a jerk." Collins insisted that his coach's compliments were "just for the press." Man-to-man Collins never felt any warmth from Nugent and felt no attachment to him. "Some guys would come up and say, 'How're you feeling today?' or put an arm around you. Nugent didn't even know guys' names," Collins said.

Despite the lack of personal chemistry with his coach, Collins's accomplishments at Maryland were larger than life. On defense he stuffed Syracuse's great Heisman-winning running back, Ernie Davis, twice at the goal line. That led the Terps to an upset of the Orangemen. Collins picked off passes from future professional standouts such as Roman Gabriel and Norm Snead, then both playing in the Atlantic Coast Conference. On special teams he punted into the corners and blocked punts to win games.

As an offensive player he was simply spectacular, diving and darting, showing off the hands and moves that would distinguish him for most of the next decade, even among the finest pros. With Collins leading the way, in 1961, the Terps beat Penn State 21–17. That would be the only time Maryland would defeat the Nittany Lions in thirty-seven games, close to forty years.

Although Collins could seemingly do it all on a football field, his passion was reserved for catching the ball. Since early childhood it was all he wanted to do. He grew up an Eagles fan, but at Maryland he chose number 82, the same number as his hero, Raymond Berry. Collins admired Berry's preparation and meticulous attention to detail. He studied the Colts' receiver's game, and he sought to emulate him in every way.

From watching Berry he learned that a receiver's speed should be measured not vertically but by point of break. "Everybody thought I was a slow son of a bitch. I was faster than Raymond Berry. A guy doesn't necessarily have to be a 9.4 sprinter to get out there 15 yards quicker than [even a great runner]," Collins said.

Bob Hayes was a case in point. Known as "Bullet Bob," the sprinter went to the Tokyo Olympics and came home with two gold medals, each one representing a new world record. If Collins lacked speed, Hayes dripped with it. But when Collins met Hayes at his first Pro Bowl, he noticed something interesting.

"Running outs at 15 yards," Collins said, "I was getting to the sideline faster than Hayes. Don Meredith couldn't understand that."

The physics of it may have befuddled Meredith, but Collins was practically a professor on the subject. He summed up the phenomenon thusly: "If you can't break left and right as a pass receiver," he said, "you ain't worth shit."

Collins had one receiver's virtue that the nearsighted Berry lacked, and that was great vision. In that respect Gary was like Ted Williams, the Red Sox star whose magnificent hitting was often explained in terms of superhuman visual faculties. "The Thumper," it was said, could see the individual laces on the baseball as it approached his bat. Collins claimed, "With the proper break [he] could see the ball leaving the [quarterback's] hand. If I could pick up the ball at that point, I could adjust and catch [even] a bad pass," he said.

Eyesight, footwork, and great size and strength took Collins a long way. He left Maryland in style, selected number four by Cleveland in the 1962 NFL draft and also number four by Boston in the AFL draft. When he chose to sign with the Browns, he became the first player ever selected during owner Art Modell's long reign over the franchise.

So this was the man across from Bobby Boyd, the one Boyd was left out on an island to cover. The Colts' cornerback might have been overmatched on paper, but he wasn't overly concerned. He had successfully covered tall receivers before.

In '62 and '63 Boyd had to face R. C. Owens in practice every day. Before coming to Baltimore from San Francisco, the six-foot-three end with kangaroo legs famously teamed with the magnificent quarterback Y. A. Tittle. Owens and Tittle had invented a pass pattern known throughout the NFL as the "Alley Oop." The name was a phrase French acrobats screamed just before they leaped into the air. In the parlance of the NFL, it became code for an unsophisticated yet devastatingly effective pattern in which Owens ran to a spot in the end zone where Tittle would heave the ball high into the air in his general direction. Owens would simply outleap defenders to pluck the ball from the fluffy clouds as if it were a piece of fruit. R.C. was basically a modern-day NBA player in a helmet and chinstrap; nevertheless, Boyd covered him, and pretty much everyone else in the league, with great efficiency. The Colts' cornerback had no concerns about Collins, but perhaps he should have. Cleveland's end was taller, stronger, and a great deal younger than Owens.

In the Colts' zeal to cover Warfield and contain Jim Brown, Frank Ryan saw his moment. "When you're playing a man-to-man defense and particularly a blitzing defense, you get just gargantuan opportunities," he said.

Those opportunities didn't come until the second half, but they came. Early in the third quarter Tom Gilburg, the replacement for the injured Joe Don Looney, trotted in to punt. Gilburg was primarily an offensive tackle, though he was considered an excellent punter as a collegiate player at Syracuse. Kicking into the teeth of the bitter wind, Gilburg could muster only a 25-yard punt. That gave the Browns the ball on Baltimore's own 47-yard line. With that advantage Ryan called on Jim Brown, not as a runner but as a receiver. Ryan threw a flare pass to the punishing fullback, who gained 11 yards with it.

That was all the offense the Browns needed. After two more Ryan passes fell incomplete, ancient Lou "the Toe" Groza lumbered in to attempt a 43-yard field goal. An offensive tackle as well as a kicker, Lou was well acquainted with championship-game pressure. His career stretched so far back, he had been an original member of the Browns, starting when they were still in the old All-America Football Conference. The Toe was a henchman of Otto Graham's and had already won seven professional football championships (AAFC and NFL) in his long career before he faced the Colts in '64. He was a straight-ahead kicker, in the inefficient style of that era, but he was the greatest of them, unusually accurate and reliable. Unlike the Colts who had botched their field goal attempt earlier in the game, the Toe effortlessly stepped into the ball with his squared-off boot, and it twirled flawlessly through the parallel beams, painted brown and orange.

Though Unitas stood on the other sideline with the most potent offense in the game all around him, the Browns' unimpressive drive, culminating in Groza's field goal and the paltry three points it put on the board, somehow created a fissure in the supposedly impenetrable Colts.

In the Browns' next possession the game's true heroes would emerge. The Colts' worst fear was realized when Jim Brown took a quick pitch from Ryan and rumbled down the field with it. With a guard and tackle leading his way and even Warfield blocking Baltimore's defensive end, Brown rumbled for 46 hard-won yards before Baltimore's Lenny Lyles frantically grabbed him in a last-ditch effort and brought him down.

Frank Ryan knew that something pivotal had happened. The score was still only 3–0, but Brown's escape and mad dash played into Colts paranoia. Dr. Ryan might not have been a genius, as the sportswriters kept insisting, but he knew that the Colts' haunting fears of Jim Brown and a Browns running game out of their control suddenly made them more vulnerable than ever to the pass. With horseshoes surrounding Warfield on every snap, Ryan turned to the least covered man on the field, Gary Collins.

"On the very next play," Ryan said, "I called Collins on what we called 'a shake.'" In that play Collins was supposed to fake to the post and then break back out, going deep to the right. But the Colts' exertions caused a change in plans.

Ryan said that "Collins got down there, and he got bumped around by Boyd. In the meantime, I was being rushed by their defensive line, and I had to sort of scramble up into the pocket."

As Ryan maneuvered he noticed that Collins was not where he expected him. "I saw Gary changing the course of things in the end zone," the quarterback said, "and instead of going for the far-right corner, he was coming back across the middle of the goal."

With the Colts' two great defensive ends Gino Marchetti and Ordell Braase bearing down in a sort of pincer movement from either side, the only place Ryan had to go was forward. He sprinted toward the line of scrimmage, and as he did so he saw Collins coming back across the end zone and flung the ball in his direction.

"Boyd was all over him in his initial route," Ryan said. "But both [Collins] and I adapted ourselves to the circumstances of the play."

In addition to his improvisation, Ryan's play call had also outfoxed the Colts. After Brown's long run, and with the ball now residing just 20 yards from the goal line, he knew the defense had to fear the threat of Brown more than ever. So coming out of the huddle, he had the Browns line up in a formation from which they traditionally ran. The Colts, who had seen it all on film, called the setup a double wing, because it had two tight ends lining up next to two receivers, one pair on the left side of the line and one pair on the right. The Colts braced themselves for another attack by Jim Brown, but Ryan crossed them up and passed. It was a call worthy of Unitas, who often summed up successful play calling by claiming it was as simple as this: "Well, you run when they think you're going to pass, and you pass when they think you are going to run."

And, indeed, the formation Ryan showed caused some confusion on the Colts' defense.

"Our safety misread the way we were supposed to rotate," Bobby

Boyd said. "I was the deep outside, and our safety was supposed to be in the middle of the field and misread the play." In other words, the Colts' cornerback had expected help in the middle that never arrived.

"They had a tight end, and we were to rotate to him when they came out in those formations," Boyd said. Instead, "The safety went the wrong way. I had the deep outside, and [Collins] went right down the middle. I'm sure people thought I was to blame, but I wasn't."

No matter whose fault it was, the Colts' defenders were so confused, they were less of an impediment to the play's success than the goalpost.

"It hit me in my mind as I was throwing the ball that I might hit the goalpost with it," Frank Ryan said.

In those days the goalpost was set on the goal line, it had not yet been moved to the back of the end zone. This fact had thwarted Ryan and Collins's touchdown ambitions several times throughout the year. "At least twice, maybe three times that season, I threw passes to Gary Collins wide open in the end zone, and it would hit the crossbar or one of the other stands holding the goals up there," Ryan said.

Collins had the same fear as his quarterback. He wasn't sure whether the ball would reach him. "It was a broken pattern, and I almost missed it. I thought it was going to hit the goalpost, and I juggled it," he admitted.

But Collins's sure hands put an end to those worries; he ultimately embraced the ball. More important, by the time Lou the Toe put the extra point through the uprights, the Browns already had nine more points than they would need all day.

Now the sluice was wide open, and the Browns' attack was careening down the chute.

Ryan preyed upon the Colts at the intersection of their fears and strengths. As the game was slipping from their grasp, the Colts seemed to learn nothing from the success of Jim Brown on the ground or the openings that were created for Collins. Instead of adapting and perhaps loosening up their coverages a little so that they might confuse Ryan, where intimidation had not yet worked, the Colts' defense seemed to bear down even more.

Ryan was determined to use that against them.

"When you play man-to-man," Ryan said, "it is really hard-nosed football. You're right on top of the situation, and you're gonna stomp them and kick their butts. But it opens up just remarkable opportunities for doing a little finesse."

One of those opportunities came in Cleveland's next possession. A close observer could almost see Ryan's brilliant mind at work as he tried to make the desperate Baltimore defense collapse on the weight of its own aggressiveness.

When the Browns got the ball around midfield, Ryan wasted a play on a simple run that went nowhere. But the second play tipped his hand a little and revealed his desire to deceive. He called a reverse to Paul Warfield, putting the ball in the great receiver's hands as a runner instead of a pass catcher. But the play did worse than nothing and lost 3 yards.

Ryan had one more play left and one more small deception. "It was about third and 13," he remembered. "We're about on the 45-yard line going in, and I called a hook and go to Gary Collins, who was, I think, on the weak side. So he went down and did his little dip in and I faked the ball at him, and the defensive back just about fell out of his pants trying to get in front of Gary on the hook. But Gary was going south on the post pattern by the time he figured that out, and [Collins] was just extraordinarily wide open and there wasn't anybody within 20 yards of him when he caught the ball.

"That play selection was very unexpected to [the Colts], I'm sure. They had a very tight coverage out there, trying to prevent us from getting a first down, and I just made up my mind, 'Let's go for it.' There was nobody on our team [who] expected me to call that play."

The Colts clearly weren't expecting it, either. The result was another touchdown from Ryan to Collins, and the game was effectively over.

The Colt who bit on the fake was Bobby Boyd. Again he appeared to be victimized by Collins, but again he expected help from safety Jim Welch that never came. Boyd simply, sadly, said, "Our safety went the wrong way twice."

Gary Collins, of all people, agreed: "[Boyd] was supposed to get post help. I ran like a curl, then took off, and the safety, Welch, fell. It wasn't Bobby's fault, but the corner's gonna look bad."

When he reflected on his good fortune that day, Ryan was kind to all the Colts' defenders whom he had humbled. "The issue was the coverage and not the individual," he said. "Anytime we played against man-to-man coverage, we felt we could eat it up. If you've got good receivers, as we had, they're going to get away from those tightly covered situations."

All in all, Cleveland put up seventeen points in the third quarter, but the Colts' torturous day was far from complete.

The fourth quarter featured another Groza field goal, this one from just 10 yards, and then the third and final act of the Boyd-Collins duel unfolded.

Collins took off on a straight "fly pattern" that saw him streaking for the goal line. Boyd tightly shadowed him step for step in perfect coverage. But Ryan and Collins's day of perfection continued. Collins maneuvered his huge body between Boyd and the ball and boxed out his opponent, much like a well-coached basketball player would. As the pigskin approached, Boyd leaped to intercept it, but it was Collins who came down with Ryan's meticulously placed pass. Boyd almost seemed to have a finger on the ball before Collins snatched it away. After the catch Boyd bounced off Collins and just slid to the ground. Meanwhile, Collins dashed to the end zone with his third touchdown.

"It was just a big guy versus a little guy," Collins said. "I brushed him off, and he fell."

After the game the Colts were stunned, but, to their credit, they met the press. For Shula, young and emotional, that may not have been a great idea. Although the Colts had performed poorly in virtually every football category—they botched a field goal, shanked a punt, gave up seventeen points in the third quarter alone and twenty-seven points in the second half, and got shut out—he singled out just one aspect of the team.

"We sure found out about the Cleveland defense, didn't we?" he rhetorically asked reporters. "You have to, however, talk about our lack of offense with their defense. Our offense never gave our defense any break. We sure didn't execute our offense very well. You can't give up the ball as many times as we did and come in here a winner."

The *New York Times* noted Shula's words and then decoded

them for anyone who didn't get his point. "Without mentioning names Shula expressed disappointment at the performance of his offense, led by Unitas," they wrote.

There was no rejoinder from Johnny U, but a rival NFL coach who was anonymous was probably not alone when he expressed this sentiment: "Shula 'did a lousy job' in preparing his team for the game," he said.

Gary Collins, who played the biggest part in defeating Baltimore, said there was really no one to blame on the other sideline. The secret to beating the indomitable Colts was simple. "It was just our day," he said. "It was all aligned. We made only five to seven mistakes—the entire team! We're gonna be hard to beat."

The searchlight of defeat found Unitas and Shula and revealed aspects of their characters that the public had never seen before.

Unitas, the most famous, admired, and respected player in football, was photographed on the field in an unusual pose. His arms were cross-folded on his chest in dejection, obscuring his number, 19. His head hung low. His eyes faced the ground.

Unitas had thrown for fewer than 100 yards; he was intercepted twice. His passer rating for the game was only 32.3. He had been badly outplayed by his unheralded Cleveland counterpart. The sting of embarrassment must have been great for a man who had already been MVP of two previous title games and was defined by his clutch performances. Yet Unitas swallowed hard. His demeanor in defeat, whatever his private humiliation, was as gracious as it ever was in his many victories. "When you go over to the Cleveland dressing room," Johnny U said to reporters, "tell Frank Ryan congratulations for me. He was great."

Just twenty-four hours before, Shula was distinguished among his peers for his precocious brilliance and tell-it-like-it-is toughness. But in the aftermath of such an unexpected and shameful defeat, those qualities had lost their charm. In lashing out and attaching so much veiled blame to his own quarterback, his star, his city's idol, he lost something of his own status as a miraculous prodigy and, for the day anyway, suddenly appeared callow. He too was caught in an unguarded moment by a photojournalist. Under a headline that read "We Know Just How You Feel," Shula was presented with his chin up and his eyes forward but his lower lip sticking far out in the manner of a petulant boy who is caught by his father misbehaving and is about to cry.

There was an odd and somewhat sad postscript to the saga of the '64 championship game. In the waning moments of the contest, as time ticked off the official clock, jubilation built on the Browns' bench, while bitterness crept its way through the Colts.

Enjoying the moment of his own redemption, Ryan sought to reward a hardworking but unheralded teammate with a little of the glory.

"We had the ball in the last minute down close to their end zone," he remembered. "I did call a play, which would have been a touchdown play if the pass had been caught, to John Brewer, who was our tight end. He hadn't caught a ball all day, and he had a great year that year blocking for the team. He was not a great receiver, and I just felt, well, jeez, maybe he can be a part of this thing, too. That's why I called the play. It wasn't really to run the score up on the Colts. It was intended to reach out to John Brewer.

"The Colts were understandably upset about it," Ryan said.

They let him know it by crowding around him after the play and filling his ears with profanities.

Ryan took the responsibility on himself: "I've come to the conclusion that I probably should have had a little more maturity than I exhibited," he said.

Gary Collins couldn't agree more, but he didn't think Ryan was the only Brown at fault. "Frank shouldn't have done it," the game MVP said. "'Course that was also Dub Jones's fault," Collins said, referring to the Browns' offensive coordinator. "Jim [Brown] should have said something. Somebody should have said something [to prevent the play call]."

In that one ill-advised pass, Ryan awoke a magnificent anger in Gino Marchetti, a man most people would hope never to cross in their lifetimes.

The legend that emerged was that an enraged Gino followed Ryan back into the Cleveland huddle and shouted, "I'm going to get you for this."

"I don't remember Marchetti saying anything like that," Ryan said. "But when we flew into Los Angeles for the Pro Bowl game a week or two later, the headlines of the paper that very day said:

'All I Want Is One More Shot at Ryan.' That quote was attributed to Marchetti."

Any sane man would have found that pronouncement a cause for alarm. Gino "the Giant," as he was called, was a notorious thumper, the last guy you wanted as your enemy.

Gino played in an era when quarterback sacks were not yet an official statistic. Nevertheless, the Colts' coaching staff examined game film after one season and informally counted the number of times Gino the Giant had brought down enemy quarterbacks. That number was forty.

Gino was not big by the standards of future generations of behemoth defensive linemen. He was only about six feet four and 245 pounds. Nevertheless, he had catlike reflexes, tremendous speed, and an arsenal of moves. He was also the unquestioned leader of the Colts.

Ryan was the Eastern Division's starting Pro Bowl quarterback that day. "In the first play of the second half, it wasn't just Marchetti. Four guys hit me simultaneously and sort of ground me into the ground," he remembered. "I was knocked out as well as having my shoulder separated. [Marchetti] must have had a delicious feeling about that."

"It was obvious Marchetti tried to hurt him," Gary Collins said. "He slammed him, chicken-winged him."

The league reported that Ryan had suffered a "slight muscle separation." The fact that he was knocked out cold and probably suffered a severe concussion didn't even rate a mention.

For Ryan that terrible moment of Marchetti's revenge and that "slight muscle separation" were only the beginning of a long, painful journey. He claimed that his injury might not have been as serious as it became had not the Pro Bowl physician treated him improperly, causing even worse damage.

"I realized my right shoulder hurt a little bit, and I'm a right-handed thrower," he said. "They had a team physician who was more or less a society doctor. What he did was counterproductive to the proper way to care for this injury. He bound it up in the wrong way or something like that. He had put a heavy bandage on my shoulder to sort of hold my shoulder bone down into my socket."

The rest of the story tells a gruesome tale of the primitive sports medicine that existed in the 1960s.

"The next day, when they took that [bandage] off to make a more thorough assessment of what had happened," Ryan said, "they could not get the adhesive off my skin without lacerating my skin. Because my skin was lacerated where they were going to operate, they refused to operate. Instead, they put me in a body cast—a cast around my body that I couldn't take off! They put a belt that went up from that cast over my right shoulder and down to my back that could be [cinched] up really tight and hold that bone down in place.

"So for the next six weeks I had this body cast on, trying to get this trauma to correct itself in a natural way since they couldn't operate. Eventually, I got out of the cast and started throwing the football again," he said.

Ryan was given an exercise regimen to help him regain his arm strength. Instead, it created even more unnecessary damage, this time to his elbow.

"It was a determining feature of my career," he said, "because as soon as I got into a program to restrengthen that shoulder, I began inadvertently to tear a tendon in my right elbow. In doing the exercises that were imposed upon me to get my shoulder better, they ended up pulling the big muscle that is on the inside of your right arm away from that little point in your elbow. Inside of your elbow has a little point to which a lot of tendons are attached, and this thing was tearing that tendon away."

He played the next two seasons with terrible pain in his throwing arm. This was possible only because the Browns' physician, a man Ryan secretly suspected was a chiropractor, was always ready with a syringe.

"He kept injecting a painkiller in my elbow so that I could practice on Wednesday. And it was injected on Sunday so I could play. That went on for two seasons," he said.

After scouring the country, flying both east and west, looking for the right medical solution, Ryan finally found a surgeon in Oklahoma City who could repair the damaged tendon.

So in his moment of vindication and redemption, just as he

emerged as one of the best quarterbacks in the league, one bad decision on the greatest day of his life changed everything.

"If I hadn't had that injury in that Pro Bowl game, my career might have been very different," he said.

Unsentimental as ever, Gary Collins agreed that Ryan's career had taken a disastrous turn.

"Ryan wasn't effective after that," he said. "He couldn't throw. He was inaccurate to begin with, and [the injury] really made him inaccurate."

Despite his lost career, Ryan never let bitterness cloud his thinking about what happened, or who was responsible.

"[Marchetti] was a great player, and I had no malicious feelings toward him whatsoever, and I don't to this day," the quarterback said. "He was right and correct in having the reaction that he had. I was improper and a little bit on a cloud about calling that play."

All things considered, the '64 title game was almost as painful for the victors as it was for the Baltimoreans. Whatever Ryan's faults and limitations, however he had offended Marchetti and the gods, the curse or cost was that the Browns would never again develop another quarterback of championship caliber.

A half century has passed, and in northern Ohio, the very cradle of professional football, they are still waiting for another Frank Ryan.

# NINE

# The Conflict

Unitas was a devout Catholic who regularly attended Mass as a congregant at Immaculate Conception in Towson. One Sunday he took his young daughter Jan with him. They left at the conclusion of the early service and were making their way through the parking lot when they ran into another worshipper who was heading inside for the morning's second Mass. They were about to pass him when Unitas suddenly stopped to greet him.

"Hey, Shoes. How you doing?" Unitas said.

After that the other congregant disappeared into the building, and Jan asked her father, "Who was that man?"

"That's Coach Shula," Unitas told his eight-year-old little girl. "He's an asshole."

Johnny Unitas and Don Shula did not get along. There is no question about that. In their day the strain between them was carefully hidden from the fans by the Colts' incomparable PR machine, but it was a plainly visible fact to members of the team, to the two antagonists, and to their families and friends.

In the stress of battle the secret would occasionally leak out to the press as well. When Shula blatantly criticized his team's offense in his comments after the 1964 championship game, the *New York Times* read between the lines and divined a broadside aimed at Johnny Unitas.

Shula and Unitas should have appreciated each other. Each one had done a great deal to enhance the other's career. In 1963, Unitas's first year under Shula's tutelage, the quarterback enjoyed a renaissance and posted his best statistics in four seasons. In his second season with Shula he was named league MVP, and he returned to the championship game.

On the other hand, Unitas's performances were the key factor in Shula's success. The Colts had the top-ranked defense in the NFL, but Unitas was Shula's marquee player and the team's touchdown maker. Unitas was the propellant that took the young coach from obscurity to fame. A few years earlier Shula was a failed player and then an anonymous assistant coach. Now, with number 19 at the controls of his offense, Shula was surpassing Vince Lombardi and dominating the league. All that despite the fact that he was almost a generation younger than Lombardi and many of the other head coaches he faced.

If the friction between Unitas and Shula was hidden from the fans, it was in plain view of the many camera lenses that were aimed in their direction. When the shutters clicked they accurately captured the emotional distance and the irritation between the two men. In those shots Shula's face is inevitably grim and concerned. His intensity and determination are conspicuous. There were few smiles in his Baltimore photos and few lighthearted moments, especially in his snapshots with Unitas.

There is a pronounced difference between the photographs of Unitas with his first mentor, Weeb Ewbank, and the later shots with Shula. With Weeb there is visible and obvious warmth as Unitas and Ewbank squarely face each other. The coach sometimes drapes a fatherly arm around his protégé's shoulder.

Unitas's and Shula's body language is oppositional. They rarely stand face-to-face or look each other in the eye. There is no evidence of camaraderie or emotional partnership. There is only a cold, hard business between them, and judging by their faces it appears to be as dreary and joyless as the partnership of Scrooge and Cratchit.

One shot, in particular, sums it all up. In a photo from training camp Shula leans over Unitas's shoulder right into the offensive huddle, his head craning as he eavesdrops on the play call. Unitas looks pained and irritated by the intrusion, his flattop bristling like the hair on a provoked dog's back.

Charley Winner saw the contrasts in the two men and their approaches to dealing with others. Unitas was humble and in touch with who he was and where he came from, he said. In Shula Winner saw a self-promoter.

"Unitas's disposition was always the same, always positive," Winner said. "When John Unitas looked at you and said something, you believed it. A lot of the players told me when he called the play in the huddle, you knew it was going to work."

But Winner felt that Shula's approach was less about "we" and more about "he." "When you sit down and talk with Shula, he is it and that's it," Winner said. "Every speech he makes, he talks about the perfect season.

"Shula is the kind of a guy who won't take any bullshit," Winner said. "If he sees something, he is going to call a spade a spade. Heck, he would get on me. Boy, I'd be the defensive coach, and it would be a third and short and I'd tell him I wanted a certain defense, and they would make the first down and he would say, 'Why the hell did you do that?' I'd say, 'Don, it was third and 1,' or something like that. He'd get on me, and I'd known him ever since he was in college. But that's the way he was."

Initially, Unitas wasn't the only player who didn't care for Shula's brusque manner. The coach rubbed many of the Colts the wrong way.

"He took to the title of head coach instantly," running back Lenny Moore later wrote. "At times it seemed as if [Shula] went too far. . . . I knew many guys on the team wanted to take a shot at him."

"Don Shula was the kind of guy who could look you square in the eye and call you an asshole," tackle Jim Parker said.

These initial reactions faded for most players, and as time passed Shula gained the respect of the team. Bobby Boyd actually felt a sense of kinship with his coach since, as a cornerback, he played the same position on the field that his coach once had. Boyd was also Unitas's close intimate and, later, his business partner in two restaurant ventures. He described Shula as a highly aggressive coach and Unitas as a player who simply wouldn't tolerate overt criticism.

"Shula was a great coach. He knew what he was doing. I didn't always agree with him, but I had a lot of respect for him," Boyd said. "But he would get on you if you didn't do it the way he thought you should. Shula was very consistent. He treated everybody pretty much the same. He would jump on anybody, and he would give a little praise to everybody.

"Shula would yell at [Unitas] just like he would any of the players. . . . [T]hat was his nature. He would correct you and sometimes put you in a situation in which you got embarrassed. John didn't go for that, didn't go for that at all."

According to Boyd, the tensions between Shula and Unitas didn't lead to dramatic displays in front of the other players, but it would cause the men to square off in private.

"I never did see [Unitas] lash back at [Shula]," Boyd said. "But I know they would have some private conversations about John and how he reacted. Shula treated all of us that way; that's the way he coached. It didn't bother me that much, but I think John really resented it. They just didn't get along."

Jan Unitas knew it wasn't in her father's nature to tolerate disrespect. "My father told me he never liked the type of coach who screamed and yelled. He didn't respond well to that," she said. But she also knew better than anyone that beneath her father's impenetrable public facade was a fragile ego. "He felt like, 'I'm John Unitas. What is somebody going to tell me about playing quarterback?'"

Shula had to contend with that ego and rein it in to be successful. But he was also self-aware and knew that his own personality was, at times, an issue. Others perceived him as tightly wound and volatile, and he knew it.

"I never would mask my emotions," Shula said. "What you see is what you get. I was so intense in what I was doing, sometimes I didn't handle it as well as I should have."

While the mysteries of personality and chemistry dogged the two men, they also had disputes about tangible things: they vehemently disagreed about how to run an offense.

Dan Sullivan, a talented young guard on the offensive line, believed that the problems between coach and quarterback were based on diverging offensive philosophies. Unitas's style of play foreshadowed NFL offenses of the twenty-first century. He had a pass-first mentality that resonated with the fans. In Baltimore they joyfully paraphrased United Airlines' famous advertising tag line of the '60s and urged everyone to "fly the friendly skies of Unitas."

Shula still liked to travel by stagecoach.

"John played a different game than Don Shula wanted to play," Dan Sullivan said. "John Unitas was a pure passing quarterback. John, left to his own devices, would like to throw the ball three-quarters of the time and run the ball as a 'waste' play, if you will.

"When Don Shula came to coach the Baltimore Colts, his desire was to have a 50-50 offense—50 percent running and 50 percent throwing," Sullivan said. "[Shula] was a strong advocate of 'win first down,'" which was defined as getting four yards or more.

"Once you get four yards or better on first down, you've put the defense in a very defensive position," Sullivan said. "Now it's open for a pass. It's open for another run. And, if you get another 4 yards, it's third and 2, and it makes it a lot easier. If you don't win the first-down battle, and it becomes third and 9 or third and 10 or longer, then you're stuck in that zone where you have to pass the football. John Unitas thrived in that zone."

Sullivan knew Shula would have a tough time getting Unitas to see the wisdom of his approach. Johnny U had made his fame by defying easy-to-read tendencies. In 1958 Tom Landry, then defensive coordinator of the Giants, easily shut down Paul Brown's offense in a special playoff game against Cleveland. By examining the famous coach's inclinations, Landry and the Giants read his offense like it was a schoolboy's primer. But the next week Landry and his disciplined players were befuddled by Unitas and were utterly unsure of what he would do next. In essence New York's top-ranked defense was powerless against Johnny U, who carved them up to tie the score in the waning moments of the game and then sliced through them again in overtime.

Unitas unapologetically passed when the prevailing wisdom would have him run, and that's the way he liked to play the game.

Sullivan saw the seeds of conflict in these divergent views.

"I knew Don thought the world of John and thought he was a great quarterback," Sullivan said, "but I think if he had any desire, he would have loved to have turned him a little bit more to his way of thinking. I don't know how you could've done that. I don't know of any coach in professional football that could've done that with John."

This struggle for control of the play calling was a key issue for both men. Nancy Winner, Weeb Ewbank's daughter and Charley Winner's wife, understood the problem.

"John called all the plays [under my father]," she said. "That's what he loved, and that's why he hated Shula."

Under Ewbank Unitas had been empowered to steer the ship on Sunday. That was Weeb's method, and the team thrived under it.

"When [Unitas] said something in the huddle, that was it," Charley Winner said. "[The players] all respected him. They knew that he was going to produce. He could see things. We [the coaches] didn't call the plays.

"Weeb would more or less go over the game plan as far as the quarterback is concerned," Winner said, "and he gave John a lot of freedom. We had a group of plays. These are good for first and 10. These are good for second and long, second and short, third and long, third and short."

Winner said that under Ewbank the coaching staff offered its thoughts to Unitas about what would work in the game, but those suggestions were proposed in the spirit of collaboration only. On Sunday, though, the ball and the fate of the team were both in Johnny U's hands.

During games Ewbank's coaching staff reserved the right to converse with Unitas and remind him of things they felt were important. "The [assistant coach] on the telephone or the head coach would talk to him and say, 'Now, we haven't tried this yet,' or, 'No, try this,'" Winner said. But it was left up to Unitas to make the calls in the huddle based on what he was seeing in the game. "John and Raymond came up with a lot of suggestions because they looked at those films," Winner said. "Weeb trusted John, and they had a real good relationship."

Collegiality wasn't in Shula's repertoire with Unitas, and he wasn't about to give away control of the game.

Jimmy Orr knew that the heavy hand of Shula wasn't in concert with the way Unitas operated. "John didn't like Shula sending in the plays," he said. "John liked to look to Raymond or me and say, 'Where do you want to go?' If you took that away from him, he didn't like it. It wasn't his game anymore. He was just a stool pigeon."

That didn't stop Shula from using running back Tom Matte as his messenger to the huddle, sending Tom in with the play he wanted to see. But this served only to put the young player on the cutting edge of the dispute. Like a child in a divorce, he was used as a pawn by both power figures.

When Matte arrived with Shula's play Unitas would listen closely and then say, "I don't want to call that."

When Matte got back to the sideline the coach was seething.

"Why didn't you call that play?" Shula would ask him.

"John didn't want to call that one," Matte replied.

"Well, I told you to tell him to call it."

"I did tell him," the weary Matte would say over and over again.

Matte felt that the problems between Unitas and Shula were bigger than the play calls.

"John thought that Shula was defensive minded and John was offensive minded," Matte said. "And I really think that's where the rubber hit the road. [John's feeling was], 'You take care of the defense, and I'll take care of the offense.'"

Shula was under the impression that he was the head coach of the entire team.

Not surprisingly, then, Shula felt a certain discomfort in dealing with Unitas. While he didn't mind taking command of the many other great players on the team, men with whom he had played or who were close in age to him or who were far better players than he was, Unitas was different. It was as if the two couldn't get past their old pecking order as teammates who were going in opposite directions.

"In the beginning it was tough," Shula said. "[Unitas] thought about me as a defensive back that was just fighting to stay in the league, and he was a superstar. I just felt that I really had to prove myself [to him], every meeting, every practice, every point. I had to make sure that he understood that [what I was doing] was the right thing to do to get ready to play."

Shula made other decisions that also may have exacerbated his problems with Unitas. For one thing he added active players to his coaching staff. Gino Marchetti and Bill Pellington, the two defensive stars who had recommended Shula to Rosenbloom, were named player coaches. So, too, was offensive end Jim Mutscheller, who had only recently retired. All were Roman Catholics, giving credence, perhaps, to Weeb Ewbank's old conspiracy theory that papists had wrested control of the team. John Constantine Unitas, for all his on-field wizardry and Roman Catholicism, remained strictly a player. It was an arrangement almost guaranteed to provoke resentment.

While these issues explain a lot, they don't really delve too deeply into the one factor that makes marriages and workplaces alike work or fail—personal chemistry.

Colts center Bill Curry was, literally, the closest player on the field to Unitas and the great man's henchman. He got an up-close view of the quarterback Shula found so hard to get along with.

Curry said that the players "all worshipped" Unitas, and so did the fans, who erupted in decibels "louder than a jet engine" when Johnny U was introduced before games in Baltimore. He remembered how oddly the pressures of game time affected Unitas. As kickoff neared Johnny U's eyes began to blink with great rapidity. His teammates recognized this quirk as a sign that Unitas was in deep focus.

Curry said the one trait that really drew the Colts around their leader was his ability to remain serene in the face of disaster.

"We're playing the Bears one day," Curry said, "and after five minutes in the game it's 17 to nothing. He's thrown three interceptions, and they've picked him off in the end zone. Butkus is out there kicking everybody, knocking everybody's teeth out, and John jogs off the field after each interception, and there is no change of expression, none.

"Someone said to me, 'Doesn't this bother him?' He shows no emotion. He doesn't say, 'You guys block for me.' He might come by the O line and ask, 'Do you need a screen, Billy, something to slow down the pressure?' No change of expression. No pain in his face.

"The last play of the game was [a 54-yard pass] to John Mackey to win, 21–20. And I swear he comes off the field, and there is still no change of expression. Nothing."

That portrait of Unitas as stoic hero was the one that everyone knew. Hidden behind the iron facade, however, Curry saw another side of his nature, a man deeply burdened by both his past and his lonely, pressure-filled career.

He remembered one game against the Browns that offered

another chance for Unitas's last-second heroics. Instead, it ended in a bitter disappointment and a terrible misunderstanding among friends.

"We're playing Cleveland one day, and it's fourth down," Curry said. "It's our last chance to win the game. It's like fourth and 4, I think. Unitas threw the deep ball, trying to win the game, and they intercepted it. The guy who intercepted it, the defensive back, made a terrible mistake. He caught it at his 4, somewhere around there, and so our defense went back on the field. We had such a great defense, there was a real good chance we could knock the ball loose or intercept or get it back with a chance to win. It was a big mistake. He should've batted the ball down.

"So [offensive guard] Glenn Ressler came over to me and said, 'Can you believe that guy caught that ball?' And I said, 'Yeah, I hope he lives to regret it.' Well, we didn't win the game. I think they made a first down or something and ended up running the clock out.

"We go in the locker room, and I'm standing in the shower. You're always beat up, and you're finding your wounds and cuts in the shower. Finally, it's just John and me in there, buck-naked.

"He said, 'I heard what you said about me.'

"I said, 'What are you talking about?'

"'"You'll live to regret it." Yeah, I know I threw the damn interception, but for you to be talking like that about me.'

"I said, 'I wasn't talking about you. I don't ever talk negatively about you.'

"'Don't give me that shit, Bill. You talk too much, and I heard you this time, and I know exactly what you said.'

"I followed him in, and while he shaved I stood there and harangued him, but he never budged. 'I know what you were doing. You were talking trash about me.'

"I said, 'That's the one thing I won't do if I live to be a thousand, and I'm horrified that you would even insinuate that.'

"'I'm not insinuating a damn thing. I know what you were doing.'

"He was convinced that I was capable of talking down about him. So there was that kid who grew up expecting to work in the coal mines, and he got out of there thinking, 'People were going to look down their nose at me if I make a mistake, even my best friend, even my guardian and protector.'"

Curry never convinced Unitas that he was referring to Cleveland's defensive back and not the man he revered. In the end it all passed without further incident.

"By Tuesday everything was fine," Curry said. "He was out there slapping me on the butt, and that was his way, I presumed, of saying, 'Let's drop it.' It bothered me. It bothers me to this day that there was an element, a place in his heart, that would even think I would say that. It really hurt my feelings. But I'll tell you what, I never said another word about him that wasn't in his presence."

Shula's psychology wasn't quite as complex, but he had his own problems and pressures to deal with. Dan Sullivan knew how hard it must have been to be the head coach of the Colts with a gunslinger who chucked interceptions without remorse and then hoped to pull off miracles at the last second. That kind of thing wasn't good for a young coach's job security, especially if he worked for Carroll Rosenbloom.

"You had to win under Carroll Rosenbloom. The buck didn't stop anyplace other than there," Sullivan said. "All he cared about were wins and losses. He didn't care how you got there or how you did it. So I think to say that Shula was under the gun . . . would be a true story."

So were Unitas's and Shula's tight windings the source of their mutual contempt, or was there something else?

Bill Curry came close to finding out one night when he was drinking with Johnny U at the Golden Arm, the quarterback's restaurant. Unitas himself brought up the subject.

"Friday night was beer-drinking time at John Unitas's place," Curry said. John would come over, and he would start in on Shula. I would say, 'Hey, don't even do that. Don't do that, John.' And he'd say, 'Man, you don't understand.' And I'd say, 'I do understand. He's our head coach, and let's just leave it there.'

"As time went on John, who was a very private person, came to confide in me," Curry said. "A lot of the things we talked about are nobody else's business and never will be. But when he tried to talk about Don Shula, I would not let him. I said, 'Look, I will not go there. You talk about my coach, and I owe him everything and so do you.' He said, 'I don't owe him a damn thing.' But I didn't want to get into it with Johnny Unitas. I loved and admired him, and all I wanted to do was take care of him, keep someone from hitting him. I didn't want him creating divisions or talking about my coach, our coach, like that. And so he said, 'Okay, okay . . .'"

The spritely wide receiver Jimmy Orr had enormous chemistry with Unitas on the field.

"I asked him one time what was the thing between [him] and Shula," Orr said. "He didn't really want to talk about it. All he said was, 'Shula lied to me.'"

Did Unitas tell Orr what Shula had lied about?

"I asked him," Orr said, "but he never really answered."

# TEN

# Love Is Also a Collision Sport

I f Unitas's most important relationship at work was a strain, his most important relationship at home wasn't ideal, either. Behind the scenes, far from the sleight of hand of press agents and the adoring gaze of features writers and fans, John Unitas's marriage was failing.

The dynamic young quarterback who had changed football and his wife, Dorothy, were often presented in the press as the ideal couple. The newspapers ran features of them in their modest but nicely furnished home. Accompanying photos showed Dorothy, beautifully attired in pressed dresses, her immaculate and growing brood spread around her like vast wealth. The shutter also clicked on the dutiful Johnny U mowing the grass, puttering around in the basement, admiring his sporty American-made automobiles, and attending to his babies, still in the crib. Every year, it seemed, a new child graced the bountiful Unitas home.

Their marriage began with a story that was incredibly simple and sweet. John Constantine Unitas and Dorothy Hoelle were classmates at Pittsburgh's St. Justin's, a parochial school. He was an undersize basketball player, and she was a pretty young fan.

"They were going to a game he was playing in," Jan Unitas, their first child, said. "He offered her his seat on the school bus. When he got off the bus he told her to save him a seat next to her for the ride home."

Unitas and Dorothy were married in 1954, even before he left the University of Louisville. They pledged themselves to each other in Pittsburgh. With that small ceremony Dorothy became a part of and witness to one of the most interesting and improbable stories in the history of professional sports.

She bore him his first baby, Janice, the summer his career began and thus provided him with his motivation for success. She was there for him when the Steelers broke his heart and cut him from the squad. And she was the one who answered the phone when Don Kellett, Baltimore's general manager, came calling to offer him a tryout with the Colts. When the team sent him his first contract, Unitas was out on the construction job, and it was she who received it, read it, and signed it before he even saw it.

Dorothy was an unlikely football spouse. She was a pretty young woman but far from the cliché of a player's wife. For one thing, she was no little Barbie stick figure with blonde hair or vacant eyes. She was a real woman with a voluptuous figure. She was also independent, outspoken, and even profane in an era when women were expected to be primarily ornamental.

In Dorothy's world gender roles could be as confining as prison bars. She was labeled a nonconformist, a loud and brassy woman who simply couldn't be fathomed within the couple's social circle.

Pert Mutscheller, former teammate Jim Mutscheller's wife, considered herself Dorothy's friend, but she was adamant that Dorothy was a difficult woman in marriage.

"Everybody felt sorry for John. They'd be out in public, and she would swear and down him," Pert said.

Dorothy's outspokenness included a bawdy and unfiltered sense of humor. "John was friends with a famous singer who was friends with Rock Hudson," Pert said. "This singer was visiting Dottie and John in Baltimore, and he said to Dorothy, 'I'm friendly with Rock Hudson.' She said, 'I don't believe you.' So he called Rock Hudson up and put Dorothy on the phone. And she said, 'I heard you're gay.' John was just about ready to shoot her. She would just come out with things like that. You never knew what she was going to say."

"Every other word out of her mouth was *fuck*," Colts running back Tom Matte said. He remembered one evening when he and some of the other Colts and their wives were invited to an elegant dinner party in Washington, hosted by Vice President Spiro T.

Agnew and his wife. The evening was great fun, until it took an embarrassing turn.

"We were invited with a whole bunch of dignitaries like the secretary of state and others," he said. "It was a beautiful party. Anyway, we're having cordials afterward, and the men went to the library, and we're having a couple, when all of a sudden my wife comes in and she's crying. She motions me over to her. I said, 'What's wrong?' She said, 'Tom, you won't believe it. You can't believe what Dorothy Unitas just said. We were just talking about John [Unitas], and Dorothy gets up and says, "My husband has a restaurant called the Golden Arm that does very well in Baltimore. Well, my son was just living down at the beach this summer, and he got the nickname of the Golden Penis."'"

Jan Unitas said that Matte's story had made the rounds over the years but couldn't possibly be true. "My brother never lived at the beach, and he was only about twelve years old when the story was supposed to have taken place," she said. "My mother could tell a dirty joke as well as any man, but she was adamant about acting like a lady in public, among people you may not know."

In that era and social class women and men were still "ladies and gentlemen." For an evening out the gentlemen sometimes wore tuxedoes, while their ladies were adorned in furs and long gloves. In a formal world such as that one, in which poise and control were considered prime assets, a horrifying story about a revered man's wife was, of course, irresistible fodder, even for his best friends.

But Dorothy's frank sense of humor made her only a little ahead of her time. Soon Americans would find that every trip to the family food market, the most wholesome place on earth, would end in a checkout aisle where multiple mainstream magazines openly dealt with women's sexual proclivities, the possibilities of multiple partners in a single encounter, the merits of toys in the bedroom, and the pleasures of bisexuality. Not long before, any hint of homosexuality was considered the most aberrant if not detestable of behaviors. In retrospect, considering all that would soon come, Dorothy's wry observation, even at a formal party, even conveyed to the vice president's wife, seems tame and innocent by comparison.

If the story about Dorothy was intended to convey some explanation for why Unitas's marriage failed, it didn't touch on Unitas himself or the barriers he presented to a happy and successful home.

He was, from the earliest days of his marital union, a serial cheater. In that he was not unlike the other "great" men of his era. President John F. Kennedy was a handsome young husband and father, but also a well-known, if protected, womanizer. Civil rights leader Martin Luther King Jr. was perhaps the country's greatest moral leader since Abraham Lincoln, but on multiple occasions the prying Federal Bureau of Investigation recorded King in hotel rooms all over the country with many different women. In some of those recordings he could clearly be heard engaging in spirited sexual intercourse. FBI director J. Edgar Hoover feigned disgust at this behavior and referred to King as a "tomcat." Nevertheless, the director himself was widely believed to be a closeted gay man and cross-dresser whose longtime lover, Clyde Tolson, was the number-two man at the bureau. The authorization for these intrusions into King's privacy came from the president's brother Attorney General Robert F. Kennedy, whose rumored infidelity with actress Marilyn Monroe, the sexiest woman in the country, later became well known to the public. Monroe was thought to be just one of Kennedy's many dalliances.

The regular churchgoing folk forgave the peccadilloes of their great men. Indiscretions were viewed as the reward earned for the terrible burdens and pressures those men had to endure.

Right or wrong, there is no question that Unitas sought sexual comfort outside of his home. His daughter Jan said that her mother knew that "he was never a faithful husband, not from the beginning."

One teammate acknowledged, "Johnny U and I used to chase pussy together."

A professional woman who had wandered into Unitas's orbit learned about both his appetite and his ego when they collided with her desire to procure an autograph for a nephew. She approached him at practice one day and asked him if he would be kind enough to sign a ball for her. When he agreed she said she would buy a clean new football and bring it to practice the next day. Unitas magnanimously offered to save her the trip and instead come to her apartment that evening to sign it. When he arrived he sat down in her living room and engaged in a little small talk with her before getting down to business. "So, are we going to fuck or what?"

"What? No!" she said with astonishment.

With that Unitas immediately got up and beat a path for the exit. When he got to the door he opened it, swung around, and said, "Next time you'll ask me."

Another young Baltimore woman, a teen then working as an operator at the old c&p phone facility on York Road, also learned something about Unitas's activities. "We could listen in on any phone call we wanted just by flipping a switch," she said. "One day I knew Unitas was on my line, and I couldn't resist. I flipped over to his line, and he was talking to a girlfriend, not his wife. Let's just say it was obvious."

If Unitas's private behaviors were ultimately a calamity for his wife and five children, they weren't out of step with his times. Male sexual behavior that was once considered immoderate and immoral was quickly making its way into the mainstream.

Samuel Roth, a Greenwich Village writer and bookstore owner, made this possible. By 1957 he had done three different stints in jail, all for merely selling books and pamphlets that were then considered "indecent." Fed up with this never-ending threat to his freedom, Roth challenged the constitutionality of an old U.S. law that declared mailing "obscene, lewd, lascivious, or filthy" material punishable.

"It's not that Roth was engaged in higher learning and wanted, as an intellectual, to change [things]," the writer and social critic Gay Talese said. "He was a smut peddler, and he wanted to make money, and he wanted to not have his business interfered with by sensors. He was interested in making money, and, parenthetically, he changed the law."

Roth's aims and ends may have been sketchy, but he won his case and thereby profoundly changed American culture.

Hugh Hefner was one conspicuous beneficiary of Roth's case. His magazine, *Playboy*, was free to package women in its slick, glossy pages. It opened minds by publishing groundbreaking interviews with some of the century's most fascinating newsmakers and published great short fiction from the masters of that craft, all beside photographs of women with their breasts and vaginas on display.

If that seemed like a curious combination of elements to blend under one cover, it was certainly a successful recipe. Hefner, or "Hef," as he was called, lived in a mansion and hosted a never-ending orgiastic party there. His signature look was silk pajamas and a contented smile.

"Because of the *Roth vs. USA* decision, movies like *I Am Curious (Yellow)*, a nude movie from Sweden, [were made legal]," said Talese. "Language that put [profane comedian] Lenny Bruce in jail in 1954–55 was allowed in 1959 and 1960. What Lenny Bruce suffered for in the late 1950s was perfectly allowed in 1965. Amazing."

Talese said nudity was showing up in even more surprising places than the newsstands or movie houses. *Oh! Calcutta!* was a Broadway musical with frontal nudity, men and women totally nude," he said. "You'd see penises dangling out there onstage. I mean, this was unheard of. Fashion went from the miniskirt to nudity in advertising," he said. "You would see a perfume ad, maybe in *Vogue* magazine, and the model would be pretty much nude like had been [only] in *Playboy* before."

The trend "moved into the slick middle class or even the upper class," Talese said. "A great photographer named Helmut Newton, here's a guy in *Vogue* magazine who had women nude, some of them in bondage. I mean, Christ! He was an amazing guy, and he never would have existed as an artist were it not for that *Roth vs. USA* obscenity case."

Talese had his own place in this drama. He was one of a few serious literary figures who explored and stretched the post-*Roth* rules with work that was far more explicit than anything that had been created for the mainstream before.

Talese grew up in Ocean City, New Jersey, the son of Italian immigrants. Like good boys everywhere, he followed in the religious traditions of his parents.

"The Catholic Church where I was an altar boy was made up of Irish-born priests and Irish-born nuns, mainly, condemning immorality and condemning writers and filmmakers for presenting sex explicitly and in a dirty fashion. I grew up with books

LOVE IS ALSO A COLLISION SPORT

called dirty books, dirty films, 'Watch your dirty mouth,' and all that idea of censorship. More than that it was underlined with the threat of going to hell if you continued with your dirty ways. That's why I wrote *Thy Neighbor's Wife*," he said,

It was, Talese said, "about the changing definition of morality" in America. It took him ten years to write it or, as one journalist noted, "longer than it took Tolstoy to write *War and Peace*." He not only examined the subject matter with exhaustive research but lived it himself.

Though he was happily married to a beautiful wife, Nan, and had two young daughters with her at home, he threw himself into the sexual experiences he wrote about. He traveled to California and took up residence at the Sandstone Retreat, a community where the inhabitants were dedicated to open sex. He stayed for six weeks, but each night he would call home like any dutiful husband on a business trip, only while he was speaking to his wife about his day there were naked bodies all around him. His "research" also included trips to massage parlors and live sex shows.

Even before he finished the book, Talese was accosted by those who questioned his respectability and wondered aloud or in print about the embarrassment and humiliation he was heaping on his wife and children, let alone his parents.

Whatever the controversy, he had captured the imagination of the American public. There was something intensely alluring about a brilliant mind and insightful social critic describing and explaining those things that had only recently been the sole province of the sick, the fringe, the fevered, and the grammatically challenged.

If it all wasn't in good taste or even moral in the conventional sense, it was, at least, spectacular business. Doubleday paid him $1.2 million for *Thy Neighbor's Wife* and a second book. United Artists paid him a record $2.5 million for the film rights. All told, with foreign and paperback rights, he earned more than $4 million from the project before it ever arrived in bookstores or sold a single copy to the public.

*Thy Neighbor's Wife* was amazing if for no other reason than that more than forty years after it was completed, Talese was still married to Nan. If he was eventually going to hell, as the priests and nuns of his youth had warned him, at least his life on earth was happy, productive, and enjoyable. He managed to accumulate great wealth, fame, and prestige as well as the continued devotion of his children and wife.

Far from being ostracized for his work, Talese was greeted with praise and respect; he was showered with attention. In the powerful world of New York publishing, his sojourn into the seamy and the tawdry had made him a grand eminence.

If anything, Talese was a little late to the game. Many years before *Thy Neighbor's Wife*, fiction writers were already describing infidelity and "grotesque" sexual acts in great detail. These writers were among the nation's most respected artists.

In Philip Roth's 1969 novel, *Portnoy's Complaint*, his protagonist, Alexander Portnoy, masturbates with inhuman zeal and variety. Australia banned that book, but in the United States both *Time* and the Modern Library included it on their lists of best English-language novels of the twentieth century. Down in New Orleans an unknown novelist named John Kennedy Toole was dreaming up Ignatius P. Reilly, another character obsessed with his own equipment and, in his case, rubber dishwashing gloves.

Toole's brilliantly comedic novel managed to capture the weirdness of deep southerners in much the same way that Roth found the strange essence of the Jews of the Northeast. The two tribes couldn't have had less in common except, it seemed, that their young men spent too much time alone in the bathroom.

And somewhere tucked away in New England was John Updike. Like Lenny Moore, he was born in Depression-era Reading, Pennsylvania, and much like David Halberstam he traveled the distance from a modest upbringing to Harvard University.

After college Updike started off writing for the *New Yorker*, where he published one of the most memorable baseball stories ever written, "Hub Fans Bid Kid Adieu," about the last-ever at bat of Ted Williams.

Updike's artistic ambitions were high-minded, and he wanted to make a permanent impression in fiction. So he and his wife, Mary, picked up and moved to Ipswich, Massachusetts. In that picturesque New England coastal town, founded by a Puritan, Updike discovered the witchcraft of adultery. It was the one subject that would dominate his work and ensure his literary and financial fortunes.

If Updike had been a ditch digger or a truck driver instead of an internationally celebrated intellectual, he would have been described as a guy who couldn't keep it in his pants. He was intelligent and charming enough to end up in bed with several of his neighbors' wives, though he had a sharp, pointy face reminiscent of small rodents.

Whatever feelings of freedom Updike's behavior provoked, he was in fact confining himself. One of his affairs necessitated that he temporarily leave the country. When that exile ended, he entered into an affair with permanent consequences. He left Mary and his kids to pursue a relationship with Martha Bernhard, another neighbor, who had three children of her own.

If Updike thought his life would go on much as before only with a different woman, he was sadly mistaken. His relationship with his friends and children would never be the same. Only two of his kids and one of his friends were in attendance for his marriage to Martha. When Updike won a prestigious medal from the National Book Foundation, none of his children came. Many believed that Martha blocked him from his family and friends.

The new sexual freedom allowed men to live out their fantasies but at the expense of the realities that had once characterized a stable and comfortable life.

In 1960 Updike published *Rabbit Run*, an autobiographical novel set in a thinly veiled version of his hometown. The story follows a former high school basketball star who runs away from his wife and children to pursue a relationship with a part-time prostitute. Updike doesn't waste his sex scenes on self-gratification; *Rabbit Run*'s graphic descriptions include two people. His big contribution to the new literature was to make that sex oral.

Had Unitas been the literary type, he might have felt a certain kinship with Rabbit Angstrom, not to mention Updike. He was an athlete living the new morality, regularly stepping away from his family to pursue needs that superseded them.

Pert Mutscheller, a beautiful young woman in the 1960s, noticed that her friend Dorothy didn't like Unitas talking to her. She took it as a sign of Dorothy's aggressive hold over the husband. If Dorothy was in fact losing her grip on all that was reasonable, it might have had something to do with the sickening tangible evidence of her husband's infidelities that she was regularly forced to confront. As Unitas's laundress she found "[menstrual] blood in his shorts," according to her daughter Jan. Even that was far from the worst. After a trip to the ob-gyn she came home with medicine for a condition her specialist declined to specify.

"My father had given her venereal disease," Jan Unitas said. "Her [gynecologist] treated her but didn't tell her what he was treating her for."

The chauvinistic specialist had another way of breaking the news.

"He called my father and told him about it," Jan said. "[My mother eventually] found out from her family doctor. She got a sinus infection or something and went to the family doctor. While she was there she told him about the medicine the [gynecologist] gave her. He told her what it was for."

No matter how mortifying the consequences of Unitas's reckless behavior, it might have been explained away as part of the lifestyle of a superstar. Many of the other football wives dealt with the same, or worse.

But much like Updike, Johnny U's years of out-of-control sexual behavior eventually ended up with him emotionally ensnared by another woman. One of his teammates introduced him to Sandra Lemon, a stewardess in her late twenties.

Unitas's liaison with "Sandy" quickly grew into something more serious and permanent than his many other transitory relationships.

"My brother John went to Calvert Hall [high school]; it's right next to the Glenmont Towers apartments," Jan said. "One day my mom got a call from Calvert Hall, and they said, 'You need to come pick up your son. He's sick.' It was noon or whatever. He was the type of kid who was never sick, never missed a day of school. So she goes and picks him up, and he couldn't look at her, couldn't look her in the eye. And she said, 'You want to tell me what's going on? You're not sick because you have an illness. There's something else going on.' And he told her that he heard in the hallways of the school that Dad had gotten an apartment for his girlfriend at the Glenmont Towers," adjacent to the school.

That girlfriend, living like the don's *goomar* in the love nest Unitas paid for, was Sandy. Soon the entire Unitas family would know her name all too well. Dorothy could see it in black and white in her own mailbox. She opened an official-looking envelope one day and found a statement that revealed her own name had been removed from one of the couple's financial instruments and was replaced with Sandy's.

Even baby Kenneth (called K.E. by the family), a proficient talker at the age of two, had Sandy on his lips. One Saturday morning Unitas readied to leave the house to run errands when, at the last second, Dorothy made a suggestion: "Why don't you take K.E. with you?"

So father and son both left.

Later that night Dorothy, Jan, and K.E. sat in Jan's room when the young child innocently said something surprising.

"Sandy cried on Daddy's green shirt today."

Unitas had apparently planned to tryst with Sandy, but the unexpected presence of the little boy from another woman provoked intense emotion in her.

Sandy was also starting to become well known to Unitas's friends, a fact that intruded itself on Dorothy. The reigning wife was forced to field phone calls from family friends telling her of social events Unitas attended with Sandy by his side instead of her.

That kind of information was soon accompanied by pleas to "let him go." People she once considered among her best friends were calling to tell her incredibly hurtful things. "He's in love for the first time in his life," more than one "friend" told her.

These many humiliations naturally made the situation in the house incredibly tense. The couple started to fight, and Unitas could be quite cruel in verbal combat with his wife. He criticized her looks, focusing on her nose, which he considered too prominent.

"If I had your nose full of nickels," he told her in an especially mean exchange, "I wouldn't have to work so hard."

All the conflict and controversy seemed to be heading in just one direction—separation and divorce. But Unitas surprisingly told Dorothy that he didn't want to leave.

Jan, then about seventeen, secretly listened in to a key exchange between her parents on the topic.

"One Saturday morning Mom and Dad sat in the living room, and Mom confronted him on everything," Jan said. "Mom told him, 'I know about Sandy. I'm being told by people that you are in love for the first time in your life, and I should give you the opportunity to go be with her. And I know about the apartment in Glenmont. So here's my proposition for you. Go live with her. You've got a place to live with her, go live with her. See how long it takes to figure out what you want. You either want to be here with us, married with me, to be with your kids, or you want to be with her. Go figure it out, if it takes six weeks or six months. All I ask is that you continue to support us as you've been doing.'"

Unitas's response: "I shouldn't have to leave. I should be able to do what I want and come and go as I please."

Dorothy wondered aloud what she got out of such an arrangement. "You can have the privilege of being Mrs. Johnny Unitas," he told her.

As almost any married man could imagine, Dorothy didn't respond too well to that outrageous proposal.

"She told him that he forgets that she has known him since he was a bowlegged, bucktoothed kid, and he could take his footballs and shove them up his ass," Jan said. "He never understood. She didn't like being 'Mrs. Johnny Unitas.' She loved being Mrs. John Unitas. She was still in love with the skinny fifteen-year-old boy she first met. She didn't care at all about being the wife of a superstar."

Whatever Dorothy liked or disliked seemed to be beside the point. Unitas, finally if reluctantly free from his obligations to her, briefly moved with Sandy to Nevada, where he achieved legal residency and benefited from that state's more liberal divorce laws.

He married Sandy only hours after he thought the divorce papers were finalized.

"When Dad came back," Jan said, "I'll never forget, it was the summertime; it was June. I'm walking out to the car, and Dad pulls up in the driveway, and he gets out of the car and he says,

'I just want to let you know your mother and I are divorced and I am married again.' The whole time he was in Nevada he never called or made the effort to really be a father during that time. He was all wrapped up in his own little world."

Like Updike, though, Unitas found that the transition from one woman to another was far more complicated than he had bargained for. His separation agreement with Dorothy allowed him to visit the children at his pleasure, but he simply didn't. He stopped interacting with his five offspring from Dorothy as soon as he moved out.

"He had access anytime he wanted it," Jan said, "but he didn't take advantage of it. He didn't come over, didn't call. Only Kenneth ever went to stay with him for any amount of time. But Dad constantly disappointed him. It was heartbreaking to see that little kid all dressed and ready to go with his little suitcase packed, waiting for his father who would sometimes never show up."

From the perspective of his first wife and family, Sandy didn't want them around. The kids' photos disappeared from their father's wallet. For many years they were never invited to their father's new home.

"Many years later I became involved with a great guy named Michael [who was divorced with children from a previous marriage]," Jan said. "Eventually, I fell in love with him. As we were starting to become serious, he told me something he felt I needed to know: 'My kids will always come first,' he said. I loved hearing that. It really impressed me. With my father not only were we not first, we weren't even on his totem pole."

Dorothy, as blunt and acerbic as ever, even in defeat, delivered an unassailable truth to her husband. In what must have been a rueful moment for the former Sports Father of the Year, she said, "You are a hero to every child in this country, except your own."

# ELEVEN

## Unprecedented Success

Johnny Unitas signed his tenth contract with the Colts in June 1965. In his decade of professional football he had enjoyed an unprecedented rise, from an obscure long shot rejected by his first team to the most famous and celebrated player in the game. He didn't go to the top alone; he took Baltimore, the Colts franchise, and the entire enterprise of professional football with him. After a decade of brutal beatings on the field and even bounties issued against him, he had enough game left to be the reigning MVP, and he had just led Baltimore to its third championship appearance of his tenure. Since the day Johnny U came walking into the Colts' starting lineup, Baltimore had never known a single losing season.

In New York Unitas's old coach and mentor Weeb Ewbank, now the leader of the AFL's Jets, had also just signed a quarterback to a new contract. His soon-to-be protégé was a rookie with a bum knee who had not yet played a single down of professional football. Nevertheless, at the press conference announcing the deal, Ewbank gushed profusely about his new gem and applied the word *Unitas* to him like a superlative.

"I see in this young man the same qualities that are found in Unitas," Weeb told the scribes. "He has size, quickness, a wonderful arm, a quick delivery, courage, and the ability to make the big play."

The subject of all that adulation was Joe Namath. Even if he shared all the similarities with Johnny U that Ewbank saw, there was one key difference between the two quarterbacks: Namath, a former shoe-shine boy, had just affixed his signature to a three-year deal worth $400,000. Unitas's new agreement with the Colts, according to the *Baltimore Sun*, was a one-year deal for about $65,000.

Unitas couldn't help but take notice. Namath had done nothing in professional football yet, but he had already financially eclipsed the game's biggest star.

At home, perhaps with envy, Johnny U referred to the Hungarian-derived Namath as "the green-eyed Gypsy." It wouldn't be long before the press and fans across the country were reverentially referring to him by another name, "Broadway Joe."

If Namath's contract supremacy wasn't a reflection of ability, it said a lot about old-fashioned business leverage. Namath was the beneficiary of the war for players between the established NFL and the upstart AFL. The two leagues were fighting to sign draft picks. But veterans like Unitas were victims of an interleague détente in which the two sides agreed to refrain from going after each other's established players. So guys like Unitas, no matter how skilled, had no cards to play.

As the 1965 season dawned that humiliation wasn't Unitas's only problem. Soon after reporting to camp he complained of soreness in his arm. He had also done so just prior to last winter's championship game. Though his elbow constantly pained him, like a "toothache," he was still making every throw on the field with as much power, touch, and accuracy as he ever had.

The Colts were a transitioning team, trying to recover from the sting and stain of their inglorious loss to the Browns. They had no choice but to do so with two potential massive holes in their defense.

Gino Marchetti and Bill Pellington had both announced their retirements. The Colts felt relatively sure they could replace the irreplaceable Marchetti, since they had two excellent football players in Ordell Braase and Lou Michaels to man the defensive-end spots. The linebacker position, on the other hand, presented Shula with some problems.

Pellington had a reputation as one of the meanest and toughest linebackers in the game. In addition to that he was the "quarterback" on defense, calling all of the Colts' plays. Shula's first step in filling the void Pellington's absence created was to use the team's number-one draft pick to select Mike Curtis, who was both a linebacker and a fullback at Duke.

The Colts' coaches quickly determined that Curtis would be more valuable to them on offense, running the ball instead of tackling the runner. (Curtis would later permanently return to defense.) That meant they still needed a linebacker. And in order to attract one, they used Joe Don Looney as the bait.

Joe Don was still in his early twenties and starting only his second season in the league. His potential combined with his evident strength, speed, and size made him a valuable commodity. As the Colts and Giants already knew, Looney was a misery but one you could easily unload on some other sucker. In this case the Detroit Lions, desperate for running help, filled the bill. They proffered Dennis Gaubatz, a ferocious young middle linebacker stuck on the bench behind their beloved All-Pro Joe Schmidt. The Colts gratefully accepted.

When the astonished Joe Don heard what Baltimore had obtained in exchange for him, he commented as only he could. "I think the Colts made a hell of a deal," Looney said.

He was right about that.

Gaubatz developed into a key piece on the Colts' defense. Meanwhile, Looney spent less than two seasons with the Lions, despite the fact that Detroit coach Harry Gilmer had hailed Joe Don upon his arrival as the team's missing piece to a championship. In fact, Looney performed admirably for the Lions, scoring five rushing touchdowns in his first season with them.

But he quickly ran afoul of Gilmer anyway. When the coach ordered him to deliver a message to the huddle in a game, Looney refused and told his boss to call Western Union instead.

Needless to say, Joe Don was soon the property of the Washington Redskins.

Every single coach Joe Don had in college and the pros rejected him, and they all cited the same reasons—his immaturity and mental instability. In the 1960s there was only one place left to turn for a man like that. Too unpredictable for football, he was given guns and grenades and sent to Vietnam.

The experience somehow bestowed a prescience on Looney that was still lacking in America's great men. While the president, congressmen, and business and military leaders were all still in denial about the war, telling the country it could be won, Looney was speaking a despised truth.

"Guys are dying like flies in Vietnam, a war we couldn't win if we sent 10 million men over there," Joe Don told *Sports Illustrated*. "It's tragic because it's such a waste. We're going to pull out of Vietnam as soon as we can, and what have we accomplished?"

That was the American question of the decade, of course, posited and framed with perfect clarity by a man named Looney.

Meanwhile, the marshal-like Shula seemed to be having better luck than the Pentagon. The Looney-for-Gaubatz deal was just one of his many brilliant moves. Under his direction the Colts became a mighty repository for talent—in the front office, the coaching ranks, the scouts, and the players.

Shula's machine lifted Baltimore to great heights. For four seasons of his reign (1964, '65, '67, and '68) the Colts averaged little more than one loss per year. His sharp rise and sustained success quickly put him in a league with the greatest coaches of all time. Shula was the peer of successful but grumpy old men like Paul Brown, Lombardi, and Halas—even though he wasn't even forty yet.

The fans respected, admired, and appreciated Shula. They identified with his working-class roots and felt a kinship with his brusque, take-no-prisoners approach. He was at once one of them and better. He was a winner.

Shula's populism aside, however, their focal point was Johnny Unitas. He was so associated with the Colts and their long period of sensational play that the horseshoe on the team helmets no longer represented the franchise, horse racing, or even good luck. In a city where the industries were all moving out, where the blue-collar jobs were gasping and the headquarters all fleeing, the horseshoe took on an immense meaning. It was a symbol of town sanctity despite the rejections and humiliations.

But for all intents and purposes, the horseshoe was Unitas's own initial. The team and the city, the players and the citizens, drew their strength and power, their very identity, from U.

The Colts' loss in the 1964 championship game, and Unitas's incredibly poor play against the Browns, all seemed like some strange anomaly that could never be repeated. Unitas was indomitable, and, because of their connection to him, so were *his* men and his city.

So the falling of the leaves in 1965 came to Baltimore with incredible optimism. In the season's first game Unitas outplayed Minnesota's Fran Tarkenton, another future Hall of Famer, and threw two touchdown passes. The Colts torched the Vikings, 35–16.

In week two they traveled to Wisconsin to meet the Packers in Milwaukee. Green Bay seemed to bring out the worst in the Colts. With the game almost over, Baltimore had already fumbled three times and Unitas had thrown two interceptions. Those five turnovers had led to seventeen Packer points. With only about a minute left to play, it should have been a disaster, but, in fact, the Colts were only down by three and in possession of the ball. Unitas knew what to do with it.

Facing the best defense in the NFL, he masterfully advanced his Colts 45 yards in five plays. With fifty-three seconds still left on the clock, and the Colts needing only a field goal to tie, he had Baltimore comfortably perched on the Packer 37.

Green Bay might have reasonably expected him to run, but Johnny U crossed them up and put the ball in the air. He hit Matte, a famously reliable receiver out of the backfield, with a 15-yard bullet. Tom caught the ball, but then he fumbled it away for Baltimore's sixth, and fatal, turnover.

The Colts lost 20–17, but the circumstances underscored the razor-thin difference between the two teams. The Colts wouldn't lose again for another two and a half months, ten more games, and the Packers would dog their heels the entire time. The long winning streak was all the more impressive as some of it was accomplished without Unitas, who missed a game and a half due to back spasms. The problem first surfaced in a contest against the Rams, but Johnny U soldiered on through the pain for a couple more games. Finally, at Wrigley Field in Chicago, the Bears advanced his pain to the unendurable stage with blitzes and brutal hits. Unitas left the game for good in the third quarter and missed the next one as well. Those were the first games he missed due to injury in about seven years.

In the meantime, Shula inserted Gary Cuozzo, Unitas's well-regarded understudy, to take his place. Cuozzo did more than fill in for the famous man; he eclipsed him. The quarterback lit up the Vikings and threw five touchdowns passes against them in a 41–21 Colts victory. Even Unitas had never done that.

The next week Johnny U was well enough to return to action and face the Eagles in Baltimore. The Philadelphians came limping down 1-95 with a measly 3-6 record, but they put up a hell of a fight. Just before the half they roughed up Jimmy Orr so badly, he had to be rushed to the hospital for shoulder X-rays.

Since Orr had come to Baltimore in the famous trade that sent Big Daddy Lipscomb to the Steelers, he had been a kind of Colts talisman. By his own admission he was relatively small and slow, but for him that was no liability. He led the league in yards per reception on three different occasions, averaging more than 20 yards all three times.

If Orr's greatness suggested a sense of purpose, well, that was purely coincidental. Jimmy utterly lacked a serious side. He spoke in an exaggerated southern drawl so deep and gargled as to be almost unintelligible. A listener could tell that he had reached the end of a sentence only because he used laughter like punctuation. His mission, it seemed, was to go through life with a twinkle in his eye and to make joking, drinking, gambling, and romancing his chief occupations. Football just happened to be something he was superb at doing, and it provided him with pretty good money for all the fun he wanted.

Orr was unquestionably among the best players of his era. Nevertheless, he found he could live without certain aspects of the game. He didn't like to practice, and he didn't like the contact. Once, in a film session, Shula berated him for missing a downfield block. But Jimmy took the criticism with good humor.

"Why in the world would you send a thoroughbred to do a mule's work?" he asked.

Baltimore was clinging to a slim three-point lead against the Eagles in the fourth quarter when an ambulance came speeding up to Memorial Stadium. The back door flung open, and Jimmy dramatically hopped out in full uniform. Buckling his chinstrap like a fighter pilot, he ran through the tunnel and incited an eruption of thunderous applause.

Shula, hearing the cheers, looked over and saw Orr's arrival on the sideline. Without saying so much as a single word, he motioned for Jimmy to join the offense on the playing field. Unitas didn't waste any time, either. On the second play from scrimmage he heaved a 22-yard pass to Orr, who snatched it out of the air, in the end zone, for a touchdown. After the extra point the Colts were ten points ahead, and the game was all but over. Orr remangled his shoulder making the catch, but the Eagles had lost their wings.

After the game reporters asked Unitas why he waited until the second play to throw Jimmy the ball. Why not the first? "I thought he might be out of breath after running from the hospital," Johnny U said.

When the euphoria ended, the Colts still had hard issues. Despite the theatrics of their victory, they were an exhausted and hurting team. What was worse, their next game was only four days away, on Thanksgiving, in Detroit.

Behind quarterback Milt Plum, the Lions weren't much. With the season nearing its end they had managed only a .500 record, and they were trending downward, having lost their last two games.

Yet the Colts were ripe for a trap. The Lions were always tough to beat on Thanksgiving, a holiday that seemed to belong to them. On top of that, eight Colts starters were either playing injured or not playing. Evil omens.

Indeed, it all portended bad things. Unitas had a terrible day, completing only fourteen passes for 188 yards. He was picked off two times. Both of his misfires led to Detroit scores. It might have been Thanksgiving, but the Colts left Motown like a dad on Father's Day. They came out of it with a tie (24–24), and they felt lucky to have it.

Meanwhile, the Packers were still in hot pursuit. They went to Los Angeles, where the Rams unexpectedly beat them, 21–10. The Colts had dodged the bullet and were still in command of the West, but that feeling of well-being wouldn't last long.

The very next week a disastrous and thrilling sequence of events unfolded. In Baltimore the Colts faced Chicago, a team that always administered a thunderous beating to Unitas.

"The Bears had bounties on us, there's no question," running back Tom Matte said. "Johnny U, they wanted to knock his ass out."

First, Chicago took away Unitas's short passing lanes. Then, when he attempted to go long, they blanketed his receivers with double coverages. In the second quarter, with Unitas only three for nine and 24 yards gained, he stubbornly faded back once more. It was a decision, as it turned out, that was hazardous to his health. Just as he flung a long, vain pass in John Mackey's direction, two Bears slammed into him. One collared him around the head and shoulders, while the other crashed into his legs. The torso of the great Unitas was bent in half, backward. Even if his "ass" wasn't knocked out, as Matte said, his leg was. He was badly injured and removed from the field.

Cuozzo, who had performed so admirably earlier in the year, was summoned to stand in. But he, too, was powerless against the barbaric Bears. Unable to recapture the magic he'd shown against the Vikings, Gary fired two interceptions, and the Colts lost the game, 13–0.

The worst news of the day was yet to come. Johnny U's knee ligaments and cartilage were torn. His injuries required immediate surgery, and his season was most likely over. But when Shula spoke to the reporters after the game, it was more about insults than injuries. "It was the worst game I think I've ever seen our offense play," he said.

He also wondered out loud about something that few others had yet to consider. What would happen in the unlikely event that Cuozzo also went down? "We have Tom Matte who can go in," Shula said, "and a band-squad member, [George] Haffner, we could activate."

Matte, of course, was a backup halfback, and Haffner was "Mr. Irrelevant," the very last player chosen in the NFL draft just a few months before. Haffner still hadn't played a single real down of football in the pros.

By raising the point Shula showed that even in the face of swirling and disappointing events, he was rational and in command; he was already planning ahead. In any event, there was very little time to philosophize about what had happened or what it all meant. Lombardi and the Packers were looming. They would be in Baltimore in a week.

If the Colts could overcome their injuries and beat Green Bay,

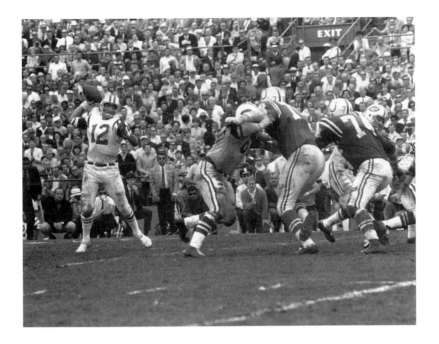

**1.** Joe Namath had been on Weeb Ewbank's radar a long time. The canny coach knew all about Namath from his assistant Chuck Knox, who'd scouted Joe all the way back to junior high school. Bear Bryant, Namath's college coach, convinced Ewbank to draft Namath, and he helped convince Namath to sign with Ewbank. AP PHOTO/NFL PHOTOS

**2.** (*opposite top*) The Colts were leading the Western Division in 1965 when Unitas tore ligaments in his knee in the Chicago game. With immediate surgery scheduled, his season was over. The next week Johnny U's backup, Gary Cuozzo, suffered a separated shoulder playing against the Packers. Baltimore's season would hinge on a running back playing the game's most important position. AP PHOTO/DAVID BOOKSTAVER.

**3.** (*opposite bottom*) One of the most highly anticipated games in history took place in Green Bay when the Colts and the Packers tied, forcing a special one-game playoff to determine the champion of their division. With both Colts quarterbacks on the bench with injuries, Shula used Tom Matte at quarterback. The Colts lost only on a disputed field goal at the end of the game that looked clearly bad on film. In overtime Packers kicker Don Chandler kicked a "good" field goal to win it. AP PHOTO/VERNON BIEVER.

**4.** (*above*) To their fans the Colts appeared to be a merry band of brothers, but that was far from true. Black players like Lenny Moore felt disrespected by the era's segregation laws and by informal agreements in the NFL to limit the number of black players on team rosters. In 1963 Moore was injured most of the season and felt as though he was being pushed off the team. AP PHOTO.

**5.** Vince Lombardi's iron will to win was hard for even Johnny U and the Colts to overcome. At one point the Packers won five games in a row against Baltimore. But the two teams carried on a rivalry of unmatched intensity. Lombardi's Packers won five titles in the decade, but the Colts had a higher winning percentage under Shula than Green Bay did under Vince. AP PHOTO/ NFL PHOTO/VERNON BIEVER.

**6.** (*opposite top*) Unitas was known for two things: he was fearless even in the face of the toughest players, and he was almost impossible to beat in the clutch. The Rams' Merlin Olsen once explained how unnerving Unitas could be, even after driving him into the ground. "I knew—we knew—he was going to get us sooner or later," Olsen told Bill Curry. AP PHOTO/NFL PHOTOS.

**7.** (*opposite bottom*) Earl Morrall played for four teams before being traded to Baltimore and considered retiring instead of reporting. Playing under Shula changed everything for him. As a Colt he led the league in passing and was named league MVP. But Joe Namath disparaged Morrall before Super Bowl III and ticked off the names of AFL passers he considered better, including his backup on the Jets, Babe Parilli. AP PHOTO.

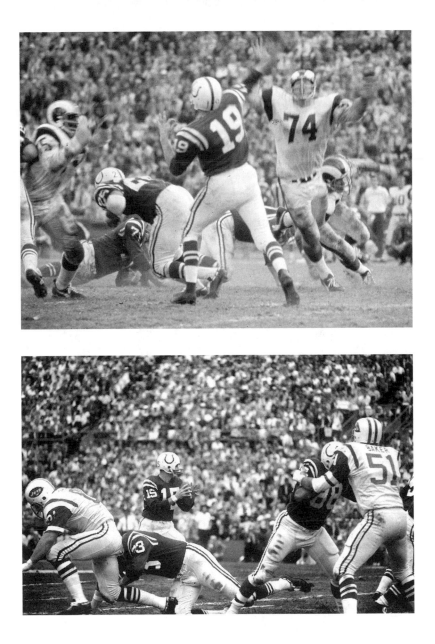

**8.** Unitas and Morrall became good friends off the field. They were so inseparable, and looked so much alike, their teammates jokingly called the slouching Unitas "Hump" and the big-assed Morrall "Rump." AP PHOTO/ WILLIAM SMITH.

**9.** (*opposite top*) Johnny U and Merlin Olsen of the Los Angeles Rams shake hands with President Lyndon B. Johnson in Washington. In the 1960s professional football players had an effect on the culture. In the 1968 presidential race both Democrats and Republicans considered football coaches for the top of their national tickets. AP PHOTO/JOHN ROUS.

**10.** (*opposite bottom*) Part of the secret of Johnny Unitas's success was the chemistry he had with his receivers. Here, he reviews a play with Jimmy Orr, a supposedly short and slow receiver who nevertheless had a flair for making huge gains and clutch touchdowns. AP PHOTO/WILLIAM SMITH.

**11.** Unitas, pictured here with his first wife, Dorothy, and their first four children, was voted "Sports Father of the Year" in the early '60s. He looked like the all-American family man, but the definition for that was rapidly changing. AP PHOTO.

they would most likely cruise into the postseason. A loss would be all but fatal.

The Packers had their own problems. They didn't seem to be exactly the same team that went to three straight championship games earlier in the decade. They still had a punishing defense, with middle linebacker Ray Nitschke at its core. But it had been more than two years since Green Bay had last won the West, and in that time their offense had lost a great deal of its swagger. Where once their pounding ground game had put them at the top of the league scoring tables, now they were mired in the lower half.

Looking for a spark in the unlikeliest place, Lombardi announced on Wednesday that Paul Hornung would start at halfback. In years past the Golden Boy was one of the most famous and celebrated of all the Packers, a Heisman Trophy winner and triple threat who could run, pass, and kick. Even in the glory days Lombardi thought Hornung was only an average back in the middle of the field. Inside the opponent's 20-yard line, however, the coach believed he was a different man, one with an unusual instinct for finding the end zone. Indeed, in 1960 Hornung led the league with thirteen rushing touchdowns.

But in 1963 the Golden Boy was suspended for gambling and didn't play a single game all year. In '64 he had a painful nerve problem and couldn't perform well. In '65 his steep decline had only continued. The fans looked upon him as a major cause for Green Bay's offensive miseries, just as they had once seen him as the prime catalyst for Packers domination.

But Lombardi always considered Hornung a big gamer, and he had a hunch that Sunday, with the pressure more intense perhaps than it had ever been, the Golden Boy would finally regain his luster.

In Baltimore they were unconcerned with the Packers' machinations. They were still grieving the fallen Johnny U, whose damaged knee joint quickly went under the surgeon's knife. The fans were also evaluating young Cuozzo, wondering whether he might be able to live up to their impossible standards for a quarterback.

The *Baltimore Sun* indulged this curiosity. They dialed long distance to speak to Cuozzo's mother and father in New Jersey, as though they held the keys to his character and fitness for duty.

Mrs. Cuozzo *kvelled* over her suddenly famous son; she bragged about his grades and his membership in the "Ravens Society," an intellectual group at the University of Virginia, where he went to college. She also noted that he had been accepted to Yale Medical School but chose instead to study dentistry at the University of Tennessee. She said he wanted to follow in the footsteps of his father, "the doctor," who was also a dentist.

The fans would have to wait until Sunday to see whether all that maternal love and toothy brilliance would make Cuozzo an effective passer with the terrifying and bald specter of Ray Nitschke chasing him down like a loan collector.

These high stakes and compelling story lines made the second Colts-and-Packers matchup of 1965 an extraordinarily anticipated regular-season game. And that was before one more spellbinding factor wound its way into the picture.

On the morning of the game a thick fog rolled off the bay and enveloped Memorial Stadium in a translucent shroud. The hazy mists lent the festivities a dreamy quality. From the stands the players shimmered in a silvery glow, looking like mere shadows of reality as they emerged from and disappeared into the low-slung clouds. For angst-riddled Baltimoreans, those dreams weren't wish fulfillments; they were more like fever hallucinations. Looking to the Packers' sideline, they could see the imperial Lombardi, standing like an obstruction in his fedora and thick black glasses. But on the Colts' bench there was no sign of the white number 19. Instead, there was only the suddenly small figure of the unadorned Johnny U, leaning on his new crutches, his damaged pin tightly wrapped in a cast, his bristled head bereft of the gleaming white helm. In place of the dramatic cold-weather cape typically slung across his shoulder armor, there was only a long and forlorn London Fog raincoat, barely concealing his business suit and tie. He wasn't clothed for heroics; he was cloaked in the garb of secret identity.

At first the game seemed to live up to its expectations. The action careened out of the gate. Early on the momentum swung back and forth, with mistakes and great plays. The game didn't become really interesting, however, until just before the end of the first half. The Colts were behind by only one point, 14–13, when they recovered a Packer fumble at the Green Bay 2. Baltimore had a great chance to go to the lockers at halftime with a six-point lead, but young Cuozzo got greedy. Instead of allowing his line and running backs to do the work with a charge at the goal line, the quarterback ran a play-action pass, faking a handoff to Lenny Moore and then throwing in the flat to fullback Jerry Hill.

The experienced and wily Packer defenders smelled the deception, and one of them, linebacker Dave Robinson, picked off the pass and returned it 88 yards to the Colts' 10. Starr didn't waste the opportunity. He quickly hit his flanker, Boyd Dowler, in the end zone, and Green Bay skipped into halftime eight points ahead instead of six behind.

Curiously, Shula, who had endured so much tension for his attempts to send plays into Unitas, left Cuozzo alone to make the call himself. He offered no suggestions from the sidelines to the inexperienced quarterback. The very poor play call was Cuozzo's, and his alone.

The afternoon belonged instead to Paul Hornung. That was apparent in the first quarter, when he ran for a 2-yard touchdown and caught a 50-yard pass from Starr for another.

In the third quarter Cuozzo's shoulder was badly injured. He went down to the locker room so that he could be pierced with a needle that injected a painkiller deep into the joint. He missed seven plays.

Paul Hornung, meanwhile, scored two more touchdowns, to give him four on the day with a quarter still remaining.

Cuozzo returned to action in the fourth and gamely led his teammates to two touchdowns. His work pulled the Colts within eight points of the Packers with six minutes left to play.

But then Bart Starr hit Hornung with a 65-yard touchdown pass, and it was all over.

So the story of the game was not the emergence of a sensational new player but the reemergence of a has-been. Vince Lombardi's hunch had proved prophetic. All told, Paul Hornung scored five touchdowns, three on the ground and two as a receiver. His pair of receptions gained 115 yards.

The humiliations kept coming for the Colts. With the Packers' victory the two teams flipped places in the standings. Green

Bay, at 10-3, was half a game ahead of the 9-3-1 Colts. Even worse, Cuozzo had a badly separated shoulder that would require him to undergo an immediate and gruesome surgery. Steel wires had to be inserted to reattach the prodigal arm to the shoulder. Gary's football career, which had seemed so promising just twenty-four hours prior, was now in danger.

Although there was still one game left to play, Baltimore appeared doomed.

For their last game of the year the Colts had to travel all the way to Los Angeles to face the surging Rams. LA had had a terrible season, losing eight in a row at one point. Nevertheless, the Rams had turned things around and were moving in the right direction. They were in the midst of a three-game winning streak that included an easy victory over the Packers, 21–10, and a thrashing of the defending-champion Browns, 42–7.

Even if the Colts could beat the Rams on the road, a dubious proposition in their depleted state, the Packers surely wouldn't stumble in their game against the 49ers. San Francisco had not only been humiliated by the Bears just the week before, losing 61–20, but they had also given up six touchdowns to just one player, the sensational rookie running back Gayle Sayers.

In Baltimore there was only one question worth considering: With Unitas and Cuozzo both injured, who was going to play quarterback for the Colts? George Haffner was added to the active roster, and Shula made a trade with Pittsburgh for the veteran Ed Brown, who was near the end of a long, unremarkable career.

The era's restrictive rules froze the roster where it was before the next-to-last game of the season. So neither player was eligible for postseason play, even in the unlikely event the Colts should make it to the championship game.

All things considered, Shula made the best decision he could and elected to go with his backup halfback Tom Matte as the signal caller. Matte had already stepped in when Cuozzo went down with his shoulder injury in the Green Bay game, and he had performed well.

Before that all his prior experience at quarterback was in coach Woody Hayes's Ohio State program. Woody was famous for saying, "There are only three things that can happen when you throw the ball, and two of them are bad." Needless to say, Matte wasn't slingin' it around in a prostyle offense in Columbus, Ohio.

Before handing over the reins of the Colts to Matte, Shula did his due diligence and called Woody for a scouting report on how Tom performed as a quarterback.

"He's a great kid," Woody told Shula. "He did everything I asked him to do."

"Were there any negatives that might help me out so I can be alert for them?" Shula asked.

There was a long silence on the line. Finally, Woody said, "Well, he had trouble taking the snap from center."

In other words, Shula only had to teach Matte everything about being an NFL quarterback. And he had a week to do it.

Tom Matte came from the type of background that suggested he was ripe for a challenge. He grew up in a tough neighborhood in Cleveland, a place he later described as the "worst crime district in Ohio." He was raised to be a very tough man, by a very tough man. His father, a Canadian with elements of Iroquois, was a professional hockey player who made very little money.

After his athletic career the old man worked as a union mill-wright who traveled around the country for his profession. He was well known for his extraordinary balance, a skill he attributed to his Indian blood. "He was one of those wackos who walk on the high beams," Matte said. "He fell one time about fifty feet and almost killed himself."

Because Matte's father was a professional hockey player, Tom was raised on skates. He was an all-star, all-everything, on the ice. His father recognized his son's obvious potential and wanted him to concentrate on hockey and didn't want him to play football. But in the ninth grade his mother secretly signed him up anyway, and all his father's apprehensions came true. On the very first play of his football career, a kickoff, Matte got clipped, and his knee was shattered. His father was so angry, he didn't speak to him for three months. Meanwhile, the doctor told him his injury was severe enough that he would never play sports again.

It wasn't true. The tough Matte bounced back from his knee problem and quickly developed into a talented and multifaceted high school athlete. He filled out to 190 solid pounds and combined that power with agility and speed. As a member of the track team he ran the quarter mile in 47 seconds flat; he ran the 100 in 9.9 seconds. He also pole-vaulted and topped out at around thirteen feet. That was impressive for a high school athlete, considering Bob Richards, the best pole-vaulter in the world at that time, was hitting about fifteen feet. Matte also averaged fifteen points a game on the basketball team.

At Ohio State Matte played football, ran track, played ice hockey, and even found time for fraternity basketball. That versatility paid off in professional football. The Colts drafted him as a quarterback, but with Unitas in his way he quickly decided to play running back.

His NFL playing weight was around 220 pounds in an era when the average offensive lineman was only about 245. Nevertheless, he was agile and gained Unitas's eye with his outstanding ability to catch the ball out of the backfield.

Matte idolized Johnny U. He followed the quarterback's example of study and hard work. He became a devoted watcher of game film and recruited his wife to help him. The two of them sat on their sofa at night and ran the projector back and forth as they charted plays and tendencies late into the evening. More than forty years after his career had ended, Matte still had reels and an old-fashioned projector in his home.

Matte learned his own assignments and the assignments of every player on the field. He conferred with his offensive linemen and learned how to regulate his speed to use their blocking to his greatest advantage. Like Unitas and Raymond Berry, he stayed long beyond the formal end of practice to continue to work on patterns and timing.

In the hard realities of professional sports, however, Matte's work ethic didn't always pay off exactly as he had hoped. His playing time was limited due to the fact that he was stuck behind an athlete who was even far more talented than he was, Lenny Moore. Even Matte conceded that Lenny was "probably the best all-around back-receiver who ever played the game."

Talent notwithstanding, Matte resented the fact that Lenny got the attention and opportunities without trying as hard as he did. Matte thought Moore used injuries as an excuse to duck practice.

"All week long," Matte said, "I had run every play in practice. And then on Saturday morning, guess who would come bouncing out of the fucking locker room?"

Moore's unwillingness to work through pain, if that's what it was, offended Matte. In the ethos of the day Tom soldiered through a multitude of gruesome injuries. In 1964 he played with bleeding ulcers. After an operation to correct the problem, he had to receive seven and a half pints of blood. The human body holds only about nine.

After another operation at a local hospital, he suffered a staph infection. That caused him to lose about fifty pounds in a month and brought him close to death. His years of playing football in the sun also took their toll. When Matte was being treated for another condition, a physician noticed a growth on his nose. A biopsy determined that it was cancer; what's more, it was only a sixteenth of an inch away from a tear gland. "If that cancer hits the tear gland," the specialist told him, "you'll be dead in about three months."

Later on Matte's appendix burst. All told, he endured about eighteen different operations, including one to the heart, during his career.

This man who had endured so much was now going to step into the crucible and hot spotlight of playing quarterback for the Colts, in the biggest of games against the greatest of teams, with almost no preparation. It was a role no one else would relish.

Unitas was a reassuring presence. He and offensive coordinator Don McCafferty devised a whole new offense just for Matte. To aid Matte's recall, Shula outfitted him with an armband that had the key plays and formations written on it.

"Unitas said, 'Do what you can do best: roll out; do the quarterback draws. You'll really screw everybody up,'" Matte remembered. "John was instrumental in helping Shula and McCafferty design plays around what I could do."

Although it was easy enough to see what the Colts were lacking without Unitas or Cuozzo, the circumstances, in their most optimistic light, also presented Baltimore an unanticipated opportunity. No one knew what to expect from Matte and his new playbook. There was a school of thought that saw it as a strategic advantage for the Colts.

Back in Baltimore, reduced to the role of spectator, Gary Cuozzo sat up in his hospital bed in his pajamas and watched the game on TV. A patient at Children's Hospital recuperating from his shoulder operation, he looked like a kid home from school with a cold. Sitting next to him, watching the game on the old tube with its rabbit ears, was a twelve-year-old little boy, also a patient.

In Los Angeles, that city of dreams, Matte and his teammates also lived out a fantasy. Although Matte did not complete a single pass in his Unitas-designed offense, he bulled his way to 99 yards on the ground, running from the quarterback position. Lenny Moore, in the midst of a season of decline, scampered 28 yards for a touchdown. And Ed Brown, the quarterback Shula acquired only one day before, who had only one practice with the Colts under his belt, came in intermittently and threw a 68-yard touchdown pass to John Mackey.

While all were obsessed with the Colts' offense and its problems and possibilities, Baltimore's extraordinary defense turned in a clutch performance. Bobby Boyd intercepted the Rams' Roman Gabriel twice. The first one led to a Colts touchdown, and the second one sealed the victory with Los Angeles on the Colts' 9 and only seconds remaining in the game. Boyd stepped in front of Gabriel's bold shot at the end zone and ended all Rams hope. The Colts won 20–17.

Despite the great victory, the Colts' players believed their season was over. Instead of returning to Baltimore to begin preparation for the next week in the unlikely event there was one, Unitas, Dan Sullivan, Matte, Jimmy Orr, and about four or five other players flew to Las Vegas to unwind and have a little fun. The players took time out to watch the Packers-49ers game, and, like the rest of the country, they couldn't believe their eyes as they watched San Francisco tie Lombardi in a big game.

Baltimore and the Packers were now tied in the standings. Sitting there in Las Vegas, the Colts weren't even sure of the tie-breaking procedures and didn't understand the implications of what they had just watched.

But someone back in Baltimore knew exactly what it meant.

About an hour after the game the phone rang in Unitas's hotel room. "Get those sons of bitches back on the plane and get back to Baltimore," Don Shula told him. "We've got another game to play."

Some didn't believe the Colts even deserved to be on the same field with the Packers. They had already lost to them twice in the regular season, and the second meeting was an embarrassing blowout in their own house. And now Baltimore's once mighty offense was limping into Wisconsin, held together with little more than Scotch tape and moxie. Even creaky Ed Brown, the one-day wonder who threw the big touchdown pass against the Rams, wasn't eligible to play in this "postseason" game.

Regardless of their relative merits, the Colts and Packers had identical records, and in the tie-breaking rules of the day, that called for a one-game playoff.

The only way Baltimore, with Matte at quarterback, could beat the highly disciplined Packers was to get the lead on them and then hope their own superb Colts defense could shut down the struggling Green Bay offense.

On the very first play from scrimmage it seemed that scenario might actually play out. Bart Starr, Green Bay's superbly accurate quarterback, faded back to pass and hit tight end Bill Anderson, but so did Leonard Lyles, Baltimore's cornerback. Anderson fumbled upon Lyles's impact. Don Schinnick, the Colts' outside linebacker, scooped up the ball and raced toward the end zone with it. Starr dutifully pursued Schinnick to try to tackle him before he could score a touchdown, but Colts safety Jim Welch drilled Starr. The great quarterback's ribs were severely bruised, and after only one play he was done for the day. His backup, Zeke Bratkowski, would play quarterback for the Packers the rest of the day. Starr's only action would be to hold for kicks.

With their 7–0 lead Baltimore would now attempt to hold on for dear life. Matte attempted twelve passes and completed only five of them. He ran for 57 yards against the stout Packers, and he did just enough to give Baltimore a chance to win.

In the second quarter Matte drove the Colts 68 yards so that Lou Michaels could kick an easy 15-yard field goal. At the same time, the Packers were highly frustrated in their own attempts. When they had the ball on the Colts' 1, the Baltimore defense manhandled the famous Packers line and stuffed attempts by both Jim

Taylor and Paul Hornung to cross the goal line. And Baltimore went into halftime with a 10–0 lead.

But in the third quarter the charm left the Colts, and the curse set in. Punter Tom Gilburg took a high snap and had to run instead of kicking the ball. The Packers tackled him and took over on the Colts' 35. Bratkowski passed the Packers to the 1. Again, Baltimore stopped Jim Taylor on the goal line. But on the next snap Paul Hornung took the ball in. The score was 10–7.

And then the unkindest cut. After an exchange of the ball, Colts lineman Billy Ray Smith zeroed in on a sack of Bratkowski. Instead of merely tackling him, however, he clubbed the Packer quarterback across the head with a forearm, not an unusual play in that brutal age. Ironically, however, after the beating Unitas took against the Bears that left him crippled and on the sidelines, the officials were protecting the quarterbacks more closely. Billy Ray was called for the personal foul, and instead of an 8-yard loss, the Packers had the ball on Baltimore's 43-yard line as the time continued to tick.

Bratkowski moved the ball to the Baltimore 22. And then one of the great dramas in all of football lore unfolded. Don Chandler, the Green Bay kicker recently acquired from the New York Giants, trotted in to attempt the short tying field goal.

His kick approached the rickety, wooden uprights and at the last moment appeared to sail right. But the official posted beneath the goalpost threw his arms in the air, signaling the kick was good.

But was it?

The Green Bay long snapper, Bill Curry, said he didn't see the kick, but he had a couple of friends who did. "Don Chandler, who is very good at keeping his head down, looked up, saw the ball after it passed the upright, and it was clearly wide, so he turned around and kicked the ground. However, I have an unimpeachable source, Bart Starr, who simply doesn't tell lies, who was the holder that day. Bart says it went directly over the upright, and therefore it was good. My face was in the mud at the bottom of the pile. Someone had jumped on my head."

Fair or foul, the kick was ruled good, and the game went into overtime. It ended only with another short Chandler field goal, this one clearly good.

UNPRECEDENTED SUCCESS

Baltimore's one-year reign over the West was over. Photos of Lombardi with an exuberant, jubilant smile filled newspapers from coast to coast. No one loved victory more than he did. Nevertheless, he was old school and poised, and in the locker room after the game he attempted magnanimity.

"Tom Matte is a great athlete," Lombardi said. "I have great admiration for Shula and all the Colts."

Carroll Rosenbloom, the man who demanded championship success from his coaches, professed great satisfaction with his men—and irritation with the referees. "I was never more proud of any team I've had," the magnate said. "We didn't deserve to lose. There was no justice out there today."

In a sense officials' mistakes and winners and losers were irrelevant that day after Christmas 1965. The Colts lost, but professional football enjoyed a huge victory. The Colts and Packers represented a high-water mark for the game.

Lombardi and Shula were perfecting what Unitas and Berry had started in the mid-1950s. They were all raising the bar of intensity and competition and unlocking the potential of the game, demonstrating how suspenseful, unexpected, and compelling it could be. Every game all year had crackled with import, culminating in the high-stakes playoff.

It was only football, but it was being played at a higher and far more dramatic level than anyone had ever seen before. It was all spurred on by coaches and players with a manic sense of competition, men who were driven to incredibly long hours of work and to seek every possible edge. The two coaches almost seemed to be from different eras, but there they were on the same field, opposing each other. One, Lombardi, was the greatest champion in history and in the heart of his great run. The other, Shula, was the coach who would one day win more games than any other, but he was only at the beginning. Both sidelines teemed with future Hall of Famers. The game was played in the harsh winter elements, on real grass, in light provided by nature. The uniforms were ruggedly crafted from natural fibers with numbers stitched onto the material. The players were courageous and dedicated to their work. And the referees were participating in the same big-game pressure as the players, making their decisions on the spot, trusting only their eyes. There was no replay yet to review, stopping the action and removing the human element. Officials' errors and interpretations of the rules only added to the drama of a show in which no one could predict the ending.

Professional football had many great moments ahead of it. It would grow and go in directions its founders never could have foreseen. But it reached its crescendo in Green Bay that day, and it would never be quite as good again.

The Packers, of course, went on to beat the same Cleveland Browns team in the championship game that the Colts had lost to the year before. In the long off-season the officials' errors, especially the call on the disputed field goal, greatly irritated the Colts and their fans. One newspaper published a photo purporting to unequivocally show the kick was wide.

Matte was rightly enjoying his moment in the spotlight and his well-earned position of respect with the nation's sports press and fans. At one point he attended an awards banquet at the Minneapolis Touchdown Club. He shared the place of honor at the head table with Vince Lombardi. When Matte got up to speak, he came prepared with a model goalpost he'd made. It had a gimmick that slid out to make the goalposts much wider. To the delight of the Minnesotans in attendance that night, he called it "the Green Bay goalpost." As usual, however, Lombardi feigned delight at the joke and then had the last word.

"Tom, I don't know if the field goal was good or bad," Vince said, "but when I went to the bank on Monday morning my check said we were the champions."

Lombardi was referring to the winners' share of the postseason money. One of the Colts had done the math and figured that the disputed field goal cost each Colt about $10,000.

The league didn't have much to say about the officials' calls and whether the field goal was actually good. But before the next season started, the NFL mandated that the goalposts be standardized. Among the changes, they were to all be painted yellow, and the uprights were all to be twenty feet above the crossbar. Everyone in football informally referred to these new taller goalposts as the "Baltimore extensions."

It was a second disappointing ending to a season in a row for Don Shula, but also a rebirth of sorts. After the game he told reporters how much the loss of Unitas had hurt the Colts, how limited they had been without the great man's ability to move the ball But the reality was that Shula had just shown the world that he could stand toe-to-toe with the greatest coach who ever lived and perhaps the greatest team ever assembled without Unitas stepping a cleated toe on the field or taking a single snap.

Shula didn't need Unitas, and, what's more, he had proved that cold day in Green Bay that he might not even need a quarterback at all.

## TWELVE

## Changing Times

After three years Unitas and Shula had accomplished a great deal together—everything, it seemed, except what they had set out to do. They made themselves famous and the Colts one of the most feared and respected teams in the league. But to their mutual embarrassment, they still had failed to win a championship.

Meanwhile, the team was evolving and changing. Charley Winner, the Colts' defensive coordinator since the mid-1950s, announced that he was leaving to become head coach of the St. Louis Cardinals. Few men had ever done as much for a franchise as Winner had for Baltimore. Charley was the man who brought Weeb Ewbank to the Colts' attention. Winner had scouted Don Shula in college and greatly aided his development as a pro player. Charley was there when Johnny U walked through the doors for the first time, greeting him and accurately evaluating his talent. Later on Charley worked with Unitas late into the night to teach the young quarterback all about defense.

Charley Winner was an unlikely football player or coach. He was small, intelligent, articulate, and genial. At only five feet six and less than 150 pounds, it was hard to imagine him competing in a uniform, let alone bossing around the behemoths who did. But he was a lot tougher than anyone realized.

Charley came out of a hardscrabble German American family in Summerville, New Jersey, about a half hour south of New York City. His father was poor and uneducated but possessed a keen understanding of machinery and could take an automobile apart piece by piece.

That skill landed the elder Winner a job as a laborer for the town. He drove and repaired street cleaners for the magnificent sum of $26 per week. Charley was as energetic and physical as his father; in fact, he could barely sit in a chair. But his passion wasn't for labor; it was for football, and his austere parents didn't approve of the frivolity.

"I could hear [my mother and father] in their bedroom, arguing," Charley said. "They never wanted to sign my consent slip so that I could play football. Then, when I got to the point that I was playing pretty good, they would argue about who I took after."

In fact, football offered Winner a chance to move beyond his parents' life. Though he was small of stature, Charley had powerful legs and jackrabbit speed that attracted the interest of college recruiters. Southwest Missouri State, in particular, was interested and formally offered him a scholarship.

"I went down to the barbershop," Winner remembered, "and my dad was sitting in the chair. I walked up to him, and I said, 'I have a chance to go to college, and it won't cost the family anything. What do you think?'"

Winner's father took a deep breath and said, "I think you ought to go out and get a job and help the family."

The young man and the old man simply disagreed. The very next morning Winner lit out for Missouri. He was eighteen and had $150 of his own money in his pocket.

When Charley got to Springfield, coach Red Blair didn't appear to be any more impressed with him than his parents had been. He told Charley to get down in his stance so he could evaluate his fundamentals.

Seeing the reluctant kid squatting awkwardly in front of him, Red screamed, "Winner, what're you going to do? Take a shit?"

The advent of World War II suspended Southwest Missouri's football program, and Charley joined the service. A radio operator and a gunner on a b-17, Winner flew seventeen missions, taking off in England to fly over enemy territory. He was shot down by Nazis over Hamburg, and he was taken prisoner for nearly two months before Russian troops liberated him.

Reentering civilian life, he returned to college football, but in a fortuitous decision he left Southwest Missouri and enrolled at

Washington University in St. Louis. That's where he played for the young head coach Weeb Ewbank.

Charley became so close to Weeb, he married the coach's daughter, Nancy. To support his new wife, Winner took an assistant coach's position at nearby Case Tech. When Weeb left Washington U to become an assistant with the Browns, he got Charley a second job scouting for Cleveland. And then, of course, the duo eventually moved on together to Baltimore.

Winner was an ongoing asset to Weeb and, later on, Shula. In 1958 his Colts defense was the second best in the league in points allowed. In both '58 and '59 the Colts were one of the greatest intercepting teams of all time, stealing seventy-five enemy passes over the two years.

In 1964 Winner's Colts defense was not only best in the league but considered one of the best in history, or at least it was before it collapsed in the second half against Cleveland in the championship game.

Now Charley was headed back to where it all began for him, Missouri. In St. Louis he would try to find success as head coach of the Cardinals, a team beset by poor ownership and deep racial divides.

Shula's difficult job was finding a replacement for a man so capable. He didn't shrink from the task. In fact, he may have seen opportunities in Winner's departure. He now had the chance to bring in his own man, one who wasn't connected to his predecessor.

In a larger sense this one key hire would demonstrate for the world one of Shula's great talents, an incredible instinct for unearthing coaching and front-office brilliance.

Shula's hires included Bill Arnsparger, a future defensive coordinator on multiple Super Bowl teams and, later, a major college and professional head coach. Shula also provided a first professional football opportunity to a Baltimore high school history teacher named George Young. Young taught and coached football at Baltimore City College, a public but highly prestigious institution located in a castle-like edifice right across the street from Memorial Stadium. Eventually, the fat, bald, and bespectacled Young would build Super Bowl winners for the New York Giants, where he drafted Lawrence Taylor and gave Bill Parcells his first head-coaching job.

Shula's most brilliant hire, however, was his handpicked successor to Charley Winner, a young coach named Chuck Noll. In Noll Shula couldn't have found a man more similar to himself. The two were close in age (Shula was two years and a day older), and both had played for Paul Brown in Cleveland, though not at the same time. They came from working-class families, attended Northeast Ohio Catholic grammar schools, and had great high school football careers. They both played their college ball at Ohio-based Catholic institutions. Both men made it to the professional level, relying more on intelligent play than imposing athletic ability. After their playing careers were over, both went quickly into coaching.

It was no wonder, then, that Shula told the respected football historian Michael MacCambridge that he wanted to hire Chuck Noll "five minutes" into his interview. Noll was interested in Baltimore, too.

Chuck Noll was a defensive assistant on the San Diego Chargers' famed coaching staff that also included head coach Sid Gilman and future Raiders coach and owner Al Davis—all future Hall of Famers. Nevertheless, the Chargers were financially hamstrung, seriously affecting the quality of their on-field personnel. As head coach Sid Gilman explained it, the team listed college players on two different draft boards. The first board featured the players the Chargers wanted; on the second board were the players the Chargers thought they could afford to sign. More and more, the Chargers were forced to draft from that second board.

Noll didn't consider that a suitable situation for his own career ambitions. His goal was to become a head coach. To achieve that, he felt, he would have to move on to a stable, well-stocked organization that had a legitimate chance to succeed. That perfectly described the Colts.

Shula was intrigued by Chuck's mastery of the more complex pass coverages employed in the AFL. Far more progressive than the older league, the AFL was utilizing many varieties of sophisticated zone defenses, while in the NFL they were largely guarding pass receivers in archaic man-to-man schemes.

Noll was a pioneer in the new tactics, and his teams were incredibly successful in employing them. In 1961, working under defensive coordinator Jack Faulkner, Noll's defensive backs picked off an incredible forty-nine passes or, on average, three and a half interceptions per game, a professional football record.

The Colts' players immediately felt the difference. Defensive back Jerry Logan told Michael MacCambridge, "Before Chuck got there I knew my job but I didn't really understand how my job fit in with everybody else."

Explaining how a player's task fit in with the larger defensive philosophy was one of Noll's strengths, and it said a lot about how he viewed football. He believed that trust was the key to success; as long as everyone covered his own assignment, his own area, his own man, all would be well. If there was a root to trouble, Noll believed, it was a player who lost faith in the guy next to him. Just a small cheat step or two in the direction of a weakness was the ruination of even a great defense. So Noll insisted that his players know how their role fitted into the whole scheme.

Noll could accept the fact that there were times when one player was physically outclassed by another. After all, it was impossible to keep a lid on a Jim Brown or a Paul Warfield all of the time. Sooner or later, they would rise up and get you, simply because they were superior men. But Noll had no patience for players who repeatedly made mental mistakes.

"He was relatively less interested in guys who were just fast, just big, or just physical," Michael MacCambridge said. "He wanted guys who were rational."

There was no doubt that Noll's methods worked. Charley left behind a top-tier defense, yet under Noll the unit steadily improved. In Winner's last year in Baltimore, 1965, the defense was ranked fourth in the league and gave up 284 points. In 1966, Noll's first season, the Colts gave up only 226 points and were third defensively.

The 1966 season dawned with a great deal of anticipation. The Packers were the defending champions. After they defeated the Colts in their overtime classic, they went on to beat the Browns for the title in Jim Brown's last-ever game.

For many football fans, however, the two best teams in the NFL were the Colts and Packers. The previous season's scintillating three-game series between them was the crescendo to an operatic season filled with implausible plot twists.

The league clearly knew the marquee value of Baltimore and Green Bay. The two teams were scheduled to kick off the season for the entire league on a Saturday night in Wisconsin.

Unitas was back from his leg injury. Though his knee still required rest and regular draining, his return added to the intense drama of the Green Bay–Baltimore rivalry. There was still a lingering sentiment among Colts fans, perhaps it was a certainty, that the Colts would have won the playoff game had Unitas been healthy. At least one of the Packers, however, didn't agree. Speaking anonymously to *Sports Illustrated*, he said, "It may be easier [to beat the Colts] with Unitas. When they went to Tom Matte in the playoff we had no idea what to expect. We know what they do with Johnny Unitas."

Vince Lombardi, who'd known Unitas to torch his teams and many others through the years, certainly didn't see it that way. "It boils down to this," Vince said. "If Johnny Unitas is hot, no one can beat them. If he's just good, we have a chance. If he's only fair, then we'll take them."

In the season opener the rusty and creaky Unitas was something less than fair. He threw three interceptions, two of them were returned for Green Bay touchdowns, and the Packers beat the Colts 24–3.

And thus began another bitter and frustrating season of trying to unseat Lombardi. The opening-night loss put the Colts behind the Packers right from the outset, and the rest of the year was spent chasing them down as they promenaded through the league in their green jerseys.

Unitas had his most challenging season to date under Shula. He battled a number of injuries, including a sore throwing shoulder. And for the first time in years, he tossed more interceptions than touchdown passes.

The Colts lost to all their major Western Division rivals at least once, going down to the Bears, Lions, and Rams in addition to their season-opening loss to the Packers.

Despite his physical problems and propensity for turnovers, Unitas was still an extraordinary weapon. That point was driven home in early December when the Colts met Chicago at Memorial Stadium. Coming off two straight losses, one to Detroit and

CHANGING TIMES

one to the Rams, the Colts looked like they would be Bear casualties, too. They were down by two points with less than two minutes left in the game.

There was a glimmer of hope when Chuck Noll's defense sacked Chicago quarterback Rudy Bukich on third down. The Bears were forced to do the one thing they didn't want to do: they punted and put the ball back in Johnny U's hands. Unitas maneuvered the Colts into scoring position in just five plays. When he finally hit Raymond Berry in the end zone with the winning score, he still had thirty-nine seconds to spare.

Those theatrics gave the Colts a jolt of faith heading into the season's penultimate game, December 10, in Baltimore against Green Bay. The Colts had four losses, but a mathematical chance and a lot of optimism. But it wouldn't be easy. The Packers had only two stumbles all year, one to the 49ers and the other to the hard-charging Vikings.

Even if the Colts could beat Green Bay, they would still need the Packers to lose the next week in Los Angeles just to tie them. If the Packers beat the Colts, they would be crowned Western Division champs right on the spot and punch their tickets to the NFL Championship Game.

The day was cold and wet, offering hazardous footing and an element of danger to every snap. Bart Starr severely bruised his ribs early and left the game, never to return. His understudy, Zeke Bratkowski, was a wily veteran who offered the Colts no breaks. He came off the bench and hit Elijah Pitts with two touchdown passes.

Unitas had a tough time matching that performance, struggling even to handle the ball. He threw three interceptions. Luck wasn't on his side, either. At one point he hit John Mackey right in front of the end zone. The big tight end backed in for the apparent touchdown, but after crossing the goal line he fell to the ground and the ball popped out of his hands. Though he had clearly caught the ball, possessed it, and easily broken the plane of the goal line with it, the referees called it an incomplete pass. And with that odd decision six hard-won points came off the board.

Despite the setbacks, the Colts, as usual, were still in contention to win the game at the end. The score was 14–10 with five minutes left. Baltimore had possession. Facing the best and most disciplined defense in football, Johnny U electrified the crowd of more than sixty thousand screaming Colts fans with three straight completions. Lenny Moore played wideout so two fullbacks could patrol the backfield and protect Unitas.

Like old times, Johnny U hit Lenny twice. On third and 7 Unitas put the ball in Berry's hands right in front of a Green Bay cornerback for a 22-yard gain. And just like that the Colts had the ball on the Packer 15 with a minute and a half still on the clock.

Every football fan in the country knew that ninety seconds was an eternity for Johnny U. He huddled with his men and decided it was time to go for the jugular. He instructed Jimmy Orr to run a down and in. As always, it was a prescient call. The small receiver was open for the touchdown that would have won the game, but Unitas inexplicably couldn't find him. Instead, the quarterback, sensing pressure in the pocket, took off, holding the ball in his massive hands. In his haste he never saw Packers defensive end Willie Davis skulking in his direction. But Davis found Unitas and cracked him hard. The explosive blow jarred the wet ball loose, and a linebacker recovered it. Before anyone in the stadium could process what they just saw—the stunning reversal of fortune and its implications—the game and the entire season were over.

The usually hypercomposed Unitas lay facedown in the mud for an extended moment. He was, for once, crushed under the weight of his own failure. When he finally returned to the bench, his best friend, Berry, and his pupil, Cuozzo, both came over to offer him comfort and support. One more man also dared approach number 19. It was Shula. In the face of past disappointments he had criticized his quarterback. But today he crouched beside the bitterly distraught man, barely balancing himself above the wet and filthy ground. With cold rain remorselessly pelting both of them, Shula pushed away his own frustrations and bitter disappointments and consoled his anguished and defeated player.

This loss to the Packers, the Colts' fifth in a row, was particularly painful. Not only was it frustrating to lose to the same opponent time and again, not only did the loss end the chase for the title, but it also cut off the Colts' hopes of making history.

The Packers, by virtue of their victory, clinched the West and ascended to the NFL Championship Game. Two weeks later Green Bay vanquished the Dallas Cowboys and won the right to go to the inaugural AFL-NFL World Championship Game in Los Angeles. The Packers faced the Kansas City Chiefs, and, as virtually everyone expected, they beat them too. In other words, Green Bay became the first Super Bowl champions before anyone even knew what that meant.

When the 1967 season dawned there was every reason to believe things might be different for Baltimore. For one thing, the NFL had realigned, and the Colts were no longer in the same division with Green Bay. They wouldn't have to outduel the Packers anymore to make the postseason. This change was brought on to accommodate the many new franchises the NFL added in the '60s when Dallas, Minnesota, Atlanta, and New Orleans all joined the fold.

With so many new teams, the league felt it was best to retitle the old East and West "Divisions" and call them "Conferences." Starting in 1967, each conference had two divisions. The East Conference had the Capitol and the Century Divisions. The West Conference was composed of the Coastal and Central Divisions.

The Colts were placed in the West's Coastal Division, along with Atlanta, Los Angeles, and San Francisco. Meanwhile, Green Bay was in the Central Division, with Detroit, Chicago, and Minnesota. Both the Colts and the Packers remained in the West Conference.

This new arrangement added a level to the postseason. Previously, barring a tie, there was only one postseason game. The winner of the East would meet the winner of the West for the NFL Championship. Now the two "division" winners would meet in a playoff game, and the winner of that would go to the NFL Championship Game. The league champion would then face the AFL champion in the Super Bowl (though it wasn't yet called that).

In a sense the game would never be the same. Separating the Colts from the Packers ended an era of rugged football in which teams fought with incredible ferocity for a lone postseason spot. With rivals like Green Bay and Baltimore playing at such a high level, every game crackled with import. Nevertheless, the Colts may have been relieved to get some distance from the Packers. Year after year under Shula, Baltimore fielded championship-worthy teams, only to suffer some new form of bad luck that would allow the Packers to cuckold the championship from them. Moving to a new division would offer the Colts a seemingly clearer path to the postseason. Baltimore still had Green Bay on the schedule, but they would play them only once instead of twice. The Packers' ability to keep Baltimore out of the postseason seemed to be severely curtailed.

The biggest worry the Colts had in their new division came from Los Angeles, where the Rams were a different team under new head coach George Allen. In his first season in Los Angeles, 1966, he had improved the club, taking it from a four-victory team, the Rams' record the year before he arrived, to an eight-win season his first year on the job.

George Allen, like Shula, was young, highly ambitious, and effective. Shula found him quite different from the bombastic Lombardi. "Allen was quiet, but always trying to gain some kind of edge to win," Shula remembered.

That edge would include calling Shula at home in the middle of the night to discuss a little business. "He would want to call and talk trade with me, but he said he didn't realize there was a three-hour time difference. I'd say, 'George, do you know what the hell time it is?' He'd say, 'Oh, I forgot about the time difference.' So the next morning I would give him a call. 'Did I wake you up, George?'"

Even without Lombardi in his division, Shula could clearly see that the obsession with winning was spreading. To keep up with these fanatics, Shula had to constantly improve the Colts. Despite the disappointments he and the team had suffered so far, no one doubted Don's leadership or ability. The Colts came to play every single week, and at the end of the year they were always in the thick of it.

But 1967 brought greater reasons for optimism than usual. For one thing, Shula pulled off a blockbuster trade just about a week before the annual draft. He sent backup quarterback Gary Cuozzo and taxi-squad guard Butch Allison to the New Orleans Saints. The second-string quarterback was understandably dissatisfied sitting behind Unitas, a state of affairs that didn't look to change for years. The Colts had long touted Cuozzo as a starter-quality player, although no one really knew exactly what he was capable of. He had performed both well and poorly in infrequent relief of Unitas.

Running back Tom Matte's memories of Cuozzo were mixed. "Cuozzo was not star material," he said, "but he was a good, sound quarterback."

Matte's abiding memory of Gary was not a happy one. He recalled a young man who was overzealous to show the coaches what he could do.

"We played a game up in Detroit, a preseason game, and [Cuozzo] got to come in," Matte said. "Shula told him to take a knee and run the clock out. I came in, someone got hurt, and I don't even have my helmet buckled because [Gary's] just supposed to take a knee. Well, he sees a certain defense and calls '36 Trap.' I say, 'No, no, no.' I come across, and some rookie grabs me by the helmet and lifts me up, and this guy comes in and hits me with the forearm and knocks out four of my teeth. I have to stay in Detroit overnight because all of the nerves are dangling. I wanted to kill Cuozzo."

Matte's grillwork notwithstanding, Shula had a plethora of potential trade partners for Cuozzo. None was more willing, or more giving, than the fledgling New Orleans Saints. In exchange for Gary New Orleans gifted Shula the very first pick in the upcoming draft and also threw in versatile Bill Curry, who was a linebacker, center, and special teams player. Plus, the Saints threw in another draft pick, too.

The deal, Saints coach Tom Fears said, "makes it possible for us to have strength and experience at football's most vital position."

In fact, he had just been fleeced.

Bill Curry had not spent even a single day with the Saints. New Orleans had only recently picked him up in the expansion draft, something the NFL instituted to stock the new team with talent even before the college draft. Most of the players in that draft were washed-up veterans who had seen better days. Curry was an exception. He was a fine young player who had been in the league only two years, but who had already played in historic games, including as the starting center for Green Bay in the first Super Bowl.

A highly intelligent and articulate man, Curry had the polished manner and bearing of a U.S. senator and the thoughtful and kindly demeanor of a small-town Baptist minister. He was chosen by the Packers in the twentieth round of the NFL draft, the next-to-last man selected.

Despite his conventional appearance, Curry had a rebellious streak. He was raised in College Park, Georgia, where football is akin to religion, but as a young man he disliked the game and had intended to quit his high school team. Only the stern presence of his father prevented him from doing so.

Curry's dream was to pitch in the big leagues for the New York Yankees. He stuck with football anyway, and despite his antipathy for the game he played it at the highest levels.

Though Curry didn't look like a stereotypical NFL lineman, he had a past that prepared him to meet even the most difficult challenges. His paternal grandfather had been crippled by polio. His mother's father had been murdered. And Curry's father, "Willie," did not take weakness lightly. Willie Curry was a good boxer and an early evangelist of physical fitness and weight training who won the junior national lightweight championship in three different Olympic lifts.

Willie Curry eventually coached boxing, weightlifting, and gymnastics at the Georgia Military Academy. Young Bill was only about six years old when he started going to the gym with his dad and learning how to lift weights.

Willie and Bill didn't exactly see things eye-to-eye. The gym was sacred to the father, a place that demanded discipline and adherence to the proper techniques. And although Bill would later describe his dad as an almost godlike figure to him, he also didn't mind aggravating him. Willie regularly threw Bill out of the weight room for laughing at the solemnity of his workout routines.

Irritating the men he admired would become something of a habit for Bill Curry. From time to time, Curry spoke out against his mentors, bluntly telling them or others how he saw things. He learned the hard way the toll an indiscreet truth could exact, however, and his habit was to express regret at some later date.

In Green Bay Bill was introduced to a father figure who would take him on a journey from respect to loathing to remorse. That man, of course, was Vince Lombardi.

The two did not get off to a good start.

The day before reporting to the Packers training camp for his rookie season in 1965, Curry played in the College All-Star Game against Cleveland, the defending professional champions. He played every down in the game and along the way suffered a concussion. Less than twenty-four hours later he was in Wisconsin, where Vince Lombardi met him with a weak handshake and a demand.

Lombardi informed Curry that he would probably play in that night's intrasquad scrimmage. Without regard to his head injury Bill was taken to a classroom and tutored in a few rudimentary plays. Even without the injury Curry was just a twenty-two-year-old kid who was asked to play his second game against top-level pros in two days.

Curry was still concussed and aching from his game the night before, travel weary, and utterly lacking professional experience when he was thrown out on the field in a driving rain to play later that night.

That was his first real taste of the demanding Vince, but not the last.

In his second year Curry played in a preseason game against the Steelers. He was kicked in the head with a blow so violent, he dropped to the grass as if gunshot. In fact, he had just suffered another severe concussion. He attempted to regain his senses and continue playing, but when the quarterback signaled for the ball, Bill failed to snap it two times in a row.

After the game he wasn't even capable of dressing himself. His wife had to be called to the locker room to put his clothes on for him.

Later that night, at a team dinner, Lombardi checked on Curry's health by asking him a series of questions:

"Curry, do you know where we are?"

"No, sir," Curry answered.

"Do you remember how you got here?"

"No, sir. I sure don't."

"Curry, who won the game?"

"We did, Coach."

"Good!" Lombardi screamed, and everyone erupted in laughter at the sight of an intelligent young man reduced to the state of an advanced geriatric patient by a serious brain injury.

Two days later Curry still had a "splitting headache." He was sitting in the locker room holding his head when Lombardi walked in and ordered an assistant coach to take the young player out on the field in full pads. Ray Nitschke, one of the most feared men in football, was already outside waiting for him. The two were instructed to smash each other at full speed, over and over.

Curry knew the cynical reason for the brutal exercise: Lombardi wanted to see whether the Packers should pay his salary for the year—about $12,000—in light of the brain injury. They decided to keep him on the roster, and he became the team's starting center.

Not surprisingly, Curry didn't look back upon those stories with fondness. When his career was nearly over, he collaborated on a book, *One More July*, with the famous sportswriter and literary icon George Plimpton. That book has faded into obscurity, even in the Plimpton canon, but it was a brilliantly conceived and executed piece of long journalism. It took the reader on a drive with Plimpton and Curry as they made their way from Louisville to Green Bay for Curry's last-ever summer camp as a professional football player. It was kind of like a jock's version of John Steinbeck's *Travels with Charlie*, with an offensive lineman standing in for the eponymous standard French poodle.

Curry would later call it an "angry" book and betray some embarrassment at his involvement in it. But *One More July* was engrossing and insightful. It displayed the chemistry between Plimpton and Curry through the male magic of the American road trip, while it illuminated on a sport that was at turns brutal and beautiful, violent and intellectual. They recorded their conversations, and Plimpton put it all down in delightful writing.

Of course, the central figure of their discussions, the recently deceased Lombardi, wasn't even present in the car. Curry described his old coach in unsentimental terms.

Lombardi had the "ability to shock, to frighten, to overpower other people with whatever means he had to use," Curry said. The Packers didn't lose often, but when they did, Curry said they were serenaded with verbal abuse from their coach. "I'm sick and tired of being father confessor for a bunch of yellow, no-good punks," Lombardi would scream at his Packers. "The whip! That's the only thing you understand. And I'm going to whip you again, and drive you, make you!"

In Curry's eyes Lombardi was almost like a dog trainer for human beings. He elicited a desired response by utilizing a man's intense or base motivations. "I'm going to make you afraid," Curry quoted Lombardi. "I know you're not afraid of the physical aspects of football or you wouldn't be here. You're not afraid of scrimmaging or anything like that. But you are afraid of embarrassment in front of your peers. That's what I'm going to do to you. I'm going to embarrass you, humiliate you . . . until you do the job."

Lombardi was scarcely more charming if his Packers won. He would "always let us know it was a one-man show," Curry said. "If we got on a winning streak he'd say things to us like, 'Don't think you're responsible for all this success. Don't let it go to your heads and become impressed with yourselves because I want you to understand that I did this. I made you guys what you are.'"

Such a fierce, competitive, and abusive personality naturally brought vitriol boomeranging back toward itself. The players' insults could be crude. If the Packers noticed their coach was in a rage on a particular day, they said he was "on the rag," referring to the female cycle.

Alex Karras, the great Lions defensive tackle, also took aim at Lombardi. One game, when Detroit intercepted a Green Bay pass and ran it back for a touchdown, "Karras came walking back up the field. He glanced over and noticed Lombardi standing there, just livid with rage," Curry remembered. "Alex said, 'Hey, how ya like that, ya fat wop!'"

The Cleveland Browns players didn't take anti-Italian swipes at Lombardi. Instead, in his thick glasses and fedora, and with his broad, toothy smile, they saw a Charlie Chan figure. "We called him 'the Jap,'" Browns receiver Gary Collins remembered.

The Colts, by virtue of their trade with the New Orleans Saints, had the first selection in the 1967 draft. There was a lot of sentiment that Florida quarterback Steve Spurrier was the best player in the entire group, but with Unitas still playing at a very high level, Baltimore had no interest in him.

In fact, in one of the deepest drafts of all time, Baltimore had its pick of future Hall of Famers. Bob Griese, Gene Upshaw, Alan

Page, Lem Barney, Floyd Little, and Willie Lanier were all there for the taking.

But Shula had his eye on someone else.

Up in Michigan an American tall tale was unfolding. Playing for the Spartans was a young man with the innocuous name Charles Smith. When he was still a toddler his sibling tried and failed to call him "brother," and instead it came out "Bubba."

Bubba Smith was a name that would stick.

The son of a Texas high school football coach and a schoolteacher, Bubba didn't grow up; he grew skyward. He topped out at around six feet seven and 265 pounds. He needed glasses, according to his ophthalmologist; because he grew so fast, his eyes couldn't keep up.

Bubba went to college in East Lansing, Michigan, because the segregation in Texas and throughout the South would have kept him off the field at any school that wasn't historically African American.

But even at Michigan State Bubba's size and demeanor made him something of an oddity. When Smith arrived on campus and got out of the white Buick Riviera his father had given him as a gift to use at college, his new coach, Duffy Daugherty, marveled at the specimen and asked, "Are you going to drive that car, or just carry it around with you?"

The fans would also learn to revel in his hugeness and ferocity. Electrified by his tackling and pursuit of the quarterback, they took to chanting, "Kill, Bubba, kill!" That bloodlust echoed from the stands every Saturday. Bubba ate up the attention. But even as his legend grew, he backed it up with substance. His Michigan State teams were undefeated in both 1965 and 1966; they won the national championship twice, sharing the second one with Notre Dame. Bubba was a two-time All-American and a major contributor to all of that success.

Shula wasn't even the only coach in Baltimore to draft Smith; the Baltimore Bullets of the NBA also selected him. Smith stuck with football and got off to a great start in the pros. When he played the world champion Packers in the College All-Star Game, he lined up directly over the Packers' perennial All-Pro guard Jerry Kramer. Treating the great Kramer like a mild diversion, Bubba sacked Bart Starr twice. In his first day at Colts camp, he gave another substantial All-Pro offensive lineman, Dan Sullivan, the same treatment. Smith chopped Dan in the neck and shoulders and immediately knocked him face first into the dirt

By 1967 the Colts had been so good for so long, there was a belief by some fans and writers that they were an aging team poised for decline. The indicator was the previous season's five-loss campaign. But it was quickly apparent how wrong those assessments were. The Colts leaped out of the gate and won their first four games. In the last three of them Chuck Noll's defense didn't give up more than a single touchdown per game.

Baltimore didn't make its first misstep until the Rams came to Memorial Stadium for game five. As expected it was tightly contested. Unitas played well but suffered a difficult day anyway. His receivers dropped perfectly thrown passes in important situations, and one sure touchdown clanked off Ray Perkins's hands and fell to the ground. These mistakes seemed inconsequential, as the Colts enjoyed a 24–14 lead with only ten minutes left to play.

That margin quickly evaporated in the most improbable way. A late Rams drive stalled when Roman Gabriel, their quarterback, rushed for a single yard on third down. That left Los Angeles with one option. They had to attempt a 47-yard field goal. In those days, before the proliferation of so-called soccer-style kickers, that was considered a long distance and a risky attempt. In fact, as the kick from Bruce Gossett plummeted from the sky, it looked like it might fall short of its target. Instead, it hit the crossbar and then improbably bounced through the uprights. In that light Gabriel's 1-yard rush loomed large.

And then Unitas made a terrible miscue. In a drive designed to run out the clock, he gambled and attempted a short pass into traffic. That poor decision culminated with the ball in the hands of linebacker Maxie Baughn. The Rams had one more chance, and they cashed it in when Gabriel hit Bernie Casey with a perfectly thrown 16-yard spiral in the corner of the end zone.

There were a few saving graces. The score was tied. There was time on the clock. And the ball was going back to Unitas. In his inimitable way he marched the Colts all the way downfield. But then things started to go wrong. He targeted Matte, and Matte dropped the ball. Next he looked to Willie Richardson, and Willie too could not hold on. But then, on the next play, Unitas came right back to Richardson. Johnny U fired to his receiver near the 25-yard line as the Rams dragged the quarterback to the ground. Unitas alertly signaled time-out from the turf, which the officials granted. An easy field goal would give the Colts the victory. But then, unexpectedly, a referee near the play ruled that the ball had been stripped from Richardson before Johnny U requested his time-out. It was a fumble, the referees said, and the ball belonged to Los Angeles.

Instead of the Colts winning in the last seconds, they left the field with a bizarre tie. Afterward, George Allen, Los Angeles's maniacally driven and focused coach, expressed a great deal of satisfaction with the game's inglorious outcome.

"If we finish the season in a tie with the Colts," he said, "the title will go to the team which scored the most points in the series."

The next battle between them wasn't scheduled until the last game of the year, in LA. The Rams at 3-1-1 were only a half game behind the Colts, 4-0-1, but there was still a very long way to go, Allen's premature thoughts notwithstanding.

The next week Baltimore traveled to Minnesota and fought both the Vikings and a vicious midwestern wind. They escaped, barely, with their second tie in a row. But after two straight frustrating games, after six total games, they were still undefeated, the only team in the league that was.

After a victory against the Redskins in Washington, the Colts came back to Baltimore to meet their nemesis, Green Bay. The Colts were 5-0-2 and the Packers 5-1-1, but the psychological edge belonged to Green Bay, the winners of five straight against Baltimore.

The game was another close and physical contest. The only points of the first half came on a Packer field goal in the second quarter. Green Bay finally put the game's first touchdown on the board late in the fourth quarter. With a 10–0 lead, it looked like they would defeat the Colts again.

Impossible situations, of course, were Unitas's stock and trade. There were about six minutes left when he finally took command. Though the Packers had stymied him all day, it was as if a lightbulb had suddenly gone on. Finally, he moved the ball with ease, going 62 yards in ten plays. The drive culminated with a 10-yard touchdown pass to the unexpectedly redoubtable Alex Hawkins. Lou Michaels lumbered in and missed the extra point. So with a little more than two minutes left in the game, Baltimore had to kick the ball away and somehow close a four-point deficit.

Shula had no choice but to order the onside kick. It was a desperation tactic that rarely worked, and everyone in the stadium knew it was coming. The kick was poorly executed. Michaels booted it a little too hard, but it worked out in the Colts' favor anyway. The ball pushed past the first line of Packers to the Green Bay 34, where Baltimore's rookie defensive back Rick Volk found the ball and pounced on it.

Now the Colts had the ball on the Packer 34, and they had a chance. But they were in trouble again when they were only able to gain 4 yards in three plays. They faced fourth and 6 with only a minute and fifty seconds left on the clock.

Unitas faded back to pass. In an echo of the previous season's frustrating loss to the Packers in which he ran and fumbled away the season, Johnny U bolted again. This time there were two Packers standing between him and the first-down marker; with no choice but to go forward, he lowered his head and rammed through them. This time he held onto the ball and gained the first down.

Sick of the cat-and-mouse games and the danger lurking around every corner, Johnny U decided to strike. He faded back and looked to the end zone. Willie Richardson was waiting there, though Herb Adderly, Green Bay's cornerback and a future Hall of Famer, was right there with him.

Unitas disregarded the danger and flung the ball right into Richardson's hands.

With all of the weight of the past on his shoulders and, of course, the pressure of the moment to contend with, Unitas hung thirteen clutch points on the proud Packer defense, and he did it all in the tense waning moments of the game.

The Packers were stunned, but Lombardi didn't alibi or protest the result. What little wrath he had, he aimed at Baltimore's fans. During the game one of them, a man with flammable breath, wobbled his way from the stands to the Packers' sideline. He stood shoulder-to-shoulder with Lombardi himself and engaged the great man in banal conversation. He asked Vince to sit down and requested that the coach ask all his Packers to sit, so that the drunk and his friends in the cheap seats could see the game better.

"The sideline stuff in this stadium is terrific," Vince said, smiling, after the game. "They come up and poke at you and yell at you, and most of them are drunk. The cops just stand there and let them do it."

It was as if the Colts had asserted their primacy by beating the defending-champion Packers. After Green Bay Baltimore blazed its way through the league. They crushed Atlanta and Detroit by a combined score of 90–14 and then beat the 49ers, 26–9.

And then came Dallas.

The Cowboys presented problems that few other teams did. Led by coach Tom Landry, a glaring man underneath a sharp-brimmed fedora, Dallas was leading the NFL into the future. Like the Colts, they suffered some hard times at the hands of the Packers' archaic attack, losing to Green Bay in 1966's NFL title game. But the Cowboys were also pioneering new and interesting approaches on both offense and defense, where their stellar personnel labored to keep up with the complex schemes of their coach. In the end, however, in Dallas as everywhere else, the fundamental virtues made the biggest differences.

Dallas had a compelling quarterback in Don Meredith, two tough running backs in Dan Reeves and Don Perkins, and speed to burn on the outside with Olympian Bob Hayes receiving the ball. On defense the Cowboys' most formidable weapon was a line that featured the twin pillars of Jethro Pugh and Bob Lilly. They shut down opponent running games and pressured quarterbacks. In short, Dallas was a highly balanced outfit.

The night before the game a hard rain fell, and Memorial Stadium's barren field succumbed to a swamp. Unitas ignored the obstacle and helped the Colts jump out to a 10–0 lead. But Dallas scored seventeen quick points, first on a 35-yard strike to Bob Hayes, then on a Unitas interception returned 26 yards for six by Dallas's Dave Edwards, and finally on a field goal.

The Colts were behind in the fourth quarter, 17–10, but once again hard conditions and a shrinking clock became a Johnny U showcase. He rallied the Colts for two field goals (aided in part by a Don Meredith interception) to pull within a point.

Then the Colts' defense held Dallas one last time, and Unitas returned to the field. He masterfully mixed the run and pass to move the team to within spitting distance of the goal line. He handed to Jerry Hill, who was tackled for no gain. Then he threw to Richardson in the end zone, but missed him. Finally, he called Lenny Moore's number.

Like the hero of a western, Lenny went where he pleased without a single Cowboy laying a finger on him. He scored the six that won the game.

Landry had come into town praising the Colts as "the best" team in football, but he left with a different point of view. "We had the best team," he said after the game. "Even Baltimore admitted it was lucky to win."

No one in the Colts' locker room had said any such thing.

Landry, so often described as a stone-faced stoic, was in the midst of losing his composure. In his frustration he pinned all the failure on one man, a man he'd be counting on. "You will have to blame Don Meredith for the loss," Landry said.

All those histrionics came despite the fact that on the day Dallas lost to Baltimore, they also punched their ticket to the postseason. A tie between Philadelphia and Washington clinched the division for the Cowboys. So Landry had publicly insulted and demeaned the key man in his own quest for respect.

While both Dallas and Green Bay were wrapping up their divisions despite late-season losses, the Colts, undefeated and with the best record in football, were struggling to shake the Rams and declare victory.

After a stumble in midseason in which they lost to San Francisco and then tied both Baltimore and Washington, Los Angeles had yet to lose again. With only a single loss and two ties, they were right behind the Colts, still within striking distance.

The Rams beat Atlanta the same weekend the Colts punched out the Cowboys. The Colts still had reason to feel good about their chances. Baltimore faced the fledgling Saints, a team with only two victories so far on the season, while the Rams drew the

Packers for the next-to-last game of the season. A Colts victory and a Rams loss would clinch the division for Baltimore.

But it wasn't to be. The Colts handled their business and crushed the Saints, 30–10. As usual the Packers delivered Baltimore no favors. It looked like Green Bay would easily win. With only three minutes left in the game, fullback Chuck Mercein plummeted over the goal line to give the Packers a four-point lead over the Rams. The game's result seemed doubly ensured when Los Angeles fumbled the ball back to the Packers in the ensuing drive.

But Green Bay couldn't move against the Rams' top-rated defense, and the Packers had to punt. The Rams rushed everyone they had and blocked the kick. Los Angeles took over on the Green Bay 5 with less than a minute to go.

Roman Gabriel didn't waste any time. On the first play he aimed for the end zone, but missed his target. He asserted himself again and hit Bernie Casey for the winning score. The Packers technically lost, their third defeat of the year, but they felt no pain. They were already ensured of going to the playoffs. Meanwhile, back in Baltimore the Colts could barely enjoy their victory over the Saints. They remained undefeated, yet they were clearly the day's losers. Thanks to the Rams' miracle victory over the Packers, Baltimore would have to make the long, draining trip to Los Angeles for an all-or-nothing game.

Once more the Colts were at the center of a late-season matchup of intense national interest. The Rams took an early ten-point lead when Roman Gabriel hit the speedy Jack Snow with an 80-yard pass in the second quarter.

The Colts turned to the pass early to close the deficit. Without the run game to worry about, the Rams' powerful front four dominated Baltimore's line. Unitas could do nothing, as Deacon Jones and Merlin Olsen menaced him all day. In fact, his performance was dismal.

"We had Unitas pegged," Rams linebacker Maxie Baughn said after the game, "and how many times have you ever seen that done? This is a great credit to our coaching staff. They had all the Colt tendencies broken down. We got the best rush we've had all year."

Unitas was clearly outplayed by Roman Gabriel, who looked considerably younger, stronger, and in greater control than the

Colts' quarterback. Johnny U threw a touchdown and two interceptions; Gabriel threw three touchdowns and no interceptions. That, and Chuck Noll's suddenly vulnerable defense, added up to the 34–10 shellacking.

The Colts were undefeated until the last day of the season and were tied for the best record in football, yet they didn't even qualify for the postseason. Maybe most hurtful of all was the Packers' role in their defeat. They had moved away from the division in which Green Bay was so often their barrier to the title, yet somehow the shenanigans of Vince and his team still cost Baltimore the postseason. The Colts didn't even have the satisfaction of bowing to Packer dominance; Baltimore lost out thanks to a rare show of Packer ineptitude when Green Bay bumbled away the game to the Rams. Even more frustrating, the Packers easily beat the Rams 28–7 in the first round of the playoffs.

The Colts could at least take solace in a couple of personal achievements. Unitas was named MVP, again; it was his second time under Shula, fourth time overall (in one poll or another). Shula won his second Coach of the Year Award, though he shared the distinction with the Rams' George Allen. All of the Colts were forced to watch the postseason games from the comfort of their sofas. The NFL Championship pitted the Packers versus the Cowboys, two teams Baltimore beat in the regular season. The Dallas–Green Bay game was played on a frozen-solid Wisconsin field in subzero temperatures. The game entered the lore as "the Ice Bowl," and it would only enhance Vince Lombardi's rock-solid reputation. The Packers defeated Dallas in the last second of the championship and then beat the Oakland Raiders in another anticlimactic Super Bowl. After that one Lombardi hoisted the champion's trophy, which seemed so natural in his hands they eventually engraved his name on it.

## THIRTEEN

## War

Headlines about football in the 1960s ran side by side with dispatches from the war in Southeast Asia. Dark newspaper tales of jungle warfare, internecine guerrillas, and befuddled generals, once American heroes who had defeated Hitler but now drowning in a worthless and godforsaken place called Vietnam, were echoed in Baltimore by stories of the superior but sad Colts improbably defeated far from home.

Football in America provided an outlet for a fundamental human urge, the need to dominate and humiliate one's neighbors. Within the game the nation's metropolises were city-states, stadiums were walls that would repel or fall, and game fields were the battlefields where triumph or disaster unfolded. They were modern-day Athenses and Spartas speaking the same language and worshipping the same gods yet inexplicably at "war" every Sunday.

The metaphor was more urgent and poignant in Baltimore than it was in most places. Baltimore wasn't glamorous like New York or a place of great consequence like Washington. It wasn't as large as Philadelphia or as celebrated as San Francisco. It was often the butt of cruel jokes by other East Coasters who merely cruised through it on I-95, holding their noses at the smell of the smokestacks and at the sight of the grimy workers who lived and labored beneath them.

Unitas didn't exactly change that perception, but in the Sunday wars his missiles made Baltimore the lone superpower. He was an ancient warrior wielding the javelin with the skill and precision to strike from afar, and he was a Cold Warrior, a launcher of state-of-the-art weapons that could end your civilization.

Because he had been a long shot, and because his city was so reviled by outsiders yet so utterly sacred to its residents, it wasn't hard for fans to view him as a David, improbably defending his Jerusalem against hordes of the others. His right arm, of course, was nothing more than a sling.

The helmets, tactics, uniforms, and violence all made the game seem like combat, though football was not war at all, far from it. Americans were acutely aware of that because their sons were participants in a perverse lottery that dragged them from their homes when they were barely out of footie pajamas and taught them how to kill. Many returned irretrievably broken. More than fifty thousand of them never returned at all.

The war that raged on while the football games played on shared very little in common with previous American conflicts. It was dissimilar in almost every way to World War II. There was no obvious starting point. There was no villainous face to which all the blame could be attached. There was no real threat or danger to the United States. And there were no clear goals to be achieved.

Right alongside the boys who went to fight were other young men who went to tell the stories: writers, reporters, and broadcasters who would deliver the news of America's successes or failures. Many of them reported what they were told, but one in particular reported what he actually saw. In the end he would change everything.

That man was David Halberstam.

Halberstam was born in New York City and raised in the suburbs, first in Connecticut and, later, in the New York suburb of Yonkers. He was the son of Jewish parents. His father was an army surgeon, and his mother adored him so completely, she imbued him with the massive ego and utter confidence that were his hallmarks to everyone who knew him.

He had the good fortune to graduate high school not long after quotas limiting Jewish students at Harvard were lifted. So he took his brilliant mind to Cambridge, Massachusetts, but being a pioneer wasn't entirely gratifying. He didn't belong to a single club at Harvard. His free time was spent holding jobs he found demeaning, including cleaning the rooms of his fellow students.

Despite his setbacks and disappointments, Halberstam found

his life's work at Harvard writing for the *Crimson*, the school news-paper. His talent and passion were evident even then. In a place filled with brilliant thinkers and writers, he eventually rose to the position of managing editor.

After school he went south, first working at the smallest daily newspaper in Mississippi and then, more significantly, covering the civil rights movement for the *Nashville Tennessean*.

He seemed to be in a hurry to define his legacy, and while he was still in his twenties he started the significant work that would change his life and in a very real sense change the course of human events. The *New York Times* hired him, and in 1962 they made him a war correspondent and sent him to Vietnam.

If possible, he was less welcome in Indochina than he had been at Harvard. Just as the circumstances of the war were something no one had exactly seen before, Halberstam's approach to cover-ing it was also unprecedented. He refused to cozy up to power and declined to take the word of American generals at face value in an era when their prestige was unquestioned. In fact, he con-tradicted them at press conferences and in his dispatches for the *Times*, calling into question their honesty and integrity. Even worse, when Paul Harkins, the U.S. commanding general, approached him at a cocktail party, Halberstam refused to shake his hand.

The government didn't take his insults or, more precisely, the uncomfortable truths he told lying down. Eventually, Harkins and Frederick Nolting, the American ambassador in Saigon, turned to smearing Halberstam, insisting to all who would listen that he was a liar. He even got on the wrong side of the president. Ken-nedy, seeing his war undermined with every word Halberstam pecked out on his portable typewriter, insisted that the *Times* fire him. But the ownership backed their man. Not only did they retain Halberstam, but they also refused to grant him vacation time, lest anyone get the idea that Kennedy was successfully intimidating them. The *New York Times* wanted it to be crystal clear that David Halberstam wasn't going anywhere.

Halberstam was not in the least bit obsequious. His relative youth and position could not be exploited by power to intimidate him. Kennedy's glare in his direction did not prevent him from doing his job and reporting the truth that he found. "Halberstam didn't have an idea that he was currying to the Kennedys," said his close friend Gay Talese. "He didn't give a shit. He didn't care. He did not want to be in their little Harvard club. He went to Harvard, sure, but he did not want to knuckle under or praise at their altar. He didn't want that."

Neil Sheehan, Halberstam's friend and journalistic colleague in Saigon, described Halberstam as an indefatigable worker, a reporter who would fight through crippling exhaustion and work all night long at the typewriter to meet a deadline. Sheehan also described him as a man whose "physical courage in action matched his moral courage."

Halberstam went out into the field on patrol with the soldiers. He saw for himself what was happening in battle. In this he won respect. The Mekong Delta troopers initiated him into their "Blackfoot Club," a society that could be joined only if you traversed the rice paddies where the mud was so thick and pervasive, it seeped through even military boots and dyed the skin of the feet a dark and filthy black.

That hard work and intensity paid off. The young man whose credibility was questioned by the president of the United States was awarded the Pulitzer Prize for International Reporting in 1964. By then Halberstam was just thirty years old, and Kennedy was dead.

Gay Talese, another reporter at the *Times* with big ambitions, shared a lot in common with Halberstam, not the least of which was a desire to stretch the boundaries of journalism. Talese, who started as a brilliant sportswriter, had slightly different goals than his friend. He did not want to *write* for a newspaper, per se, but instead wanted to be a *writer* at a newspaper. In other words, he had literary ambitions for his nonfiction prose.

He and Halberstam where changing the medium. Talese wrote long, unflattering magazine profiles of American heroes. In one, "Frank Sinatra Has a Cold," he portrayed the beloved singer as self-absorbed, rude, and controlling. In another he eviscerated the legend of Joltin' Joe and showed "the great DiMaggio," as Hemingway called him in *The Old Man and the Sea*, as little more than a bundle of weaknesses and insecurities. That was some contrast to the image the public had of the indomitable Yankee Clipper, the successful suitor of Marilyn Monroe, who willed his team to so many pennants and World Series championships.

These pieces, so hurtful yet so obviously true, were gripping to read and in a sense courageous for showing beloved figures as they were, not as how the public wished them to be. In essence, by exposing the frailties and deficiencies of the great, Talese was doing much the same thing with popular-culture icons that Halberstam was doing with politicians and generals.

Halberstam's work was not only engrossing but having a profound effect on his country. By exposing the lies behind Kennedy's war, he was risking everything. He was standing in direct opposition to credible men who, in the case of the generals, had risked their lives over and over for their country. Others were either elected to or appointed to high office. All of them claimed Halberstam was a liar or a subversive or both. They suggested he was doing the enemy's work.

That Halberstam was ultimately proved right not only vindicated him and catapulted his career but also called into question the nation's belief in the veracity of its most consequential men. It was a loss of faith that would gain momentum as the decade careened on.

So what were these important military men and political leaders all lying about? Only the reasons young men were snatched away from their families and sent halfway around the world to kill; only about the atrocities their country was committing; only about America's realistic chances for victory.

"The fact that [Halberstam] was right was beside the point," Gay Talese said. "He thought he was right before [other] people thought he was right. He had an awful lot of confidence."

Talese felt that Halberstam's almost unbelievable ability to stand up to power at such a young age came from (where else?) his mother.

"Some of these guys grew up with mothers who were really cheerleaders," Talese said. "And their sons are seduced by their mother's high opinion. They go far. Blanche Halberstam [David's mother] was a major figure in his life. She was the supreme cheerleader. She adored him. And she thought David was the greatest figure in the world, and he believed it. She thought he was Moses, for Christ's sake."

The confidence that Halberstam had in the face of the generals was also present in front of a far more imposing figure, the blank page.

Talese marveled at the speed with which his friend worked. "He was enormously fast," he said. "I'm ten times slower than [he was]. He wrote very, very, very quickly. He didn't have a lot of self-doubt, which I do, for example, and even Tom Wolfe does a little bit. But David Halberstam had no self-doubt. Whatever sentence he wrote, he thought, 'That is what the story is.' He didn't question himself. I once wrote that Halberstam had the ego of Charles de Gaulle.

"I saw him write pieces for magazines or parts of books he was writing," Talese said. "He would sit there at that little typewriter he had, banging away. Even if there were errors, he didn't bother correcting the typos. He would do it later. I would want to correct the typos right away. Not him. He would just go ahead. His page was sloppy. My page was very careful. When I finished a page, it was pretty much ready for the printer. Halberstam needed many, many phases of correcting, typos and other things. But it didn't bother him. He had this tremendous confidence to go on. Many people who are more self-doubting might say, 'Well, maybe I should try to get it right because maybe it is not quite right.' He always thought it was quite right."

The full expression of Halberstam's self-confidence didn't come until a few years later, when he wrote his second Vietnam book. This one focused less on the war in the field and more on the men back home who disastrously conceived of an adventure that was doomed to failure. His book was called *The Best and the Brightest*.

The title referred to the men whom President John F. Kennedy had handpicked to advise him in his new administration. This eclectic group included many men who, because of their high positions of power and especially because of their proximity to the Vietnam adventure, were household names in America for the entire decade of the '60s. Their ranks included cabinet members and advisers, such as Secretary of State Dean Rusk, Secretaries of Defense Robert McNamara and Clark Clifford, and National

Security Special Assistant McGeorge Bundy, to name a few of the more prominent names. By and large, they were Ivy League educated and brilliant. For the most part, they were career academics, college presidents and professors, or business successes. They constituted a core of the most highly respected individuals in the nation and were regarded as one of the most talented teams any president had ever assembled. Yet they inevitably led the nation to a ruinous war that was anything but inevitable. They went to work every day and made the disastrous decisions for ten years that killed, maimed, divided, and destroyed. Their ideas tore America apart, separating fathers and sons, young and old, affluent and working-class poor.

Though this group and Kennedy made the terrible decisions, they didn't make them in a vacuum. French colonialists pulled them into the quagmire. Republicans who had so easily and expertly attached the "soft on communism" label pushed them. And then, of course, there was Joe McCarthy, who, just a few years before, proclaimed to find communists, like termites, infesting their ranks.

Kennedy himself, though initially skeptical of going to war in Indochina, finally was the one to initiate engagement, and for the very worst of reasons. Convinced by Averill Harriman, one of his men, to meet with Soviet leader Nikita Khrushchev in Vienna, he walked like a baby into a disaster.

Though Kennedy had been a hero in World War II and a congressman and a senator before assuming the presidency, Khrushchev viewed him as young, inexperienced, and especially soft. This view was bolstered by Kennedy's first embarrassing experience standing up to communism, in Cuba, at a place called the Bay of Pigs. That's where, in April 1961, Kennedy's Central Intelligence Agency supported an invasion of the newly communist country by a paramilitary group of dissident Cubans. All along Kennedy had hoped to act subversively and deny U.S. involvement. Eventually, however, he got cold feet. At the last minute he failed to back up the dissidents with the American military help he had promised for the invasion. The result was a humiliating defeat that was aggrandized by the Cuban communists to the humiliation of the United

States and especially the Kennedy administration. In the end the failed invasion only weakened Kennedy and buttressed Castro's revolution.

Tensions were high over Soviet aggressions in Europe, especially Berlin, but Kennedy had the bravado to go into the room with Khrushchev, his more experienced counterpart solo. The president started the meeting on a conciliatory note. "I propose to tell you what I can do, and what I can't do, what my problems and possibilities are and then you can do the same."

Halberstam wrote that Khrushchev responded with venomous reproach. "The reaction was astonishing, a violent attack on the United States, on its international imperialism, but particularly its presence in Berlin. . . . The missiles would fly, the tanks would roll, they must not doubt his word."

The meeting was a disaster for Kennedy and the United States. Khrushchev dominated the personal encounter with the president, who felt he lost a key battle.

"I think [Khrushchev] did it because of the Bay of Pigs," Kennedy told his friend influential journalist Scotty Reston off the record. "I think he thought that anyone who was so young and inexperienced as to get into that mess could be taken, and anyone who got into it, and didn't see it through, had no guts. So he just beat hell out of me. So I've got a terrible problem. If he thinks I'm inexperienced and have no guts, until we remove those ideas we won't get anywhere with him. So we have to act."

The place for that action, Halberstam showed, was Vietnam. One disaster led only to another, ad infinitum. So many lives lost and ruined not because of an imminent danger to the United States or because of a gathering storm of threat. It happened only because one powerful man had humiliated another.

Halberstam's book was so thorough, so brilliantly researched, so ingeniously conceived, so moral in its perspective that it begged one important though silent question: If it was about a "club" of men who were the nation's finest and most intelligent, how could Halberstam himself have been excluded from it?

Halberstam, too, was a Harvard man with an unassailable work ethic. He was articulate and engaged. He would have been an exceptional addition to any team who valued excellence in statecraft, yet he was an outsider. It was a position some thought was inevitable for him owing to one simple fact— he was a Jew.

The Catholic Kennedy often spoke of feeling like an outsider himself in a society dominated by Protestants. But as Talese pointed out, that was nothing compared to being a Jew.

"McNamara and those Kennedy people, including Kennedy, who went to Harvard, were of a different stripe than Halberstam," Talese said. "The great thing about Halberstam and the great thing about Jewish journalism, they brought to journalism a sense of mistrust of power, experienced from their ancestry of being abused by, excluded by, power. It brought to journalism of that period a point of view of the outside in, by people who were very, very unimpressed with power. And Halberstam was very unimpressed with those smart white guys like McNamara, typically, but the whole rest of them, Mac Bundy and all those guys.

"As far as reporting, Halberstam was always tough, and he was always willing to take an unpopular position because he felt his views were not being heard strongly enough, because he was a bit of a contrarian," Talese said.

"Halberstam, on the contrary, was fighting the generals and the general position of the State Department and the White House all the way through that war. He led [Neil] Sheehan (also a future Pulitzer winner) and numbers of others," Talese said. "He was working on the *New York Times*. If he was working at the *Baltimore Sun*, you never would have heard of David Halberstam. But he was working at the *New York Times*, and that's the biggest paper in terms of international coverage, and here he's saying, 'We're losing the war.' And the generals are saying, 'No, we're not. We're winning the war.' And Robert McNamara was saying, 'No, we're not. We're winning the war.'

"*The Best and the Brightest*, the best book he wrote, was about the reputation of these so-called experts and bullshitters in our government," he said.

Halberstam's book about Vietnam dominated the *New York Times* best-seller list for the better part of a year and became, in its era, the centerpiece of intellectual discussion. Yet despite this towering contribution to American letters, Halberstam was not above criticism. In his speed to write and demonstrate facts, his prose style suffered. His sometimes-lusterless pages were in the crosshairs for the cruel attacks aimed at him.

Writing for the *New York Review of Books*, author and noted critic Mary McCarthy dismissed him as she described his work as an effective soporific.

"I attribute my stupefied boredom partly to Halberstam's prose, which combines a fluency of cliché with deafness to idiom and grammatical incomprehensibility," she wrote with a switchblade. "Yet I have read many dull and badly written books about Vietnam with no particular effort. If Halberstam's was such a grind to get through, there must be other reasons."

All criticism aside, the things Messrs. Halberstam and Talese revealed about American heroes, patriots, and priorities uncovered corrosion in the nation during what was supposed to be "the American Century." They didn't invent the corrupt leaders or create those deeply flawed heroes. They weren't the policy makers who engaged in inglorious war or defended its gauzy lies or continued to turn the sausage grinder of death. They were merely energetic and engaging enough to present things that others didn't have the industry or talent to see, let alone show. In the process they stripped away American denial.

If it was all terribly unseemly, like an injudicious man telling his neighbors about his family problems, it was also true and necessary.

Before men like Halberstam and Talese, America was under the misapprehension that it was an all-white country, that it had unlimited power that could be exported anywhere to do anything to anyone who didn't also have a nuclear arsenal, that its heroes and leaders were sacrosanct and flawless, that marriage was inviolable and average Americans were sexually moderate.

Halberstam's and Talese's work disabused Americans of all these self-generated lies. If the facts were hard for a repressed nation to swallow . . . well, at least the delusions were gone.

*The Best and the Brightest*, brilliant and flawed though it may have been, was nothing if not a primer on how the mighty lose.

## FOURTEEN

# 1968

**B**y the time summer training camps convened in 1968, the year had already been distinguished as one of the most agonizing and antagonizing in the history of the country. What wasn't causing dissension or dispute merely seemed adrift and wrong. He who was once on the bottom was on top.

In January North Vietnamese forces, once considered a ragtag army of rice farmers and carpenters, began a series of highly effective attacks against the United States and its allies in the South. This push, called the "Tet Offensive" (*Tet* being the Vietnamese word for "New Year"), resulted in huge casualties. Among the many dead were civilians executed by the North. There were casualties of a different sort back in the United States. American political and military leaders were losing their credibility with the American people. The Tet Offensive, with its flowing currents of blood, was proof that even years into the war, the North was still a potent fighting force.

Vietnam polarized the United States. Peace-minded Democrats sought to draft Robert F. Kennedy, brother of the slain president, to enter the presidential race as an antiwar candidate. Kennedy was an interesting choice, since it was his brother's administration that had started and sustained the war. In any event, RFK demurred. So the peace contingency turned to a little-known senator, Eugene McCarthy, instead. In his youth McCarthy considered becoming a Benedictine monk. He didn't seem to have the killer instincts to stand up to a combative alpha dog like President Johnson or even to make a credible run against him. But McCarthy's antiwar stance instantaneously made him bona fide and viable.

Good fortune also smiled on him. Just prior to the New Hampshire primary, the first of the election season, the *New York Times* reported that army commander General William Westmoreland had just requested an additional two hundred thousand–plus American troops. That news was not accepted well by the country, and McCarthy came within a whisker, 7 percentage points, of upsetting Johnson in New Hampshire. Though the long shot didn't win, he had nevertheless exposed Vietnam as a festering Achilles' heel for the president. The lesson certainly wasn't lost on Kennedy, who suddenly had a change of heart about both running and the war itself. He too entered the race as an antiwar candidate. McCarthy was infuriated; he didn't like Kennedy riding his coattails.

Part of the Kennedy family's legendary toughness was the stories of the supposedly brutal touch-football games the competitive and athletic brothers had on the lawn of their father's home. McCarthy sneered at that.

"[Kennedy] plays touch football," McCarthy told the nation. "I play football."

Mainstream voters knew exactly what he meant. With war out of fashion, football had become the measure of a man.

President Lyndon B. Johnson, on the other hand, had suddenly lost his taste for rough games. He told the American people on national television, "I shall not seek, and I will not accept, the nomination of my party for another term as your president." He had been one of the strongest executives in presidential history, with an irrepressible will and a knack for getting things done. He passed great and groundbreaking legislation, especially the Civil Rights Act that propelled the United States out of the shame of Jim Crow. But his political lungs took on fluid, and he and all his many accomplishments were drowned like rats in the swelling waters of Vietnam. He made many poor decisions regarding the war, starting with retaining many of President Kennedy's advisers, the very men who had conceived and advocated for the war for many years, even as it swallowed American lives.

Johnson expanded the war and sent more troops and firepower, though secret audiotapes from the Oval Office later proved that he was skeptical himself about American prospects for victory. In

1964, before all of this was evident, Johnson won the presidency with the highest-ever share of the popular vote. But in 1968 it was a different ball game. Lyndon plainly saw what everyone else did. He had almost lost to a loser of a candidate in New Hampshire, and with the opportunistic yet formidable Kennedy jumping into the Democratic race, he knew he probably couldn't even win his own party's nomination for another term.

So the dominoes started to tumble, setting in motion the inexorable rise of the bottom feeders all over the country. Johnson quit the race in March. In the first week of June Kennedy, like Martin Luther King Jr. and his own brother, was shot down by an assassin with murky goals. In August the Democrats convened for their national convention in Chicago. With no clear front-runner established, the scene was chaotic. Antiwar protesters descended on the city amid rumors that they intended to taint the water supply with hallucinogenic drugs. The demonstrators took up residence in Chicago's Lincoln Park, where they were unprotected. City police and Illinois National Guard troops physically attacked them on the premise that they did not have the proper permits to sleep there.

Passions were just as hot inside the auditorium, as delegates wrestled with whether to include a peace plank for their platform. In the end the notion was defeated. This elevated tensions to a fever pitch. Security guards started to rough up television reporters. CBS correspondent Dan Rather was assaulted in front of the entire country, prompting his respected colleague Walter Cronkite to tell the disbelieving nation, "I think we've got a bunch of thugs here." In the end it was Johnson's vice president, Hubert Humphrey, who was nominated for president. Humphrey hadn't even participated in the primaries. He was seen as the candidate most likely to continue Johnson's war policies.

And that led to the ultimate upset. In November Humphrey lost the general election to Richard Nixon. Though a relatively young man, in his early forties, Nixon had already weathered many career scandals and controversies. He had also already lost two big elections—defeated by John F. Kennedy for president in 1960 and by Pat Brown in the race for California governor in 1962.

By 1968 Nixon was washed up and left for dead. Yet he had somehow bounced back to ascend to the very throne of the nation.

Interestingly, in 1968 both major parties had considered football coaches for the top of their tickets. At the Democratic National Convention, University of Alabama coach Paul "Bear" Bryant received nominating votes for both president and vice president. On the Republican side, Richard Nixon had contemplated asking Vince Lombardi to be his running mate. Lombardi, in fact, was a liberal and a John F. Kennedy man.

African American athletes were also finding an elevated level of respect and status in the late 1960s. By 1968 black athletes had participated in professional team sports for only about twenty years. For most of that time unwritten quotas and the silent racism of team owners and executives deliberately minimized their involvement. Yet even with those impediments, many black players became stars. They revolutionized the games and raised the level of play, shifting the balance of power to those leagues and organizations that had accepted them. At the back end of the decade not only had black athletes entered the mainstream on the field, but their intellectual gifts and moral courage had elevated some of them to the role of societal leaders.

The year 1968 was an extraordinarily tense time for race relations in the United States. In April Martin Luther King Jr., the young, eloquent, and charismatic civil rights leader, was gunned down in Memphis, Tennessee. King's violent death was especially egregious because he had led the country through revolutionary change utilizing extraordinary rhetoric and the tactics of peace.

King had once preached peace from the marble steps of America's temple of freedom, the Lincoln Memorial. But in 1968 his voice was stilled as he was shot on the balcony of a Memphis motel.

King's ugly death lit a match under America's cities. Robert F. Kennedy tried to calm this storm. He delivered the news of King's death at a political rally in Indianapolis and then speaking directly to black Americans urged them to reject bitterness. Though he was a rich and privileged white man, he addressed them as a brother in tragedy.

"I had a member of my family killed," Kennedy said, referring to JFK's murder by Lee Harvey Oswald. "He was killed by a white man."

Despite his eloquence and personal revelations, the nation erupted into urban riots anyway, and many American cities went up in flames.

The Summer Olympics held in Mexico City a few months later were hardly a diversion from this combustibility. First, South Africa, with apartheid policies that extended to its athletic teams, had been invited to compete. That invitation was eventually rescinded, however, under the threat that other nations would boycott. Even after the Games were under way, things did not calm down. Two African American sprinters, Tommie Smith and John Carlos, became big news when they won medals in the 200-meter race and then scandalously used the victory platform as a stage for political commentary. As "The Star-Spangled Banner" played, the athletes dramatically lowered their heads and refused to look at the American flag; instead, they each raised a black-gloved fist as a potent symbol of "black power."

The International Olympic Committee deemed their statement inappropriate and antithetical to the Olympic spirit; the U.S. Olympic Committee, however, sitting on a tinderbox back home, took a gentle approach to dealing with the young protesters. It issued apologies to the IOC and to Mexico, hoping that would suffice in ending the matter.

It didn't.

The IOC, headed by Avery Brundage, an American, was not mollified. It demanded censure for Smith and Carlos.

"The discourtesy displayed [by Smith and Carlos] violated the standards of sportsmanship and good manners," the IOC wrote. And then they added: anyone else attempting to follow in Smith's and Carlos's footsteps "would be met with the severest of penalties."

The IOC's pious pronouncements about the Olympics and politics were all the more hypocritical considering that thirty years earlier, the organization had no trouble participating in Hitler's 1936 Summer Games in Berlin. Those Olympics were hotly debated, even in their own time, because many saw them as a massive propaganda tool for the aggressive and anti-Semitic Nazi Party.

Brundage himself was then the head of the American Olympic Committee and was a leading advocate for U.S. participation in Hitler's Olympics. When German athletes gave the Nazi salute from the victory podium, Brundage voiced no outrage, saw no scandal, and made no statement. Neither did the IOC.

Ancient Red Smith, an eminence among sportswriters, paraphrased Shakespeare when he wrote about the old men of the IOC.

"They are, as Mark Antony observed on another occasion, all honorable men who consider children's games more sacred than human decency," Red wrote.

Tommie Smith and John Carlos had their credentials revoked, and they were evicted from the Olympic Village. They were sent back to the United States in disgrace.

Dr. Harry Edwards, a young sociologist just beginning his long career focused on sports and athletes, counseled Carlos and Smith before the Games. He encouraged their public statement and assisted them in crafting it. All three of them—Carlos, Smith, and Edwards—were products of the San Jose State University athletic program.

Edwards had a point to make, and he knew that the time had come when successful athletes, international celebrities in the television age, had the platform and, more important, the credibility to speak to the world.

Edwards grabbed the moment. He linked the plight of black Americans with all oppressed people of any color. "I think that demonstration proved to *all athletes* that there is more to being a nigger than the color of a man's skin," he said. "If Smith and Carlos could be treated like that by Olympic officials, so could *any athlete.*"

It was uncertain whether Smith's and Carlos's gesture could convince some Americans about the inequities in their society. But those black fists, waving in the air, were a poignant and undeniable statement of the deep dissatisfactions that might yet rip the country apart.

If the grapes of wrath were indeed being sown, it wasn't politicians or preachers delivering that blunt and important message, nor was it poets or artists. The messenger was a man who until recently had no place at the national table, and no voice at all. It was the black athlete who was leading the way to equity and freedom.

The loudest voice of all wasn't even at the Olympics. It belonged to Muhammad Ali, a professional prizefighter who was losing his standing, his considerable fortune, and potentially his freedom because he had refused induction into the armed forces.

When the decade started his name was Cassius Marcellus Clay, and he was seen as more of a clown than a contender. Although he had won the gold medal in the light-heavyweight division at 1960's Rome Olympics, Clay was looked upon merely as a brash kid from Kentucky. He was so loud and overbearing, the conservative writers of the day referred to him as "Gaseous Cassius" or "the Louisville Lip." He wasn't deemed suitable or ready to meet the felonious heavyweight champion, Sonny Liston.

In their book *Blood Brothers*, about Muhammad Ali and Malcolm X, authors Randy Roberts and Johnny Smith showed that Liston was a menacing man, even among fistfighters. Many feared that Sonny might kill Clay in the ring, and with good reason. Liston heartily agreed. After Cassius outpointed Doug Jones in a controversial decision that ended in a hailstorm of calls of "fix" and "fake" by the fans in attendance at Madison Square Garden, someone asked Sonny what he saw in the brash young fighter.

"Clay showed me I'll get locked up for murder if we're ever matched," Liston said.

That seemed reasonable.

After the two had signed to face off for the heavyweight championship, Clay and Sonny ran into each other in a Las Vegas casino. When Cassius saw Sonny at a craps table, he immediately started shouting wildly and insulting the champion's appearance and intelligence. "Look at that big ugly bear! He can't do nothin' right," Clay screamed.

That was a bad idea. Liston was soon crowding the loudmouth and offering back his own brand of crude but effective banter.

"Listen, you nigger faggot," Sonny began. "If you don't get out of here in ten seconds, I'm going to pull that big tongue out of your mouth and stick it up your ass."

By 1968 Ali was still quick and witty, but he was no longer anyone's clown. He'd already beaten Liston in two straight title fights, both laced with controversy, and then defeated eight more men. He'd shown the world his intellectual complexity, too, when he announced that he had changed his name to Muhammad Ali and joined the Nation of Islam. The Nation had its own perception problems, as many Americans considered it a cult or hate group. Nevertheless, his involvement with the group led him into deep philosophical terrain and difficult public stances that moved him from the sports pages to the front pages.

Ali had not yet lost a single professional bout and was still in his prime, but he was defrocked of his title for defying the U.S. government and refusing induction into the armed forces. He publicly declared that he would not fight in Vietnam. The government counterpunched. His boxing license was suspended in every state, and he was sentenced to five years in prison. But the Department of Defense was about to find out something that Ali's opponents already knew—he had a granite jaw. Manhandling would not sway him. In fact, he was capable of doing more damage to them than they were to him. He desecrated the war effort when he angrily declared, "I got nothing against no Vietcong. No Vietnamese ever called me nigger."

That small statement, in its simplicity, represented a blunt truth that no one could refute. What sense did it make for a man like Ali to go to Vietnam and lose his tremendous earning potential, his liberty, and perhaps his health or life? Why would he fight for "freedom" in a country that still forced him to the back door of the diner if he was hungry?

In his simple words, Ali framed Vietnam as a war that exported that racism. He showed it to be an act of aggression perpetrated by white colonialists against dark-skinned people. In doing so he painted Americans as something they could not have even fathomed at the start of the decade. In his words the United States was no longer that righteous fighting force that had beaten Hitler's bloodthirsty Nazi murder machine or the brave Cold Warriors who confronted Stalin's naked aggression. Thanks to Ali, Americans were forced to confront a disturbing self-image, one in which they were the murderous racists and their country was the ruthless and barbaric invader. A Black Muslim, an athlete, made it clear that in Vietnam, the Americans weren't John Wayne charging westward on the back of a colt; Americans were the bushwhackers shooting at him.

Ali showed them that.

Ali's defiance and crude eloquence made him a hero to the counterculture populated by the huge "baby-boomer" generation. Their values were peace and love. They rejected materialism as they rejected war. They viewed their parents as bigoted, archaic, and sexually repressed, while they embraced civil rights, gender equality, ecology, and free love.

Ali was a symbol—to them— of their values, yet he was opposed to virtually everything they stood for. As a Nation of Islam member, Muhammad believed that an evil, bigheaded scientist named Yacub created whites from the germs of blacks to be devils. He believed a mother ship in space orbited the earth, waiting for the right moment to release bombers to kill white people. Ali didn't believe in racial inclusiveness; he approved of segregation. He wasn't in on the equality of the sexes; he believed in the subordination of women. Despite his stand against the Vietnam War, he was far from a pacifist. He was a gladiator who made a fortune by pounding other men senseless. He charmingly predicted the outcome of his fights in doggerel, but his rhetoric could also be despicable, as when he compared his formidable rival Joe Frazier, a courageous pugilist with dark skin, to a gorilla. This he did over and over again on national television and thus provided a truly noble opponent a deep and unwarranted humiliation. Ali was also hypocritical, rejecting the war on religious grounds even as he openly conducted sexual affairs that were extracurricular to his marriage.

Ali did and said things, deeply believed things, that would have doomed the careers and stained the reputations of almost any American man, black or white. But he dominated popular culture in a way that no other athlete ever had. He was handsome, funny, and talented. He was successful. For many Americans, that was simply enough.

The fighter who began the decade as an oddity without a chance for the title, who started as a clown who could not be taken seriously, was one of the most serious, famous, and admired men in the world in 1968.

White athletes, enjoying every privilege that the society had to offer, didn't have quite the same fervor for social change. They didn't use their celebrity for grand causes or to take an intellectual stand. Unitas recognized that football players could be an influence on American youth, however. Shilling for a summer camp he owned that featured NFL players teaching young people the game, he told William Wallace of the *New York Times*, "[Football players] can do a lot of good to combat the influence of the hippies and long hairs."

Like the society, professional football was also in a topsy-turvy state. In 1960 Weeb Ewbank was on top of the world. He had just won two straight titles with the franchise that he had built from scratch. That same year Don Shula was a former journeyman player and an obscure assistant coach. But by 1968 Ewbank was on the verge of getting fired from his second team, in an inferior league, and Shula was the most celebrated young coach in the NFL. And for Shula, things were only getting brighter.

At the end of 1967 Vince Lombardi had handed over the reins of his Packers to his longtime assistant Phil Bengston. After dominating the championship game and the Western Division of the NFL for the better part of the '60s, Lombardi was retiring from coaching. Meanwhile, in Baltimore, Shula was deftly handling some difficult transitions. Lenny Moore, Raymond Berry, and Jim Parker had all retired. Though each one had declined significantly, it was nevertheless a sweeping loss and a significant drain of talent. All three players were bound for the Hall of Fame.

There was an even more significant player loss coming. Shula went into the preseason with private concerns about Johnny Unitas. In 1965 Johnny U's leg injury proved that he was just as vulnerable to damage as any other mortal man. The quarterback had complained about soreness in his throwing arm, shoulder, or elbow since 1963. These issues were never the cause of too much concern, since Unitas rarely missed games and his level of play was consistently high. In 1968 Unitas was the reigning MVP coming off a 3,500-yard season. Fans across the country looked at him and saw the same old star, a player who was always prepared and almost impossible to stop. But in Shula's trained and unsentimental eyes, Johnny U was a thirty-five-year-old who had absorbed a decade of wicked beatings. Like the fans, he knew that Unitas was still the Colts' greatest asset, but as a professional he also knew that Unitas was the team's most vulnerable area of exposure. What's more, the previous season's blockbuster trade that brought Bubba Smith and Bill Curry had cost the team Gary Cuozzo, Unitas's capable protégé and backup. It left the Colts stronger across the board but with a susceptible Achilles' heel. As matters stood, if anything happened to the aging and brittle Johnny U, Shula's hopes for reaching the Super Bowl would reside in the hands of Jim Ward, a former fourteenth-round draft pick from tiny Gettysburg College.

Handing the roaring Colts offense over to Ward was like tossing the keys of a Porsche to the family's pimply driver's-ed student. It wasn't going to happen. Shula had already felt the frustration of assembling championship-worthy teams, only to see the opportunities squandered by one or another unforeseen quarterback catastrophe. The memory of the '65 season was still fresh. The Colts lost the West to the Packers because Unitas was on the sideline in a cast and the team could barely move the ball without him.

So with the preseason already under way, the coach set his sights on obtaining a quarterback with the maturity and the know-how for the job should the worst come to pass. He found one, rotting away, on the end of the New York Giants' bench.

The man Shula obtained was a good-natured, self-effacing man named Earl Morrall. Earl was the type of player that Unitas had put to shame his whole career. Johnny U attended an unheralded school and was an anonymous late-round draft pick. Morrall went to a football powerhouse, was the second pick in the draft, and came into the league with a great deal of fanfare. Yet while Unitas was a superstar of the highest magnitude, Morrall and many other former "prospects" struggled or fell into irrelevance.

Earl Morrall had been a schoolboy hero on the athletic fields of Muskegon, Michigan, his hometown. That's where he first displayed the prototypical size and booming arm of a big-time passer. When his high school career came to a close, he was at the center of a hotly contested recruiting battle that split the entire state in half. The University of Michigan and Michigan State both coveted his services, so the offers and accusations flew with equal velocity in a civil war between Wolverines and Spartans.

Morrall's father was a machinist at the Continental Motors plant. Earl turned to him for advice about where to go, but the old man had little to give. "I can't tell you what to do," he said. "I never went to college. I don't know which ones are right for you and which ones aren't."

Many in Morrall's circle derided Michigan State as a "cow college" and referred to it as "Moo U." In the end, however, guileless Earl chose State primarily because the coaches had been friendlier to him during his campus visit. At Michigan Earl was put off by coach Bennie Oosterban's demeanor. When the leader of the Wolverines called Earl into his office, he was reclining in his swivel chair, chomping on a cigar, and showing Morrall the filthy soles of his shoes.

In East Lansing the Michigan State coaches were not only friendlier toward Morrall but also more affable to each other and the players. That amiable environment was more or less the reason Earl chose State.

In addition to football, Morrall played baseball for the Spartans and was good enough to help the team to the College World Series his sophomore year. In football things didn't go as anticipated. When Earl finally became the full-time starter his junior year, it wasn't exactly the fulfillment of a dream. The Spartans slogged through their worst season since 1919 and finished 3-6. Even Earl knew that the fans associated him with that failure.

It was a foregone conclusion that Morrall would be benched for his senior year, but he surprised everyone and rewon the starting job in summer practice. But nothing came easy. In the Spartans' first game they barely squeaked by Indiana, 20–13. The following week they fell to archrival Michigan, the number-two-ranked team in the country, 14–7. The Spartans rebounded against Stanford, and Morrall scored his first-ever collegiate touchdown in the victory.

And then came number one, Notre Dame. The Fighting Irish rolled into East Lansing on an eleven-game winning streak behind star quarterback Paul Hornung. Another loss, though understandable, would have left Michigan State with a .500 record and on the brink. But playing in front of about fifty million network television viewers, Morrall was the hero, scoring a touchdown and leading his Spartans to the upset, 21–7.

Notre Dame was the turning point for both Michigan State and Earl. After that the Spartans disposed of Illinois, Wisconsin, and Purdue in quick succession. Their successful tour of the Big Ten ended with an unexpected trip to the Rose Bowl, where State defeated UCLA by a field goal at the gun. Morrall was chosen for a spate of All-American teams, beating out two future pro football Hall of Famers in Paul Hornung and Len Dawson.

After Earl's sensational senior year San Francisco selected him second overall in the NFL draft, or about 198 picks ahead of Bart Starr. The bad news was (and there was always bad news for Earl), the 49ers already had Y. A. Tittle on their roster. Tittle was an enduring presence in San Francisco, the team icon, and already recognized as one of the best quarterbacks of the century. Nevertheless, Y.A. was coming off a weird season in which he led the league in touchdown passes, with seventeen, but also heaved up a staggering twenty-eight interceptions, which placed him atop the NFL in that dubious category, too.

Morrall signed his contract for about $12,000, plus a $2,000 bonus if he could supplant Tittle as the starter. Morrall was apprehensive about competing against the illustrious Tittle, but upon arriving for summer practice his wife, Jane, got an extended glimpse of Y.A. and urged her husband not to worry. Examining Tittle's bald head, she decided that he was the oldest-looking man she had ever seen.

"He looks over the hill," Jane told Earl, though Y.A. was only then about twenty-nine years old.

If Tittle wasn't aging well, it might have had something to do with his poor relationship with 49ers head coach Frankie Albert. The two didn't see eye-to-eye, primarily because Albert wanted to call the team's plays from the bench and Tittle wanted to call the plays in the huddle. This irritation eventually erupted into an open warfare that everyone on the team could see. As a result, Morrall started four games his rookie season, while his highly capable mentor was taught a lesson on the bench. Earl wasn't really ready to start; he threw six interceptions and only one touchdown pass. Meanwhile, the 49ers dropped three of the four games.

In the next draft the 49ers selected quarterback John Brodie with their first pick in round one. They went to great lengths to assure Earl they intended to retain him, and then they quickly traded him to Pittsburgh.

Earl entered Steelertown in high esteem. Coach Buddy Parker had been a Morrall fan for a long time. Buddy also carved out his legend in Michigan, where he and his drinking pal Bobby Layne led Detroit to successive NFL Championships while Earl was performing miracles in East Lansing. Morrall was still on Parker's mind when the coach abruptly resigned from the Lions and accepted the Steelers' job. Even though Pittsburgh already had two promising quarterbacks, Len Dawson and Jack Kemp, Parker gave up a linebacker and two number-one draft picks to acquire Earl.

"You're my man," Buddy told Morrall the moment he arrived. The coach ignored Kemp and Dawson, before releasing them both. Earl considered them lucky. They both went on to huge careers in the AFL, where they won league championships and were named All-Stars. Meanwhile, Earl was stuck with Parker, which he said was akin to a misery. The coach's raging temper made every flight after a loss an aviation tragedy. Parker profanely harangued and insulted his players so badly, they'd hide in the tiny airplane bathrooms to avoid his wrath. There was no other means of escape.

Though Morrall began his tenure in Pittsburgh as this angry man's favorite, it didn't take long for their relationship to sour. In a game against the Cardinals Earl was given a quick shove from a defensive end that snapped his head sharply back like a whiplash in a car accident. He immediately noticed a burning sensation, and numbness crept down his throwing arm and into his hand. After that he had trouble gripping the ball or lifting his arm over his head, and his ability to throw was compromised. He courageously played through the disabling injury, but had to take periodic rest breaks from play. Parker had no pity or patience. Seeing only damaged goods, he traded Earl to Detroit for Bobby Layne, the quarterback Parker really wanted anyway. Even with the matter decided, the coach's mean-spiritedness shone through. "Morrall will never make it in this league," Parker told the press.

In Detroit Morrall was glad to be in his home state, but bad luck continued to plague him. Just prior to the start of the 1962 season he accidentally cut off his big toe while mowing his lawn. He eventually came back from that gruesome injury, but in 1964 the Bears' Doug Atkins, Unitas's old nemesis, hit Earl so violently, he felt like he had been stabbed with a knife. Earl wanted to continue playing, but the team doctor insisted on examining him. Putting a hand beneath the quarterback's shoulder pad, the doctor felt the jagged edge of a broken collarbone piercing through the skin.

Earl also suffered an ambivalent relationship with Lions coach George Wilson. The amiable Wilson was considered the ultimate player's coach, a man who provided his men every comfort. Wilson's quarterbacks, however, were always on edge. Every year he started training camp by declaring the competition for passers "open." And it never closed. The quarterbacks were yanked for the slightest infraction. There seemed to be no rhyme or reason to Wilson's decisions. Once he even flipped a coin just before game time to determine whether his starter would be Morrall or Milt Plum. Milt called heads; Earl rode the bench.

In 1963 Earl had a huge year. Though he started only ten games, he threw twenty-four touchdown passes and broke some of Bobby Layne's team passing records and at the end of the season was voted Most Valuable Lion. But the next season Morrall was declared the loser of the "open" quarterback competition and was planted back on the bench.

In the end Detroit grew tired of both the coach and the quarterback. In 1965 Wilson was let go, and Morrall was traded to the Giants. Earl had lasted for all or parts of seven seasons in Detroit, a highly respectable stay. Yet few of those campaigns were satisfying. Morrall started a majority of Detroit's games only once. Though he left town ignominiously, Morrall had caught the eye of the Lions' talented young defensive coordinator, Don Shula, and with time that would prove to be significant.

In New York Morrall was afforded a fresh start but found many of the same stale problems. Allie Sherman, his new coach, was an ethnic man and native New Yorker who was Lombardi's successor as Giants offensive coordinator. He and Vince were very good friends, but Lombardi's ghost cast a long shadow at Yankee Stadium and haunted Sherman many years into his tenure.

Giants fans had hoped that Lombardi would be the one to replace the unlovable Jim Lee Howell as their head coach, a fantasy they entertained long after Vince left for Green Bay. The Giants once made a bid to bring Lombardi back, but the commissioner demanded that Vince's Packers contract be honored, and Lombardi stayed in Wisconsin. All of these Lombardi longings and machinations poisoned the well for Allie, even though Sherman initially displayed something of the Lombardi touch. As head coach Sherman quickly made a deal with San Francisco and obtained Tittle. With Y.A. playing the best ball of his long career, Sherman took New York to three straight championship games, and Allie became the first man to ever win Coach of the Year honors two years in a row. But those bona fides couldn't quell the fans' disappointment at missing out on Lombardi, especially since the Giants lost all three of those championship games, two of them to Vince and his Packers.

By the time Morrall arrived on the scene, Sherman had run into hard times. The Giants were rapidly aging, and their stable of stars was declining, retiring, or departing in unwise trades engineered by Allie himself. Ferocious Sam Huff was shipped off to Washington, where he became the capital's biggest football star in a generation. Defensive lineman Rosey Grier went to LA and anchored the Rams' fabled Fearsome Foursome. Dick Modzelewski went to Cleveland and played a key role in the Browns' championship victory over the Colts. And Giants kicker Don Chandler joined Lombardi in Green Bay, where he replaced Paul Hornung as the team's primary field goal kicker. Sherman traded draft picks for veterans who didn't pan out. Perhaps worst of all, Sherman had a hard time getting along with his own assistants. "He's an intelligent man," an anonymous Giants official told the *New York Times*, "but he can't relate his intelligence to football."

In 1964 New York bottomed out and won only two games. The outraged fans serenaded Sherman from the stands, crooning "Good Night, Allie," to the tune of "Good Night, Ladies." The only thing Allie did right, it seemed, was acquire Morrall. Earl immediately ameliorated all of the Giants' negative outcomes. In 1965, with Morrall under center, the Giants dramatically improved to seven victories. Earl's twenty-two touchdown passes were only one less than Johnny Unitas's and eight more than Bart Starr's sixteen. In fact, Morrall crossed the goal line more times in the air than Jim Brown did on the ground (twenty-one). For his efforts, Earl was voted Most Valuable Giant by his teammates.

It was a big season for any individual, worthy of the best players in the game. "You can't give enough credit to Morrall," Sherman said.

But apparently you could give his job away.

Sherman came to summer practice tightly wound in 1966. The glow of the previous year's upswing had already worn off for him. Fearing complacency in mediocrity, Sherman was openly contemptuous of the previous season's 7-7 record, and, in turn, Morrall resented his coach.

The bad feelings between the two eventually surfaced on the practice field. In one chaotic episode, different assistants simultaneously screamed contradictory instructions at Morrall. When the quarterback just stood there, flat-footed, unsure of what to call, Sherman lashed out at him with a profane shout. Morrall lost his composure and screamed a few impertinent but clean words back, but Allie was enraged. The coach quickly moved from across the field to the huddle, where he gave Earl a refresher course on who was in charge. He did this in front of the entire team. Later on Morrall wrote that it was at this exact moment that he felt his relationship with his coach begin to decline.

Later in the season Earl fractured his wrist, necessitating four weeks in a cast that stretched from his elbow all the way down to the base of his fingers. The bone eventually healed, but his relationship with Allie remained fractured.

After the season Sherman and team owner Wellington Mara openly hunted for a new quarterback. They found one in Minnesota, where Fran Tarkenton, one of the best and most compelling players of the era, had just taken the unusual step of handing in his resignation.

The Giants paid the Vikings a ransom in draft picks for "the scrambler" from Georgia. Tarkenton electrified professional football with his original and unpredictable approach to the game. He dramatically extended plays with his nimble feet, looping around in the backfield and escaping the rush like Houdini cheating death. Tarkenton's athleticism was something to behold, and it was the source of endless fan fascination. It was also effective. He delivered touchdowns and victories. But his own coach, Norm Van Brocklin, didn't care for Tarkenton's style. Van Brocklin had been a great pocket passer, like Unitas. He believed in crisp timing and precise choreography between a quarterback and his receivers. Tarkenton was an improvisational artist whose receivers had to read his every twist and turn and adjust on the fly, like school-yard players.

In 1967 Tarkenton started all of the Giants' games, while Morrall had a free ticket to watch his antics from the bench. When Morrall reported to training camp in 1968, he was just one of four quarterbacks vying to back up Tarkenton. What's more, he knew he was the least wanted. He sat, while the younger passers played. Having been unwanted many times before, Earl had an occult ability to see the future. All the signs pointed to yet another trade or even an outright release.

When Sherman finally called Morrall into his office late in training camp, Earl thought he knew what was coming, but it was actually worse than he thought. The Giants had dealt him to Baltimore, the last place on earth he wanted to go. Sitting on the bench behind Johnny Unitas held no more appeal for him than sitting behind Tarkenton. At thirty-four, with a long, frustrating career already behind him, Earl was inclined to simply retire. But Sherman put Morrall on the phone with Shula, who tried to convince him to complete the trade.

"What about Unitas?" Earl asked.

"We're a little concerned about him," Shula earnestly said. "He's been having some problems with his arm."

In fact, Unitas left a preseason game in Detroit earlier in the week complaining of a sore elbow, though the press had reported it only as a "slight injury." Shula also told Morrall that Jim Ward, the Colts' young backup quarterback, had twisted his knee and would be out indefinitely.

After discussing the situation with his wife, Jane, Morrall agreed to report. He was willing to give the game that had been so bad to him one last shot. Nevertheless, both husband and wife dreaded the brutal reality of another relocation. Though the Morralls were practically NFL gypsies who had loaded the caravan many times, they had just settled into a comfortable rented home in Connecticut for the year. Now they had to find a place in Baltimore for their six-person, two-dog family, and they had to do it quickly.

Jane distributed the children with a variety of neighbors in Connecticut and went to Baltimore herself in search of a suitable home for her family. She didn't have any luck. On such short notice the type of nice rented house she had always found in the past simply wasn't available. She hoped to end their refugee status by taking to the newspapers and radio stations to ask fans if they knew of an available dwelling. She actually received a few propositions, but none of them were about housing.

"A couple of perverts called," Earl said.

With few decent options, the Morralls shoehorned their large family into a two-bedroom apartment in the suburb of Towson. It was a roof, but it wasn't exactly conducive to their comfort or their needs. Earl had a lot of hard work ahead of him, studying the Colts' offense at night, and the apartment offered him no privacy or respite from the kids.

Whatever disadvantages Morrall had to deal with, Shula threw him right into the fray. In the very next preseason game against Miami, Earl quarterbacked the Colts for the entire second half.

After the game Unitas's arm swelled and he complained of pain, though no one was too concerned. But in Dallas the following week, everything changed. Unitas played the first quarter and sat out the second. By the time Shula brought Johnny U back to start the third quarter, the quarterback's arm was cold. On the first play of the second half he faded back and found a defensive end between himself and John Mackey. In order to get the ball around the defender, Unitas flung it from a sidearm motion. Then he felt a violent pop in his elbow.

He remained in the game, but his teammates noticed his pain and his dramatic loss of arm strength.

"You could see it on his face; the narrow eyes, the tight lips," Morrall remembered in his memoir. "Whenever he threw, the ball kind of floated. It had no zip."

"I ran an out pattern," Jimmy Orr said, "and he threw me a change-up."

On the sidelines Unitas's close friend Bobby Boyd pleaded with the team doctor. "Get him out of there," Bobby yelled at the physician. "He's going to ruin his arm."

Indeed, after the game the golden arm swelled and turned black and blue near the elbow. At that time there was still no way to see under the skin for a more precise examination. Traditional X-ray was useless for the task. Magnetic resonance imaging, or MRI, the tool that could have provided clarity and helped doctors properly assess the damage, had not yet been invented. In the nomenclature of the times he had "tennis elbow," or "tendonitis." In fact, based on his symptoms, it's likely that he suffered a "Tommy John injury." Tommy John was a left-handed pitcher for the New York Yankees in the 1970s who had an issue similar to Unitas's. John had his arm successfully treated with a surgical procedure that later informally bore his name. In fact, the issue they both suffered was a serious condition: a looseness of the ulnar collateral ligament. It's a painful medical condition that is common in baseball among pitchers. Prior to the advent of the surgery, it was typically considered a career-ending injury.

Repetitive throwing and violent contact were the probable causes of Unitas's specific issue. The catastrophic portion of the injury that resulted in his failure to throw with precision or velocity probably occurred in Dallas when he attempted his "sidearm" throw. Based on the problems he had reported in previous years, it is likely that his elbow was chronically unstable, his ulnar collateral ligament was loose, and his flexor-pronator mass was acting as the elbow's stabilizer. With the sidearm throw he placed excessive stress on that area and caused the flexor-pronator mass to tear.

The plainspoken Unitas didn't know or understand any of that, but, for once, he was up front about his agony. "My arm hurts more now than it ever has," he said. "I couldn't hit a pop pass now if I had to."

Even if Johnny U could face the truth, the coaches and the fans were in abject denial. Everyone in Baltimore wondered, unrealistically, if he could return for the opener. Yet the public, the media, and even the medical community seemed to have a limited, if not medieval, understanding of his issues. The newspaper reported that Unitas was treating his extraordinarily complex elbow injury with "ice and rest therapy." The affected area was referred to as a "soup bone" by the Colts' beat reporter.

For all of the upset in Baltimore about Unitas's health status, there were many evident silver linings. For one thing, Morrall was already being hailed as the best backup quarterback the Colts had ever had. Despite his checkered past, Earl was a former starter who had enjoyed some big victories and successful seasons throughout his long career. He was clearly hardened for battle.

In fact, if Morrall resembled anyone in football, it was probably Unitas himself. The two men were only about a year apart in age. Their dimensions and body types were almost identical. They even favored the same old-fashioned flattop haircut. On the field neither was particularly mobile, and both featured accurate arms that could hit the short passes and the long bombs with great precision. Not surprisingly, Unitas and Morrall were close friends. They spent so much time together in practice and at meetings, their teammates saw them as slightly unidentical twins and gave them rhyming nicknames. Stoop-shouldered Unitas was called "Hump"; big-assed Morrall was "Rump."

Shula took a shine to Morrall. Earl may not have been as talented as Johnny U or enjoyed the same reputation around the league, but in many ways he was much more suited to working with the coach. Morrall, like Shula, devoutly believed in a run-first offense. Where Unitas had bristled about the coach sending in plays from the sideline, Morrall had no problem with it. In fact, Earl came to Baltimore so late in the preseason, he barely knew the plays and was having serious trouble learning them. It wasn't as if he was dumb or slow. He'd successfully called plays for many years and for many different teams. But the Colts' numbering system vexed him. From the Pop Warner leagues on up, the backs and the gaps between blockers are assigned numbers for the purpose of play calling. On all of Earl's previous teams the numbers were odd to the right and even to the left. The Colts were the opposite. After so many years of thinking of the offense in one way, Earl simply could not wrap his head around doing it the other.

On top of that, Shula's offensive system was considered one of the most complex in professional football. Though he had inherited Weeb Ewbank's playbook and offensive coordinator, everything changed and grew under Shula.

"Weeb was a master of a system that was totally sound but totally simple," Raymond Berry remembered. Shula "had a far different approach to the game." He vastly expanded the playbook and instituted a ponderous nomenclature for calling plays.

The tension between simplicity and complexity was a major focus in the game of the 1960s. Lombardi was the vanguard coach of the era, but his guileless offense was based on the most basic principles. Vince told his men over and over, "We're not trying to fool anyone." He had a dogmatic faith in the game's verities—running the football, blocking, and footwork—as though the proper execution of these fundamentals was a good work on the road to redemption. But some of the era's other coaches, especially Tom Landry in Dallas, Sid Gilman in San Diego, and Hank Stram in Kansas City, added layers of complexity to their playbooks in order to slow the fast and deceive the intelligent. The tension between the fundamental and the futuristic was endlessly debated.

"If I had to make a choice [between the simple and the complex]," Berry said, "I would go with not trying to do too much."

Bill Curry, who actually played for both Lombardi and Shula, saw the difference firsthand. "The Packers system was so incredibly simple," Curry said. "I went to Baltimore, and it took me months to learn how to respond quickly and in the right way."

This problem struck Morrall especially hard. "We opened with the 49ers," Curry said. "We're in Memorial Stadium, in the huddle, and Earl was saying, 'Hey, Matte, what's that formation where it's split backs with the wide receiver?'"

"Out Right, Flank Right, Split" was the name of that play in the Colts' playbook, Bill Curry said. "In Green Bay we would call that exact same formation 'Red Right.'"

The upshot was that Morrall never did get a solid handle on calling the plays. With Earl perplexed, Tom Matte took charge in the huddle. "I probably called about half the plays for the entire year," Matte said. "Earl was confused; I felt sorry for him. I'd played quarterback, too, and I knew what he was trying to do."

Incredibly, none of this slowed down the Colts. They pounced on the league as though they had a vendetta. And, in a way, they did. They took out their rage for all of the bad breaks and years of frustration they'd suffered in the 1960s, for the terrible officials' calls that went against them, for the teams they simply couldn't beat when it mattered, and even for their own self-inflicted wounds.

Morrall had only been a Colt for a few days, yet Baltimore's enemies were already his own. The schedule featured all four of his former teams, the organizations that had misused, embarrassed, and dropped him.

The revenge tour began with the 49ers, the team that had drafted Morrall. Earl torched San Francisco's defense for about 200 yards and two touchdown passes—one to tight end Tom Mitchell and the other to Jimmy Orr—for an easy Colts victory, 27–10. A couple of games later Morrall gave the Steelers, his second team, the same treatment. The Colts pounded Pittsburgh, 41–7. In the second 49ers game the Colts ran up the score, 42–14. In the most pleasing victory of all to Morrall, the Colts shut out Allie Sherman, Fran Tarkenton, and the Giants, 26–0. Finally, Earl led the Colts to almost triple the score against Detroit, 27–10. By the time the season ended, he had not only beaten all of his former employers but humiliated them.

For the rest of the Colts there was still plenty of unresolved business. They mauled the Chicago Bears, 28–7, paying back that rowdy franchise for its sadistic treatment of Unitas over the years. The Rams were the only team in football that could defeat the Colts in 1967, but they lost to them twice in 1968. And, finally, Baltimore punished the one team that had tortured them the most, the team that had stood in their way every year, the team that got the breaks and cashed the checks. That team, of course, was the three time defending-champion Packers. Green Bay couldn't even score a single touchdown against Baltimore's mighty defense, as the Colts prevailed over the Packers, 16–3.

As each game unfolded it was clear that Baltimore was much more than just another good team having a big year. They were a team for the ages. The only old nemesis with whom they could not settle the score in the regular season was the Cleveland Browns, the same franchise that improbably defeated them in the '64 championship game. The Colts' only loss in 1968 was a 30–20 defeat in week six to the Browns. Cleveland still had Baltimore's number, even without Jim Brown.

Baltimore had a potent offense, but it was the defense that made the team truly great. Bubba Smith, Mike Curtis, and Bobby Boyd anchored Chuck Noll's progressive schemes. In fact, Noll's defense eclipsed any Baltimore had ever had before, and it dominated the league. The Colts gave up only 144 points in their fourteen-game season, an incredible 10.3 per game against the best players in the world.

But the season's real marvel was Shula. The prescient young coach was on top of everything. He had anticipated Unitas's infirmity, and he had the acumen to acquire a player who could not only stand in for Johnny U but actually perform like Johnny U. It wasn't remarkable that Shula saw potential in Morrall. Other professional coaches had seen Earl's assets for more than a decade. Yet Shula was the first one who gave him the supporting cast and the confidence to flourish. Under Shula's tutelage, with Shula's players all around him, Morrall was no longer the quintessential expendable quarterback; he was the league's Most Valuable Player—Earl-goddamned-Morrall. Draft bust, second teamer, well traveled. Whatever you could call him, he had thrown twenty-six touchdown passes and was the linchpin, the very best player, on maybe the very best team ever assembled. If Earl always had it in him, no one had brought it out until Shula.

As for the man who defined the Colts for a generation, the 1968 season was painful, tedious, and frustrating. With his big reputation and aching arm, Unitas was reminiscent of Joe DiMaggio, another American athlete who had once suffered greatly while his team succeeded without him. In 1949 Joltin' Joe played in only 76 games of the 154-game season and missed significant parts of the Yankees' thrilling pennant race against the Red Sox because he was suffering from sharp bone spurs in his heel.

The Yankee Clipper's emotional struggles and pain were captured as a redemptive force in Ernest Hemingway's classic novel *The Old Man and the Sea.*

"But I must have confidence and I must be worthy of the great DiMaggio who does all things perfectly even with the pain of the bone spur in his heel," the suffering and ancient fisherman says to himself as he strives for his own inner greatness.

The book itself was the last hurrah of the aging writer who was once celebrated for his athletic prose. Hemingway shaped Joltin' Joe into a symbol of deep dignity and tremendous courage in the face of aging and declining skills. DiMaggio's persistence, even elegance in suffering, made him an example for all men who were no longer at the top of their game.

And so it was that Unitas, who had almost single-handedly catapulted football past baseball in the nation's affections, was DiMaggio-like in his struggle. There was no magnificent tragedian like Hemingway to immortalize Johnny U's pain. Nevertheless, the great comic poet Ogden Nash, an enthusiastic Colts fan who lived in the shadow of Johns Hopkins University, wrote a series of poems for *Life* that conjured up Johnny U in his salad days of 1958 when his partnership with Raymond Berry represented the game's vanguard. It was a flattering portrait to be sure, but a premature rendezvous with the past, as though the great man was already history and his career a corpse.

In 1968 Unitas was a fixture on the sidelines. Johnny U sat and watched a man with a long-shot story to match his own commandeer *his* team and lead it to even greater heights than he ever had. Unitas remained a presence. He watched the action, noted the opportunities, and offered advice to Morrall. But even as Earl's victories and great performances piled up, there was still hope among the fans that Johnny U would stride onto that field and be his old gargantuan self.

The messianic longings for Unitas's return were neither practical nor reasonable, given the nature of his injury. It was as if Baltimoreans were praying to an unseen God for a savior when, in fact, none was required. Morrall's Colts weren't the besieged Israelites; they were the conquering Romans. Even so, Johnny U was no different from the fans or coaches. He held out hope, too, and he believed he could take a team that was already just about perfect and improve it. All season long he tested his arm. The status reports of these trial runs were dispatched like war news from the front. It seemed that every practice throw was numbered and noted in the newspapers for its length, accuracy, velocity, and, of course, the amount of pain it caused him.

Unitas managed to play in four regular-season games, but with results that were unworthy of him. He threw few passes and completed fewer still. His longest stint of the year was in the Cleveland loss. He played for about a quarter and completed only a single pass in eleven attempts. Three of his passes landed in the waiting arms of grateful Cleveland defenders.

Mostly, though, Unitas just watched his teammates thrive without him. Although his patience was tried, his sense of humor remained intact. When someone asked him how it felt to stand and watch an entire Colts game, his reply was vintage Johnny U.

"I'm tired," he said, feigning exhaustion.

## FIFTEEN

# Super Bowl III

When the 1968 regular season ended the Colts stood alone as the most successful team in either league. For the second year in a row they had lost only a single game. It was a triumph for Shula and a remarkable string of success not seen in pro football since George Halas's prewar Monsters of the Midway. More spectacular still, Shula did it with two different quarterbacks. Previously, fans took it for granted that Unitas's greatness was the reason for the Colts' stunning success. He alone had been the common thread for so many victories. But in 1968 Shula had an even better record without him. In the new narrative Unitas was no longer the protagonist. His teammates spoke of how much better they played now that they no longer had him to bail them out. They spoke of an offensive line that was sharper with a quarterback who deployed the running game more frequently.

This was an all-new epic, and Shula was the man who wore the Superman cape now. The coach was the one who plugged in a backup journeyman for a Hall of Famer and actually improved the team. In the new story the quarterback was merely a part of a whole, vital, maybe, but replaceable, like any other. Now everyone could see it was a smart and prepared coach who delivered victory.

As the postseason arrived Unitas continued on as a spare part. He watched the Colts meet the hard-charging Minnesota Vikings in the divisional round. Morrall played superbly well against Minnesota's improving defense, throwing for nearly 300 yards and connecting on two touchdown passes.

The big moment wouldn't come until the following week when the Colts flew to Cleveland. Baltimore was a supremely confident ball club, but there was some apprehension, too. Nobody had forgotten the team's terrible loss to the Browns in the championship game just four years earlier. Cleveland was also the only team to beat Baltimore during the 1968 regular season. But alas, there was no stopping the Colts. Tom Matte took matters into his own capable hands and scored three touchdowns in the game. For one of them he dove forward, his thick body parallel to the ground. That one landed him in the filthy end zone of Municipal Stadium and on the glossy cover of *Sports Illustrated*. Meanwhile, Baltimore's defense shut out the Browns, and the Colts won an absurdly easy victory, 34–0.

For the first time in nine years Baltimore was the NFL champion. For many of the players on the squad it was a redemptive victory. They had been so close, so often—in '64, '65, '66, and '67. Yet all those years had ended in rank humiliation and frustration. All of that melted away in the exultation of the long-deferred achievement. Victory over Cleveland meant that they were NFL champions, and that had always been *the* goal.

In the visitors' locker room it was all fat cigars, big grins, and national media. Former jock turned broadcaster Tom Brookshire, or "Brookie," as Jimmy Orr called him, came to the lockers to interview Morrall, Matte, Boyd, and Orr. The relief of victory was palpable in the wide smiles and jovial responses of the interviewees. And then Brookshire called Carroll Rosenbloom to the microphone. The Colts' owner was beaming, but ever vigilant not to offend the football gods. "You just have to be careful what you say, as you well know," the superstitious Rosenbloom told Brookie. "You can't jinx the ball club."

And then he started to praise his coach.

"I told Shula when he came [here] I thought this would be my last coach, and that's the way it looks like it's gonna be," Rosenbloom gushed. "He's just a fine young man, a fine coach."

Only about two weeks later he would be so enraged at that fine young man, he would never want to speak to him again.

While Don Shula dazzled the football world with his brilliant moves in 1968, up in New York his old mentor Weeb Ewbank was having a rough time of it. At the dawn of the 1960s Weeb was a rock-star coach. He had won two straight titles and assembled the entire team and coaching staff himself. But by the end of 1962 he was fired and looking for work. The Browns, the franchise he came up with, had an open position at head coach, but they weren't even interested in interviewing him. When Weeb finally landed a new job it was in the "inferior" American Football League, with the hapless New York franchise, the worst organization in professional football. In 1967 the Jets under Ewbank experienced their first-ever winning season, a major accomplishment and milestone. But it was a long time coming, and it ended on a bitter note.

The Jets had jumped out to a 5-1-1 record in 1967 and enjoyed the look of a serious contender. But when they met the defending AFL champion Chiefs in Kansas City, New York's fortunes took a cruel turn. The Chiefs delivered them a humiliating 42–18 defeat. Worse than that, their star running back, Emerson Boozer, tore cartilage and ligaments in his right knee and required immediate, season-ending surgery. The Jets went 3-3 the rest of the way. At 8-5-1 they finished 1967 in second place and narrowly missed the postseason.

Boozer's injury and the team's collapse had serious and long-lasting consequences for the franchise. After five years with just a single winning season, and that one a rank disappointment, there were bound to be repercussions.

To most fans the unassailable leader of the Jets was managing partner Sonny Werblin. When Sonny and a group of four other nondescript businessmen acquired the team back in 1963, the franchise was known as the Titans, a synonym for Giants. The similarity between the franchises ended there. New York's football Giants were a premier professional sports organization in the '50s and early '60s; the Titans were a failure both on the field and off. The team's venue of operations was the old Polo Grounds, located at Coogan's Bluff, on the south shore of the Harlem River. The bathtub-shaped ballpark in Manhattan had a long and rich history in New York, mostly associated with the National League's baseball Giants. The Giants' tenure in the Polo Grounds stretched from the John McGraw era all the way to Willie Mays. Though its quirky confines had grown venerable in length of service, it was in fact a crumbling edifice and a prime catalyst for the baseball team's bolt to San Francisco in the late 1950s. By the time the Titans became lessors in 1960, it was fallow and unworthy of a modern professional sports franchise. The team drew poorly from the start, but in 1962 it hit an unimaginable low when only about thirty-six thousand paying fans clicked the turnstiles *all year*. Even that pathetic number may have been gilded, however, as it was widely believed that the Titans lied about their attendance. As one New York sportswriter pointed out, many of the fans were coming to the stadium "disguised as empty seats."

The man behind all of this dysfunction was Harry Wismer, the Titans' first president and proprietor. Wismer, a former college player and well-known national broadcaster of football on the radio, had previously owned stakes in the NFL's Detroit Lions and Washington Redskins. He was short, pudgy, and pugnacious in the extreme, and he failed to get along with just about everybody in his orbit. That included his partners; the other AFL owners; the AFL commissioner; his head coach, Sammy Baugh; and, of course, the press. To the surprise of no one, he also had a bad marriage. After being divorced by his first wife, he remarried a few years later, this time to Mary Zwillman, the widow of the notorious Jewish gangster Abner "Longie" Zwillman. Like Wismer, Longie had a short rope, just enough, apparently, to fashion a noose, as he allegedly committed suicide by hanging. There were, of course, other plausible theories about his demise.

As the team owner in the nation's premier city and largest market, Wismer should have owned a highly lucrative franchise. Instead, he was soon forced to accept loans from the other AFL owners just to stay afloat. It wasn't long before he was in full-fledged bankruptcy and selling his team for nothing more than its debts.

Wismer's descent into ignominy was nevertheless the catalyst for the rapid rise of both the franchise and its league. The Titans were purchased by a group of wealthy businessmen whose common thread was ownership stakes in horse racing tracks, especially New Jersey's Monmouth Park. The managing partner of this group was an extraordinarily clever businessman named David Werblin, a man known to all as "Sonny." Werblin arose out of Brooklyn's Jewish ghettos, where he attended the famed Erasmus

Hall High School, one of the best public schools in the country. Erasmus Hall was the alma mater of scores of intellectuals and entertainers and also had an odd legacy as educator of professional football's most prominent Jewish luminaries. In addition to Werblin, Erasmus alumni included Al Davis, the Machiavellian genius behind the sensational Oakland franchise, and Sid Luckman, the Bears legend who was considered the greatest quarterback in the game before Unitas.

Werblin gained his great wealth and success as an incredibly powerful entertainment agent with the Music Corporation of America, or MCA. He joined that company in the 1930s, starting as a messenger. From that humble position, however, he rose up to become an extremely rich and powerful agent and promoter. He negotiated lucrative contracts for huge stars such as Elizabeth Taylor and Johnny Carson. His stunning success propelled him to the leadership of MCA's television arm, and he produced both the Ed Sullivan and Jackie Gleason shows, programs that amassed huge audiences. His leadership brought MCA to a position of such industry dominance that it was ultimately targeted by antitrust investigators and broken into pieces.

When Werblin's close friend Howard Cosell referred to him as "Sonny, as in money," it was no joke.

Werblin was as formidable as Wismer had been ludicrous. No sooner had he taken over the team in 1963 than he had the entire league on the path to parity with the venerable NFL. Eschewing all tradition, Werblin renamed his franchise the Jets, a rhyme with the city's new baseball team, the "Mets." He changed team colors to green and white because they were a reflection of his own St. Patrick's Day birthday, an odd point of pride for a Jew. Like Moses, Werblin parted the waters (the East River) and led his ball club on an exodus from Upper Manhattan to the promised borough of Queens. The Jets would play their home games in the sparkling new Shea Stadium. Entering an arena where he was the heaviest hitter, he took over the AFL's television-rights negotiations. He quickly moved the contract from ABC to NBC and secured five times the annual television revenue for himself and his fellow franchise holders.

Perhaps Werblin's biggest and most important move was bringing in Weeb Ewbank, the fat little man from Baltimore, to run his team. Ewbank had a zeal for franchise healing, which he expressed in the unique vernacular of a prairie veterinarian.

"I've seen sicker cows than this one get well," he told reporters.

Under Weeb change came fast in Queens. Progress in the standings did not. After five years of the Werblin-Ewbank partnership, the Jets had lost more games than they had won. While the bottom-line results did not look good, Ewbank was in fact doing exactly what he did a generation earlier in Baltimore—he was putting together an incredibly balanced team, overflowing with coaching and playing talent. His offensive-line coach was a young man from western Pennsylvania named Chuck Knox who would go on to a long and successful head-coaching career with the Rams, Bills, and Seahawks. Knox led all three of those franchises to division titles.

Ewbank drafted and signed two sensational runners in Emerson Boozer and fullback Matt Snell, giving the Jets an inside-outside running game with both power and speed. He also developed two excellent receivers in Don Maynard and George Sauer Jr. Sauer, who was the son of the Jets' director of player personnel, was an unusually sensitive and intellectual young man who was ambivalent about football and admitted he found it "dehumanizing." Instead, he harbored hopes of having a literary career. Whatever his qualms about the game, he was nevertheless an outstanding player, an AFL All-Star multiple times who hauled in more than 1,000 receiving yards for three straight years. Maynard, meanwhile, was a seasoned veteran who went all the way back to the '58 championship game in which he was a rookie kick returner for the Giants. Maynard was the Jets' long-ball threat and Joe Namath's favorite target.

On defense Ewbank featured two fine assistants. Walt Michaels, a man Weeb had coached many years ago in Cleveland, ran the unit. Buddy Ryan was his young defensive-line coach. Ryan was Oklahoma born and grew up, much like a Steinbeck character, as a Dust Bowl Okie during the Depression. His parents' house lacked electricity and indoor plumbing. Football was his ticket up and out of that life. He went to college and played guard for the Cowboys of Oklahoma A&M (now Oklahoma State). After that he coached high school football and then left the country to go fight in the Korean War.

Upon returning home Ryan was determined to move on from high schools and began a string of jobs at the collegiate level. Always a defensive-line specialist, he coached at universities in Buffalo, Stockton, and Nashville. Ryan's defense in Buffalo posted twelve shutouts in three years and produced a player named Gerry Philbin. Philbin was, in fact, a prototype Weeb Ewbank player: athletic but also smart and dedicated to the hard work of success. The Jets made him their third-round pick in the 1964 draft, and Ryan soon followed him to New York. Philbin became a star, chasing and sacking quarterbacks, while Ryan proved to be one of the most influential theoreticians, teachers, and enduring presences in the professional game for the next thirty years.

Noticing the great pains Ewbank and Knox took to protect their quarterback, Ryan dedicated himself to disrupting the passer. He believed it was the key to winning defense. He was as devoted to the blitz as Vince Lombardi was once opposed to it. His goal was to throw off the passer's timing and, if at all possible, do him great physical harm in the process.

One of the ways in which Weeb was like a modern coach was in his understanding of the importance of having a "shutdown" corner, a man who could take an opponent's best receiver out of the game. He brought one to the Jets when he invited free agent Johnny Sample to join his team. Sample had a long history with Weeb, and much of it was not positive.

Ewbank had drafted Sample for the Colts back in '58. Johnny was an African American player from rural Virginia who found few takers for his talents when he graduated high school. So he moved one state north and became part of the very fine program at Maryland State, a historically black institution located on the so-called Eastern Shore of the Chesapeake Bay. Sample was ahead of his time in a number of ways and in fact might be considered a precursor for the modern cornerback. At six feet one and 203 pounds, he had size and strength, as well as fine speed. But even his legs couldn't keep up with his zooming mouth.

In only his second season Sample started in the 1959 championship game, a rematch between Baltimore and the Giants. He sought out New York's star running back Frank Gifford in the pre-game warm-ups just so he could hector him. Gifford, who also wrote a football column for one of the New York dailies, heard Sample impudently call out, "Hey, Gifford, when are you going to write an article about me?"

Frank meanly dismissed him.

"Kid," he said, "I don't even know your name."

All day long Sample and Gifford jawed and jousted. "Hey, Hollywood, you're too pretty to be playing this game," Sample laughed. "I'm gonna mess up your pretty face." Gifford, unused to shows of such extreme disrespect, sputtered vanilla retorts, such as calling Sample "bush leaguer." Those lame responses only convinced Sample that he was winning a psychological war with his famous opponent. Johnny might have been right about that.

Gifford not only lost the battle of words but was badly defeated on the field, too. Sample easily bested him with two crucial fourth-quarter interceptions. One he picked off right in front of Gifford and ran it back for a touchdown. Sample's other theft came courtesy of Gifford's arm, as the halfback misfired on a kind of abbreviated flea-flicker play. The Colts converted that one into a field goal. Baltimore had trailed 9–7 going into the fourth quarter, but thanks in large part to Sample's sensational performance they routed New York 31–16.

The Giants weren't the only ones who disliked Johnny. Despite Sample's fine play, the Colts also grew to despise him. This stemmed from an incident in which he was allegedly caught stealing from the players' lockers. The Colts gradually realized that small amounts of money were pilfered from them while they sat in team meetings. If a player left $50 in his wallet, he might come back to find $20.

"We couldn't figure out what the hell was happening," Tom Matte said. "So we put [team trainer] Eddie Block up in the rafters to watch the lockers and find out."

Matte said that Block saw Sample lagging behind the others. Once he was alone the defensive back sat on a stool with wheels and rolled from locker to locker in order to riffle through other players' personal belongings. Naturally, Sample's teammates were incensed by the intrusion and apparent theft. "I thought Gino Marchetti was going to kill him," Matte said.

After the season Johnny was traded to Pittsburgh, where he matured as a player. Utilizing his brilliant mind as much as his physical assets, he intercepted eight passes. He kept careful notes on every receiver he faced and was aware of each one's tendencies, compensating and adjusting for them. For instance, Sample had some success where few others did, limiting a rugged hombre like Cleveland's tall and tough flanker Gary Collins. This was primarily because Johnny was insightful enough to notice that Collins preferred to cut inside instead of to the sidelines. So Sample lined up a step or two inside of Collins and forced him to go in a direction where he was less comfortable. Collins was one of the best receivers in the game, but his effectiveness against Sample in one stretch was limited to three short receptions. Johnny had a book like that on everyone.

Unfortunately, the same acuity that made Sample formidable on the field worked against him with his employers. He noticed that as the passing game became pro football's dominant attraction, talented receivers made more money than most other players. So he complained, loudly and publicly and prophetically (as it turned out), that if pass catching was a skill worth investing in, then the ability to prevent receptions was equally valuable. He also noticed and spoke out against the unfair treatment of black players. This was a topic he discussed at length with his Steelers coach, Buddy Parker. After leaving Pittsburgh, unhappily, and taking up with the Redskins, Sample intercepted a pass against Pittsburgh and then ran to the Steelers' sideline and threw the ball at Parker's face, narrowly missing his old coach.

In his last two seasons with the Redskins Sample allowed only one touchdown pass and picked off ten. Nevertheless, at age twenty-nine, he was dismissed from Washington with no new offers in the league. He reached out to a plethora of NFL teams, but no one even bothered to return his calls. Feeling blackballed in the NFL, he reluctantly dialed up Weeb, a man he did not necessarily trust or like from past experience. Sample asked Ewbank for a job and got a position that was far better than he might have imagined. The Jets paid him more than any other defensive back in the AFL, and by 1968 he was accompanying Namath to midfield for coin tosses as the defensive captain.

All of the talent that Werblin and Weeb attracted to the Jets was ultimately overshadowed by the play and personal antics of just one man, Joe Namath. The former Alabama quarterback didn't end up in New York by accident. Before Ewbank drafted Joe in 1965, he had already scouted, vetted, and discussed him for years. Chuck Knox, Weeb's offensive-line coach, had an eye on Namath since the kid was in junior high school. Knox was a high school coach at Elwood City in Lawrence County, Pennsylvania, right next door to Joe's hometown of Beaver Falls. By the time he became an assistant on Ewbank's staff, he had extensive knowledge about Namath to pass on. In addition to that, Weeb, one of the most well-connected men in football, knew Namath's coach at Alabama, Paul "Bear" Bryant, very well. Ewbank and Bryant spoke often about Namath by phone. In one of their conversations Weeb told Bryant that he might draft the University of Miami's George Mira, a quarterback he had seen perform exceptionally well in two different bowl games. That was in 1964, the year before Namath was available. But Bryant quickly talked Weeb out of that, telling him to be patient and wait one more year for Namath. Bryant had personally schooled Joe in running a prostyle offense.

Ewbank was disciplined and took Bryant's advice. He waited for 1965, traded with Houston for the first overall selection in the AFL draft, and then selected Namath. Scouts everywhere noted Joe's quick feet, fast release, and booming arm. Like many top prospects, Namath was lavished with praise. But when Bryant called Joe "the greatest athlete I ever coached," it wasn't hype. It really meant something.

Even so, Namath was far from a sure thing. "I had an awful knee. I had a bad knee," Joe remembered. "I was surprised to get drafted. I only played the first four games and just small parts of the rest. I needed surgery. We didn't have the type of expertise we have today in dealing with joints and physiology. It was a gamble. And it turned out I was damn lucky."

Weeb and Sonny confidently selected Joe, but they were taking no more chances. In the second round they grabbed John Huarte, another quarterback, the Heisman winner, from Notre Dame. Before the day was over the Jets took two more quarterbacks. They wanted options in case things didn't work out.

Namath had his options, too. The dysfunctional St. Louis Cardinals selected him in the first round of their draft, number twelve overall. Namath would decide where he would play; he had the power to choose the deal that was most appealing to him. His peers, by and large, chose their teams based on a list of short-sighted criteria. They typically went with the team that offered them a few thousand dollars more or the city that had the more pleasing climate.

Namath was smarter than that, or at least he had better advice. Coach Bryant, continuing to council him, encouraged Joe toward the Jets just as surely as he had guided Weeb to select Namath.

"Coach Bryant told me prior to my being signed or even drafted . . . to get to know my coaches and owners . . . and to make my decisions on those lines, not necessarily based on where or the exact dollar," Namath said.

That advice easily tipped the scales in favor of Ewbank and the Jets. Weeb's Colts were Namath's favorite team growing up. His first football hero was Jim Mutscheller, Baltimore's magnificent tight end. About thirteen years older than Namath, Mutscheller was also from Beaver Falls. A local boy who had made good on the national scene, Jim was a two-way player and a captain for legendary coach Frank Leahy at Notre Dame. In the pros he was one of Johnny U's primary targets and a star of the '58 championship game. Mutscheller was one of the most underappreciated players in league history, overshadowed in Baltimore's high-flying aerial attack by the theatrics of Lenny Moore and the odd fascination that was Raymond Berry. But Mutscheller was a devastating weapon in his own right. In the championship against the Giants he narrowly missed scoring the winning touchdown in overtime when he hauled in a bold and unexpected pass from Unitas, but slipped on a patch of ice and fell out of bounds at the Giants' 1. That set up Alan Ameche's game-winning plunge, the photo of which appeared in every major newspaper in the country.

After football Mutscheller was a buttoned-up insurance agent, and his football accomplishments faded into history. But the fact was he came into professional ball about a decade before John Mackey and Mike Ditka, the two men credited with revolutionizing the tight-end position and changing its focus from blocking to pass catching. Mackey and Ditka were the first two tight ends to enter the Hall of Fame. Mutscheller was never accorded that honor, but statistically he was just as good as either one. Mutscheller scored forty career touchdowns, more than Mackey (thirty-eight) and barely less than Ditka (forty-three). Mutscheller hauled in 16.7 yards per reception, better than both of those stars.

Namath idolized Mutscheller for the rest of his life, and he admired the greatness of the Colts' passing attack. As an aspiring quarterback himself, he felt a special kinship with Unitas. When Namath was a senior in high school his team purchased new uniforms, and along with the excitement of those clean, gleaming jerseys the coach allowed his players to choose their own numbers for the first time. Joe took 19 and accepted the nickname that went with it, "Joey U."

All things considered, he was thrilled by the possibility of working for Ewbank, the man who had developed his heroes. Even all the things that Ewbank represented paled in comparison to what Sonny Werblin could give him. While the NFL's Cardinals offered Namath a contract for about $50,000 per year, Werblin wheeled in the big guns. Sonny delivered a multiyear deal for more than $400,000. There was more. The Jets' groundbreaking offer also included a luxury automobile for Joe and scouting jobs for his two brothers. Namath ran to the table to sign.

Much was made of the outlandish figure, the most money ever paid to a player up to that time. Primarily, it was a source of outrage that it was given to a young man who had a bum knee and who had yet to play a single down of pro ball.

Werblin was no fool, and he didn't get rich throwing money away. As a show-business kingmaker he knew that the size of the contract itself would attract enormous attention to Namath and his Jets. In a world in which teams still relied on the gate to make a significant portion of their revenues, marketing was essential. Paying Namath big money not only ensured his services but also guaranteed that hordes of New York and national media members would focus their attention on the Jets. They would fill their newspapers and airwaves with news about the young, wealthy, and compelling quarterback and lavish publicity and credibility on his team and its league. With that one bold pen stroke, the Jets overshadowed Allie Sherman's dismal and depressing football Giants in New York, and the AFL gained on its bitter opponent, the NFL. With Namath's contract, the Jets were even bigger news than the fading Yankees in baseball.

Namath fed the media beast by playing the part of a sex symbol. Despite appearances, it wasn't something that necessarily came naturally to him. There was a marked contrast between Joe's father and the father of his persona. He grew up in Beaver Falls, an unpretentious town located in the heart of the Rust Belt, between Cleveland and Pittsburgh. His father, a Hungarian immigrant, started working in the steel mills while he was still just a teenager. He worked at the furnace for more than forty years. Later on he supplemented his income by selling shoes. Joe remembered a childhood with a lot of parental affection, but he had no false illusions about where he was in the family pecking order.

"I had three older brothers and an older sister," he recalled. "Until I was fifteen I thought my name was 'Shut Up.'"

Sonny Werblin made sure that Beaver Falls Joe was a far cry from Broadway Joe. The man who made a fortune representing entertainers facilitated Namath's transition from modest young man to media superstar.

"If Sonny Werblin wasn't the president of the New York Jets, Joe Namath would have probably been a different package publicly," Joe said. "Sonny Werblin believed in the star system. He promoted the star system better than any of the owners prior to his coming to the AFL. He knew that stars sold tickets."

To sell those tickets Werblin exploited Namath's natural charm and good looks and led him to a lifestyle usually condemned by football coaches and owners. With Sonny's approval Joe led the league in nocturnal adventures. "I'd go out with Mr. and Mrs. Werblin three to four nights a week," Namath said. "[Werblin] wanted me to learn New York. He wanted me to get around New York. He wanted to get us on the sports pages. He wanted the Jets to get up there and get our fan base up."

Namath was certainly making fans. He was photographed at

the hottest nightspots and parties, escorting models and actresses with lustrous teeth and hypnotic cleavage. Joe's reputation as a "player" far overshadowed his skills as one of the world's best football players. It got to the point that other quarterbacks envied him more for what he did between the sheets than between the lines.

Dallas quarterback Roger Staubach even went so far as to complain about Namath's good fortune with the ladies on national TV.

"I enjoy sex as much as Joe Namath," Roger said. "I just do it with one woman."

He had to be kidding. No one in America thought anyone enjoyed sex as much as Joe Namath did.

Namath's hedonistic lifestyle was reflected in his appearance. "He was a very singular character in dress and manner," Gay Talese, a New York sportswriter in the 1960s, said. "His manner was nonchalant, very much a man of the night. Contrary to what sports preaches in terms of keeping your health and don't do this and don't do that, don't drink too much, don't take drugs, don't fuck around too much. All of this sort of Puritan ethic that's supposed to be but never really is the code of conduct of the professional successful athlete, Namath violated."

Unlike the rising tide of black players with serious issues on their minds, Talese noted that Namath was "not a political force in this country. He was a social force, a contrarian."

Joe was a shiny object. He captivated the nation and redefined the definition of a football fan. His movie-star presence in the stadium expanded the base of interested parties from paunchy middle-aged men marveling at the grace and violence of younger men to a vast new market of women who were finding a popular-culture icon in Namath. Joe's allure went well beyond the football field. He was as noted for his polish as any male in the country, leading him to author a book called A Matter of Style.

"There was a fusion between the fashion of Namath and the guy who Namath was," Talese said. "Namath dressed like Clyde Frazier," a basketball star on the New York Knicks. "Frazier was a rather colorless player, but off the field, the way he dressed and composed himself, he was cool."

Namath and Frazier both sported full-length fur coats. Clyde supplemented his ensemble with outrageously wide-brimmed fedoras. All of this personality and style had only one landing spot, and for Joe that was Madison Avenue. He starred in a variety of commercials that took advantage of his devilish persona. In one spot, featuring a naughty double entendre, Namath is "creamed" by the famous beauty Farrah Fawcett; she covers his face in Noxzema shaving foam. He tells her she has a great pair . . . of hands.

After that activity he let everyone know that he wore Brut aftershave. Why? Because "you've got to be ready to go all the way," he said.

In another commercial the steelworker's son dons a pair of Beauty Mist pantyhose to prove that the product "could make any legs look like a million dollars."

While Sonny Werblin's Jets were interesting and theatrical, delighting sports fans in New York and across the United States, they were nevertheless irritating four old men. These men—Don Lillis, Phil Iselin, Townsend Martin, and Leon Hess—happened to be Sonny's business partners and equal owners of the team. They weren't showmen like Werblin. They were businessmen, more attached to bottom-line results than the fun that could be had along the way. As managing partner Werblin had stolen the spotlight from them. It is more likely, however, that the source of their dissatisfaction was Sonny's performance. By the spring of 1968, five full years into the Werblin and Weeb regime, the Jets were a loser by almost every standard.

The team had not yet won so much as a single division title. Ewbank's overall regular-season record in New York was below .500. As for Namath, he played exactly like a man who drank and screwed too much. He threw fifty-five interceptions in the last two seasons alone.

For the Jets' owners the most aggravating statistics of all were on the ledger books. Despite leading the AFL in attendance every season since 1963, the Jets were still showing a net financial loss. The ownership group blamed Werblin and his extravagances.

Sonny's partners were done running a profligate operation, and they moved to assert themselves. The other owners demanded that Werblin either buy them out or sell his stake to them. Sonny, citing the pleasure of professional football ownership but not the return, divested. His partners paid him $2–$3 million for his one-fifth share of the club. But before departing Sonny gave the fans one last gift and signed Namath to a contract extension, consulting with no one before pulling the trigger and inking the deal.

Ewbank's continued employment was another matter. Weeb had been Werblin's handpicked choice for coach and general manager. But with Sonny gone Ewbank was at the mercy of Don Lillis, the new managing partner. Lillis's mission was for change, and he made no secret of the fact that Weeb's status was under review. Lillis brazenly met with Vince Lombardi at an Italian restaurant on Third Avenue in the Bronx and discussed the possibility of the former Packer coach taking over the Jets in 1968 as coach, general manager, or both. Lombardi, an NFL loyalist and close friend of Giants owner Wellington Mara, turned Lillis down.

Even with Lombardi's rejection still fresh, Lillis didn't bother mincing words. "We would have loved to have Lombardi," he said. "Everybody wants Lombardi, why shouldn't they?" Lillis also made it clear that Ewbank's Jets weren't performing up to expectations. "We want to have a winning team," Lillis said. "We haven't got that yet."

So maybe for the only time in history, a disappointing string of seasons led to the owner being fired and the head coach being retained. Weeb wasn't appreciated, but he was back at the helm of the magnificent team and coaching staff he had worked so tirelessly and intelligently to assemble.

In 1968 all of the turmoil and intrigue surrounding the Jets somehow led to the greatest season in their history. How far they had come was evident by how well they performed against the AFL's elite. In the first game of the year they beat the Kansas City Chiefs, only a year removed from Super Bowl I. A single point decided the game, as Namath cracked the 300-yard passing barrier and threw for two touchdowns—both to Maynard. In fact, New York would lose only three times in 1968. One of those stumbles came against the Oakland Raiders in a thrilling November game.

The Raiders had to score two touchdowns in the last minute to pull out the victory. It was a dramatic and telling contest. It also entered the public lore, not because of the great action on the field, but rather due to a decision at the television network. As the game stretched beyond the three-hour barrier, NBC switched from the game to *Heidi*, the Sunday family movie. Thousands of irate fans flooded NBC with seething calls. So many came in at one time, the network's switchboard crashed. While it was a momentary PR disaster, it provided tangible if cranky proof of how engrossing professional football was and just how passionate and numerous its fans were. The Jets lost the "Heidi Bowl," as it came to be known, squandering a heroic effort by Namath. The Raiders abused him, and on one particularly vicious hit they knocked his helmet off and fractured his jaw. But the man who would slip into pantyhose on national television for money proved that he was also one of the toughest men in football. He shrugged off the terrific pain and remained in the game to throw for 370 yards and three touchdowns against his tormentors.

From the first day of his career Namath was one of the most famous professional football players in America. Now he was also one of the most respected, even in the hallowed quarters of the game. Paul Brown, his long exile from football over, had resurfaced as both the coach and the owner of the AFL's new Cincinnati Bengals franchise. He had coached Otto Graham, brought in Frank Ryan, and lived to regret having lost his shot at Unitas. He knew that masterful quarterbacking was the key in professional football, regardless of the league.

"Because of their passer, the Jets have at least an equal chance against any team in football," the shaman of coaches said. Brown drew a short line from Namath to a possible Jets victory in the Super Bowl, still weeks away. New York could potentially beat "Baltimore, Dallas or anybody in the National [Football League]," he said. In fact, Brown saw a key difference between the Jets and all the other teams hoping to win the world championship: "They don't have Joe Namath."

On a cold and blustery day at Shea Stadium the Jets played the Raiders again, this time for the AFL Championship. In a showcase of great quarterbacks, Namath squared off against "the Mad Bomber," Oakland's dangerous Darryl Lamonica. Both teams tempted fate and threw into the squalls. Lamonica, already a Super Bowl veteran and the AFL's reigning MVP, lit up the skies. He threw for more than 400 yards and a touchdown, with most of that production going to his favorite target, Fred Biletnikoff.

Johnny Sample drew the short straw of defending the future Hall of Famer and chose to make the job an exercise in cheap shots.

All day long Sample assaulted Biletnikoff with late hits, forearming the receiver in the back of the head again and again even when the ball was nowhere in sight. In the end Fred had the last word. He torched the Jets' defensive captain for 190 yards and burned him for a touchdown when the cornerback missed an easy tackle. For Sample it was an embarrassing performance on many levels.

The Jets one-upped Lamonica's brilliant performance with a balanced attack. Snell and Boozer rushed for a combined 122 yards against the Raiders, and Namath threw for three touchdowns. The Jets were able to overcome Lamonica's sensational day, Johnny Sample's ineptitude, and a late and nearly devastating interception by Namath to pull out a thrilling 27–23 victory.

In the afterglow of such a victory, fans all over the country focused on Namath. But Ewbank, the consummate professional, knew that it took more than one man to win big football games. "There are about 50 strong hearts out here," he said. "That's where the key was."

When Ewbank looked at his Jets he saw all heart, but when the sporting press and public turned their eyes to the Colts they saw a mauler. Many referred to Baltimore as the greatest team ever assembled. The numbers would back up that assessment. Statistically, they were the equals of the 1962 Packers. Both teams went 13-1 in the regular season. With three Hall of Famers in their backfield, the Packers scored more points, 415 to the Colts' 402, but Baltimore's defense was even more formidable than the Packers' had been and gave up 4 fewer points. Although the two teams were only six years apart, professional football and the NFL in particular seemed to be light-years ahead of where it was even a short time earlier. The players seemed bigger and faster and the game more competitive than it ever had been. The 1965 draft alone was tangible proof that the caliber of athlete was improving by great strides. The Bears chose two players for the ages in consecutive picks when they snatched Dick Butkus and Gale Sayers with the third and fourth overall picks. One would develop into the most dynamic and disruptive defensive player in the history of the game and the other the most fluid, graceful, and, yes, beautiful runner. The first round of the draft was as notable for the fine players who did not make the Hall of Fame as for the ones who did. The depth of talent included Craig Morton, who eventually quarterbacked two different teams to Super Bowls; Donny Anderson, soon to be Paul Hornung's successor in Green Bay; Jack Snow, a receiver with great speed and hands to match; and Tom Nowatzke, a crunching fullback. The Colts took "Mad Dog" Mike Curtis, a fullback from Duke whom Shula developed into one of the game's fiercest linebackers. As the draft progressed beyond the first round, more Hall of Famers and superstars would come off the board. The fans saw all of this to the advantage of the NFL, but in fact the AFL was keeping pace or more likely gaining ground on its older rival. While Butkus and Sayers both went to Chicago, they came at a rare moment of decline for the famous franchise. Neither one would ever play in a single postseason game. George Halas was still in charge then, but he was fading fast. Papa Bear was born in the nineteenth century and began his own playing career in 1920 when he was an opponent of Jim Thorpe. By 1965 the world was entering the Space Age, and Halas was seventy years old and in steep decline. "By then Halas's assistants were doing most of the coaching," Shula remembered.

The stars who went to the AFL from that draft went to franchises that were rapidly on the rise. Namath, of course, landed with the Jets to play for Ewbank, a coach who was still at the top of his game and who had his greatest moments of glory still ahead of him. In the draft's second round the Oakland Raiders selected Fred Biletnikoff, a receiver from Florida State. Two years later the Oakland organization would go to Super Bowl II, and they would still be going to Super Bowls in the 1970s and '80s. In fact, the AFL had great coaches, progressive ideas, and dynamic young passers. Like baseball's National League in the 1950s, the AFL was making great strides against its more conservative and racist rival by embracing the great wealth of suppressed talent in the black communities. The new league was drafting and signing African American players with greater frequency, urgency, and enthusiasm than the NFL ever had

That the public and press still saw the older league as by and large superior to the start-up was largely a consequence of branding and public relations, two skills that were as ascendant in the 1960s as football was. Both leagues were essentially choosing from the same pool of players, but fans still believed that the jersey or helmet decal made one player superior to another. That was the branding.

The PR was provided in a couple of ways. After the first Super Bowl Vince Lombardi told the assembled press that "Kansas City is a good football team, but their team doesn't compare with the top National Football League teams." If Saint Vince said it, it was taken as the gospel. The same kind of a message was also delivered by *Sports Illustrated*, then the nation's premier sports-information venue. In the days before ESPN and the Internet, *Sports Illustrated* provided insight and shaped opinions. The leading pro football writer at *SI* was a man named Tex Maule. Maule had worked with future NFL commissioner Pete Rozelle in the 1950s when both were with the Rams organization. Maule left the league to cover pro football for *SI*, and he had many of the makings of a successful reporter. He was enterprising and intelligent, with a prose style that was in the tradition of the old-fashioned hard-boiled writer. It was spare and masculine writing that stressed facts over frivolous style. That's not to say that he was dull. Tex's stories often raised intriguing questions and answered them with open access to the players and coaches and exhaustive interviewing from multiple sources. His typewriter transported readers into the locker rooms and the homes of the players as he unlocked the secrets of the game for his readers. Tex lacked only one key ingredient of a great reporter, but it was a big one. He wasn't objective. He clearly had a bias for the National Football League that was based on something other than the empirical evidence. He showed this partisanship in both aggressive and passive ways. He might choose to ignore the newer league and its stars in pieces about the best players in the game, or he could be overtly insulting. After the AFL and NFL Championship Games, he wrote, "The pro football championship of the world was rather definitely decided on a mushy field in Cleveland on Dec. 29 when the Baltimore Colts crushed the Browns 34–0 for the NFL title." In a faux display of balanced reporting he allowed that the Colts would have to "ratify" their claim to the title in the Super Bowl, but then he ticked off a list of reasons they would easily do it.

Every time Maule praised the Jets he followed it up by damning them, too. He called Namath "phenomenal," but then discounted the compliment by predicting that the Colts' "bristling pass rush" wouldn't give him enough time to throw. He said New York had three "very good receivers" but then condescendingly called them "the key to the Jets' minimal chances."

The crooked noses in Las Vegas also bought into the hype. Jimmy "the Greek" Snyder, an infamous Las Vegas handicapper, put the Colts on a pedestal and made them seventeen-point favorites. It was a gigantic margin, hardly befitting a climactic game between two battle-proven champions. It was just another slap in the face to the Jets and their league.

It wasn't fair, maybe, but it all added up to delicious theater.

At some point, however, the game is wrestled away from the commentators and writers and prognosticators, and it is put back into the hands of the coaches and the players themselves. Usually, this happens long before the opening kickoff, as everybody experiences anew the pressure and glare of the biggest stage.

Namath took to it as though he were congenitally disposed to having two hundred million pairs of eyes watching his every move. His ability to thrive under the pressure was summed up by a press photo of him lounging around a Miami pool, his hairy chest exposed while he wore nothing but swim trunks, sunglasses, and a wide white smile.

Colts quarterback Earl Morrall was having a far different experience. Soon after the NFL Championship Game, he lived through "one of the most hectic periods" he had ever endured. The lease on the tiny Towson apartment he and Jane had shoehorned his family into was set to expire just three days after the NFL Championship Game. So immediately upon flying home from Cleveland, exhausted and aching, he had to pack his family's belongings in a U-Haul. He also had to deal with the fact that three of his four kids were suffering from a virus. The couple planned to drive back to Michigan with their possessions in tow, but Jane was worn down and couldn't bear the thought of sitting in the backseat with three vomity kids and two dachshunds for a nine-hour drive. So Morrall drove her and the children to the airport, put them on a plane, and then lit out for Michigan by himself. But that wasn't the end of the ordeal. Jane's flight landed with a swift jolt, and the Morralls' one-year-old son was jerked forward by the impact He cut his little chin so badly, blood spurted everywhere. Jane had to quickly borrow a car from a friend and rush her son to the family pediatrician's home.

When the exhausted quarterback arrived after his long drive, he had to check on his ill children, his hurt child, and his over-wrought wife; he had to unload his family's belongings; and then he had to head right back and rejoin his team. After that it was off to Miami. It was an incredible set of responsibilities and an ambitious travel schedule for any man, let alone one about to go to work in front of tens of millions of people. Earl, a loving father and committed husband, never complained.

While Morrall was mostly out of sight, Joe Namath made him-self conspicuous and entertained the press by stoking controversy. For instance, when a reporter asked him what he thought of Earl Morrall's game, Namath gave a withering response. "Lamonica is a better passer than Morrall," he said, referring to the "Mad Bomber" from Oakland, whom he'd just vanquished.

And then he really got insulting.

"You put Babe Parilli with Baltimore and Baltimore might have been better. Babe throws better than Morrall," Namath said, rank-ing his own backup quarterback above the reigning NFL MVP. And he didn't stop there. Namath bragged that the AFL quarter-backs were generally better than those in the NFL, and he ticked off a few names to prove it: "John Hadle, Lamonica, myself, and Bob Griese."

He was, in a sense, both right and impudent. The AFL cer-tainly did have fine quarterback talent. Namath might have also mentioned future Hall of Famers George Blanda and Len Daw-son. But there was no question that the attack on Morrall was also mean-spirited. Namath had heaped humiliation on a man with an exemplary character who outlasted a great deal of profes-sional misfortune to enjoy his brief moment in the sun. What's more, Namath's remarks were highly unusual in an era when the players were restrained about insulting each other, at least publicly; ballers were competitive, crude, and analytical in private, but they rarely deprecated each other's skills in the press. The players, then, looked upon each other with a respect born out of a mutual understanding for how hard it was to succeed in their violent league.

But Namath wasn't a part of their league, and he didn't care about their traditions.

"When I got asked the question about what I thought of Earl's skill set," Namath remembered, "the National Football League was still frowned upon [by AFL players]. The [NFL] still looked down on us. There was still some dislike there. And not knowing one another, I defended our league and our players."

Shula showed reporters a quick flash of his famous temper and addressed Joe's attack on his quarterback. "I don't know how Namath can rap Morrall," the Colts' coach said. "He can say whatever he wants to say, but I don't see how he can rap a guy who led the league in passing."

Morrall felt deeply affronted by the insult. Although it wasn't in his nature to take shots at other players, he offered a rejoinder. He didn't question Namath's efficacy or downgrade the AFL players or teams in general. He attacked Joe's character.

"I wouldn't want any of my kids to grow up and be another Joe Namath," Earl said.

Morrall's words had very little sting in a society where the values were changing rapidly and beyond his comprehension. Namath, of course, was neither shamed by Earl nor cowed by the Colts. On the week of the game he ran into Lou Michaels, Baltimore's defensive end and placekicker, in a cocktail lounge, of all places. Michaels and Namath were strangely connected. They were both western Pennsylvanians. Michaels knew Namath's brother; they played football together at the University of Kentucky. And Namath knew Michaels's brother Walt, the Jets' well-regarded defensive coach.

With a scotch in his hands Namath ambled over to Michaels and said, "We're going to beat the hell out of you. And I'm going to do it."

Michaels was known as "a tough son of a bitch." As a defensive end at Kentucky he was said to have injured eight players in one spring. Michaels injured so many offensive tackles and guards, running backs, and fullbacks—all his teammates—the coaches decided to hold him out of spring practice for the health of their players and the success of their program. One year, when the Wildcats had an offensive tackle they no longer wanted, they told Michaels to "beat the shit out of him" every day in practice until he quit. This was the man that Namath was blithely baiting in a barroom. Of course, Broadway Joe had no intention of fighting Michaels. Before the two could square off Namath turned on the charm, paid everyone's check, and even gave Michaels a ride back to his hotel room.

Miraculously, no one had gotten punched. But Michaels didn't care for Namath's abrasive style. The end-of-evening pleasantries didn't mollify him. The two would meet again just a few nights later at a Miami awards dinner, where Joe was honored as the "Professional Football Player of the Year." When Namath stepped to the podium to speak, a voice from the back of the room shouted, "Hey, Namath, we're gonna kick your ass."

"Who is that," Namath asked squinting into the crowd, "Lou Michaels?"

And then, again, Joe's lips got a little loose, and he uttered the words that would immortalize him and transform professional football.

"I got news for you, buddy," Joe boldly said. "*We're* gonna win the game. I guarantee it."

No one in the room saw anything extraordinary in the exchange, and only one media member on the scene, Luther Evans of the *Miami Herald*, even bothered to report it. But that was all it took. With interest in the game so intense, Namath's swagger and braggadocio were international news.

It was, in the conventional wisdom of football, a terribly stupid thing to say—but only for about three days.

While much of the country obsessed about the personal histrionics between Namath and the Colts, one of the most extraordinary stories of the matchup went underreported. It had been six years since Carroll Rosenbloom fired Weeb Ewbank. It was just enough time for Weeb to have assembled virtually the entire New York roster, but not so much time that the core of excellent coaches and players he left behind in Baltimore had eroded. Don Shula himself had been scouted, acquired, and coached by Ewbank.

One man assembling much or most of both Super Bowl participants was an unprecedented situation. It's likely that no coach in history ever had a better understanding of his Super Bowl opponent than Ewbank enjoyed that day.

Was it a major strategic advantage?

Almost fifty years later Joe Namath said that it was not. "His knowledge and our knowledge of those Colts were very good because we did a lot of studying," Joe said. "You have new faces on teams every year. You don't go back and say, 'Well, three years ago they were doing this, or this was that two years ago.' You study that team you're playing and the personnel that's on that team *now*. We were studying that year's edition of the Baltimore Colts, not what they did yesteryear."

But Namath did allow that understanding a team's historical tendencies could provide valuable information. "Sure, there are some things about coaches studying the history of other coaches and how they approach a game, or approach a team, that does a certain thing," he said.

In fact, the Colts rarely lost in the years after Ewbank relinquished them to Shula. Despite the presence of Unitas, the Colts' backbone had always been their intimidating upper-echelon defense. There were, however, two offensive teams that had notable success against Baltimore's defenders. One, of course, was Lombardi's Packers; by 1968 Green Bay had beaten the Colts seven out of ten times in the Shula-Lombardi era. The other team was Cleveland. In 1964 they engineered the biggest upset in championship-game history against the Colts, and in 1968 the Browns were the only team to beat Baltimore. The Browns and Packers had a few things in common. Number one, they had wily and experienced coaches who knew how to find even the best team's weaknesses. More important, both the Packers and the Browns ran the ball extremely well.

Lombardi consistently took advantage of Baltimore's defense over the years. The Packers knew how to tighten the Colts with the threat of the run and then snap them with precise passing. They did it with the most well-schooled offensive line in the game blocking for Hall of Fame runners like Jim Taylor and Paul Hornung.

Blanton Collier's Browns also had the right formula for taking down Baltimore. They did it in the '64 championship game with Jim Brown grinding the yards and opening the passing lanes for Frank Ryan and Gary Collins. And the Browns bested the Colts again in 1968 when Leroy Kelly rushed for 130 yards. That allowed Bill Nelson to throw three short, fluttering touchdown passes.

Passing success against Baltimore came from grinding yards on the ground. That was the only thing that could move the disciplined Colts defenders ever so slightly out of position. As Chuck Noll knew and preached, players who were cheating a step or two in the wrong direction were vulnerable to being burned by a smart quarterback like Bart Starr or Frank Ryan or even mediocre quarterbacks like Zeke Bratkowski or Bill Nelsen. And, of course, running the ball had one other major benefit: it burned the clock and kept the ball out of Unitas's dangerous hands, lessening his opportunities.

If Johnny U couldn't touch the ball, he couldn't kill you.

The hard part of the equation was actually running against the Colts' stout defense. In 1968 it was better than any Baltimore unit Lombardi had ever faced.

"That version of the Baltimore Colts was touted as the best defensive unit that ever played," Namath said. "All you had to do was look at the films and watch them and see how good they were."

Namath appreciated the Colts' defense, but he wasn't intimidated by it. "It wasn't the kind of defense that we didn't think we could take advantage of," he said.

From the very first play of the game it was clear that the Jets followed the same template as Green Bay and the Browns. After breaking the huddle the Jets lined up conventionally. But in a flash the two guards stood up and shifted two slots to the right. They created an unbalanced line, a show of force, right in front of Baltimore's left side, where young, aggressive defenders Bubba Smith and Mike Curtis roamed a ferocious patrol. Instead of running behind this advantage, Namath handed the ball to Matt Snell, who went charging in the opposite direction. He smashed into the line's weak side, away from the shift, and knifed his way for

3 yards. His massive body was brought to the ground by defensive end Ordell Braase and outside linebacker Don Shinnick. It was a simple short-yardage play, yet a highly significant and telling moment. Namath wasted no time going right back to Snell. He again attacked Baltimore's right side. This time Snell bolted past Shinnick and Braase for 9 yards. He was brought down only by the Colts' safety Rick Volk. Volk was fast and tough and a very fine football player, but at 195 pounds he was on the losing end of a physical mismatch with the massive Snell, who weighed 220. The two met in a violent helmet-to-helmet collision that put Volk to sleep. The Colts' safety was taken from the field, unconscious.

If those two plays didn't set the tone for the game, per se, they did telegraph how the Jets would approach the superb Baltimore defense. They had the choice of attacking Bubba Smith and Mike Curtis on the right or Ordell Braase and Don Shinnick on the left. Smith and Curtis represented the coming of modern football players, men who were bigger and faster than ever before. Braase and Shinnick were wily veterans, both drafted by Weeb. They went all the way back to the Colts' glory seasons of 1958 and '59. Braase had an excellent career but was overshadowed by Gino Marchetti. Shinnick was a rare and valuable commodity, a linebacker with thirty-seven career interceptions, the most in league history for the position. Both had solid careers behind them. But by kickoff of Super Bowl III, Shinnick was thirty-three and Braase almost thirty-seven.

"We never ran to their strength," Namath said.

Bubba Smith "was one guy we wanted to stay away from as much as possible," Namath confessed, "because of how good he was and because of the size mismatch."

Namath was alluding to the fact that Bubba was not facing the Jets' usual starting tackle Sam Walton. Walton, at six feet five and 270 pounds, was a massive player for that era. But he was a rookie, and not a very adept one at that. So Ewbank made contingency plans and replaced Walton at tackle with Jets guard Dave Herman, even though he was smaller.

"Ewbank, first of all, didn't think [Walton] could handle a guy from the Raiders named Ike Lassiter," Namath said, referring to Oakland's defensive end from the AFL Championship Game the week before. "And he sure didn't want to trust the rookie tackle to handle Bubba Smith. That's how Dave Herman moved out to tackle."

Meanwhile, the Jets' best run blocker was their right tackle Winston Hill. Winston was lined up right across from Braase. If the Jets looked at the Colts and saw the greatest defense of all time, at least they also saw a path.

The Colts' first possession of the game also told the story of their day. The first time Morrall touched the ball he threw a screen to his favorite target, John Mackey. The great tight end rumbled downfield, showing off his balance and power as he swatted away the Jets, who looked puny in his presence. The play went for 19 easy yards. Then Earl went to the ground and pitched to Tom Matte running a classic sweep. In an instant, on two plays designed for short yardage, the Colts had gone just shy of 30 yards. After that Jerry Hill and Tom Matte took turns rushing the ball. And then Morrall went to the air. He missed Jimmy Orr. In a third-and-13 jam, Earl calmly faded back and flipped the ball to his reserve tight end Tom Mitchell for 15 yards and another first down. The Colts were on the Jets' 19 with a fresh set of downs and incredible momentum.

But then Baltimore abandoned the running game for the remainder of the drive. Morrall barely missed on two straight passes, one to Richardson and one to Mitchell, both at about the Jets' 5-yard line. The Jets' line encouraged Earl's inaccuracies, by pressuring him and forcing him to rush his attempts. Earl faded back once more, hoping to salvage the drive, but the Jets blitzed. They nearly sacked him 7 yards deep, but Earl was strong and fast and made it back to the line of scrimmage before finally submitting.

Shula sent in Joe Namath's buddy Lou Michaels to attempt a field goal from the 26. Michaels was a left-footed straight-ahead kicker in the classic style. Booting from the left hash mark, he stepped into the ball at a severe angle. It twirled through the air but never came close to the uprights. It sailed wide right. Very wide right.

The Colts' adventure in Jets territory was a lot like Lou Michaels's barroom encounter with Namath. Baltimore menaced the Jets but failed to deliver a punch. After dominating the line of scrimmage and holding the ball for eleven plays, the Colts walked away, meekly, without a single point.

Now, with the ball back in hand, Namath decided to uncork. He faded back for three straight unambitious passes. He made a first down, but his attempts were relatively conservative. Then he faded way back for his fourth pass in a row and unleashed a long, arcing precise pass to Don Maynard. The ball traveled 50 yards through the Miami sky. It was so beautifully thrown, with a rotation so tight, it resembled nothing so much as a comet, zooming through heaven with a tail of fire. Maynard, who had beaten the Colts' safety Jerry Logan by several steps, somehow could not catch the perfectly thrown ball. If the sight of Namath, the flamethrower, napalming their defense did not strike fear on the Colts' bench, it must have elicited gasps in the row houses back in Baltimore.

In the end, it was only an incomplete pass. But it was also a calling card.

Near the conclusion of the first quarter came the game's first major break. Namath hit George Sauer with a short pass at New York's own 13. Sauer had no sooner caught the ball than the great veteran defensive back Leonard Lyles came rushing in. Lyles applied a textbook tackle, utilizing the crown of his helmet to unglue the ball from Sauer's sure hands. When the cargo spilled to the ground, Ron Porter, an alert Colts linebacker, pounced on it. With the turnover Baltimore's potent offense was only 13 yards from the game's first touchdown.

Morrall softened up the defense with Hill, who dove for a yard. And then he pitched it to Matte, who galloped all the way to the Jets' 6. Morrall decided it was time to strike. He sent reliable Tom Mitchell into the end zone on a short curl-in. It was a perfect call. Mitchell was between defenders, but open, and Morrall didn't hesitate; he fired directly at him. The ball was slightly tipped by a Jets linebacker, changing its trajectory from Mitchell's sure hands to his shoulder, where it clipped his protective armor. The ball ricocheted high into the air before descending like an easy pop-up to the Jets' Randy Beverly, who cradled it in the corner of the end zone. Instead of the touchdown the Colts deserved, it was a turnover.

While the stunned crowd and TV cameras focused on that game-changing play, far from the action Johnny Sample sneaked up behind Tom Matte and clubbed him in the back of the head with his forearm. Matte, furious, wheeled around with the intention of thumping Sample. Instead, Matte's face mask found the referee and rearranged the official's grillwork. Matte knocked out four of the man's teeth, and Sample skated away without so much as a flag.

The interception itself was a freak play that seemed to defy the laws of physics. Blame for it could not be rationally applied to any player or coach. Earl had made a sound play call. Tom Mitchell executed a perfect pattern. And Morrall's throw literally hit him. Nevertheless, Baltimore's opportunity had been squandered, irretrievably lost.

So the ball went from Morrall's hands back to Joe Namath's. For New York, something was about to happen, and at the most opportune time and unlikely place. Years of Weeb's planning, scouting, drafting, and teaching were all about to coalesce in a single drive. His protégé Namath, a man he had personally schooled and tutored in the art of reading defenses, was in command. Joe called his plays in the huddle and at the line of scrimmage and engineered a masterful drive of 80 yards and twelve plays. In a series that lasted four and a half minutes Namath continued to assert Snell where Braase, Shinnick, and Lyles struggled to contain him. When Joe read blitz from Baltimore's aggressive and speedy left, he called for a screen pass that rendered the speed, aggressiveness, and sheer greatness of Bubba Smith and Mike Curtis useless. Meanwhile, the Jets moved even deeper into Baltimore territory. With a fresh first down and the Colts chastened by the Jets' churning ground game and screen passes, Namath peered downfield and found Sauer twice in a row for a combined 25 yards. Both passes were also aimed at the Colts' vulnerable right side. Defensive back Leonard Lyles was accumulating downfield tackles on runs and completed passes, both a sign of doom.

Joe went back to the ground for a play, and then, with the blitzers once again charging into his face, he flipped another perfectly sold screen to Snell. The Colts emerged from the pile to find their backs against the wall. The Jets were first and goal to go with the ball on the Colts' 9. When another quick run by Snell picked up 5 yards, the Jets were just 4 yards from the game's first touchdown. Shula sent in Lou Michaels for Braase and substituted for Shinnick as well. It didn't matter. Namath handed the ball right back to Snell. The substitute defenders were no more effective containing him than the starters had been. Snell ran right past them and then trampled Lyles on his way into the end zone.

The drive was a tour de force, a triumph of Matt Snell's speed and brutal power, George Sauer's precise route running, and, of course, Broadway Joe's well-prepared and disciplined mind. Namath used all of his assets to overpower, deceive, and sucker the Colts. He had a battering ram fullback, but aimed him at the Colts' soft spots. He had a cannon, but fired it at open targets. If there were Colts who could do him harm, he merely avoided them. He slowed everyone down with traps and screens.

Brilliant as that drive was, it could lead to only seven points. It was a slim margin, and it was only the second quarter. Plenty of time was left for Baltimore, yet the Colts had so much expected of them, they were already, in a sense, in the loser's column. The hype that had been so excessively in their favor was exposed as a lie. They knew it, and so did millions of others. Anyone could see it. The Colts' battalion had stumbled into a jungle where the old rules didn't apply. The Colts faced men who were better trained and had greater incentives to victory than they had been led to believe. Baltimore was caught in the ravine, the enemy was in the hills all around them, and the artillery was raining down on them.

There was no quit or panic in the dutiful Morrall or, for that matter, in the emergent Matte. In a drive that featured Earl connecting with Tom on a 30-yard pass, the Colts went all the way to the Jets' 28 before the drive once again stalled and Michaels, again, missed his attempt at a field goal.

Next time the Colts had the ball Matte did his best to leave nothing to chance. He took a simple pitch for an abbreviated sweep, broke a tackle, and then sprinted his wide body for 58 yards. He took the Colts from their own 26 all the way down to the Jets' 16 all by himself. He was barely touched along the path. After Matte was tackled and lying prone on the ground, Johnny Sample came in late and kneed him in the chest and stomach. The two, again, exchanged harsh words.

The momentum provided by Matte's broad shoulders and fast legs wouldn't last long. Two plays later Morrall was back in the air. He locked onto Willie Richardson in the end zone, but there were four Jets in the vicinity. Morrall inexplicably fired into that phalanx anyway. None other than Johnny Sample picked him off. The ex-Colt covered the big and swift Richardson superbly well. Sample fell to the ground on the 2-yard line. Then he popped up and shoved the ball into Richardson's face mask.

"This is what you're looking for," Sample said to Richardson, grinding in the humiliation. With that Johnny ran off the field, exulting in his clutch play and his mean mouth.

The Jets could do nothing with the possession, however, and soon punted it back to Baltimore. The Colts had good field position—they were on the Jets' 42—and they had plenty of time to strike. There were forty-three seconds left on the clock. But the Jets were playing deep, and they were determined to deny the Colts the end zone. Hoping to pick up significant yardage underneath, Morrall dumped an outlet pass to Jerry Hill. The fullback could gain only a single yard, however, and Morrall called time-out.

With twenty-five seconds left before the half the quarterback attended a grim conference with Shula and McCafferty on the sidelines. Trying to avoid the ignominy of being shut out by the supposedly weak Jets at halftime, the Colts decided they would make it to the end zone with a deception that would beat the Jets' deep zone. Out of the sideline conference came the call for the "Flea-Flicker," a play the Colts had used earlier in the year in a surprisingly close game with Atlanta. It called for Morrall to hand to Matte, who would sweep to the right and then stop and pass the ball back to Morrall. Earl would then throw a bomb to Jimmy Orr, who ran a fake post pattern to encourage the defensive backs to flow in the direction of the "run." But then Jimmy would quickly cut back to the outside and zoom for the flag, where, if all went right, he would be all alone. That's the way it worked against the Falcons, anyway, and Jimmy walked into the end zone.

The Jets' defense ran things slightly differently than Atlanta had. They double-covered Jimmy. Cornerback Randy Beverly had the "short responsibility," while safety Bill Baird had the "deepest-widest" responsibility. But the brilliance of the play call was rooted in Matte's explosive success. At this point in the game Tom was the leading ground gainer and a threat to go all the way on every carry. Like everyone else on the defense, Baird was cheating toward Matte instead of following his assignment. So when Tom looked like he was taking off on another sweep to the right, Orr was abandoned on the left and totally in the clear. No sooner was the ball snapped than "I was 37 yards wide open," Jimmy remembered. By the time Matte passed the ball back to Morrall, Jimmy was on the goal line without a single white shirt in sight. Earl peered in Orr's general direction, and Jimmy frantically waved his hands, as if signaling a helicopter for a rescue. But Morrall never found him. Instead, Earl turned his attention to the crowded center of the field and fired an intermediate pass to Jerry Hill, a secondary choice. Jim Hudson easily stepped in front of Hill and picked off the pass.

Orr was at a loss to know what went wrong. He theorized that Matte's pass back to Earl may have been a little low, affecting the quarterback's timing and concentration. Morrall and Matte both later posited the idea that Jimmy was standing in front of the blue-and-white-clad Colts marching band in the end zone and that the smallish receiver in a blue-and-white jersey blended right in with them.

"The Colts' band was not even in Miami," John Ziemann, a percussion musician and the band's PR director, remembered. "We were back in Baltimore watching the game on TV like everybody else. Later on I saw a band in blue and white behind Orr on NFL Films footage of the game, but it wasn't us."

The first half was over, and it wasn't pretty. The Colts had been beaten in virtually every phase of the game. On special teams Michaels had missed two field goal attempts. On defense Namath's play calling befuddled the Colts. Matt Snell's bullish rushing had already produced 71 yards and a touchdown. And worst of all, on offense Earl, the MVP, looked lost. It was only halftime, but he had already thrown three interceptions.

The Colts' locker room wasn't chaotic, exactly, but it wasn't displaying the signs of a winner, either. Shula's players were pushing back on him. Middle linebacker Dennis Gaubatz lobbied to have outside linebacker Don Shinnick removed from the game.

Gaubatz argued that Shinnick simply could not set the edge and stop the rush.

But the big question, of course, was whether to bring in Unitas.

Johnny U loomed over the game like a great unsolvable mystery. So far the only time he spent on the field was at the coin toss, where he was trotted out as a Colts captain, as though the sight of his crew cut and number 19 alone would terrify the Jets. In a way it did. Namath admitted that when he saw Johnny U, "That's when things got real."

When events turned sour for the Colts late in the first half, the cameras found Unitas warming his arm on the sidelines. The NBC announcers noted his every movement. Of course, he was a hot topic in the Colts' locker room at halftime, too, where the coaches debated whether they should bench Morrall and insert him. The Don rejected the idea.

"Earl didn't have the ball that much because we turned it over so much," Shula told his assistant Dick Bielsky. "He deserves another chance in the second half."

So the Colts took the field for the third quarter with Shinnick at outside linebacker and Morrall at quarterback. Unitas remained on the bench.

Shula's battlefield decisions could be seen in two opposing points of view. In one the coach is calm and in control. He is choosing not to overcompensate in a tight game. Less charitably, Shula could be seen as a man arrogantly clinging to things that were clearly not working.

Neither view was exactly right. In fact, Shula's situation and choices were excruciating. With three interceptions in the first half, it appeared as though Morrall's Cinderella story had, indeed, hit its midnight. Yet how could a coach replace the MVP at halftime of a seven-point game? Anyway, would a badly injured Unitas have been an improvement?

Unitas believed he could play and be effective. In the days leading up to the game Johnny U had come to Shula and demanded to start.

"As we approached Super Bowl time," Shula told writer Mike Towle, "John felt that he was now ready to go and that he deserved the chance to start because of his contributions to the Colts in previous years and previous championship games. He was disappointed when I told him that I was staying with Morrall. There was no reason to relegate Morrall to a reserve roll."

Right or wrong, Shula made his decisions, and when the Colts received the kickoff to start the second half Earl trotted out with his teammates to take another shot at the Jets. But the poor guy never had a chance. On the first play from scrimmage Earl gave it to the most dependable man on the team and handed it to Matte. The big halfback bulled his way for another solid gain of 8 yards but then fumbled the ball away.

Given another opportunity, Namath didn't waste it. He put immediate pressure on the Colts. He moved the ball and exhausted the clock with a four-minute drive. And he put points on the board, as the Jets kicked a field goal to take a two-score lead. Namath gave the Colts a great demonstration of how he was going to make them pay for their mistakes. It was early in the second half and the lead was still narrow, but the pressure was really starting to mount.

Still, Shula stuck with Morrall. And again the quarterback could do nothing. The Colts went three and out. Getting the ball back, Joe hogged it, holding it for ten long plays and almost four more minutes. Everything was going New York's way until the next-to-last play of the drive. Namath briefly exited the game with a sore hand and wrist, but the Jets kicked another field goal.

Finally, Shula turned to Unitas. The Colts were down thirteen to nothing, and the third quarter was just about exhausted. When Johnny U entered the arena the fans stood on their feet and gave him a lavish ovation. But it was quickly clear that he wasn't the old Unitas. After a short pass to Matte, number 19 attempted a midrange lob to Jimmy Orr, but it didn't look good. Curt Gowdy, the NBC announcer, said the throw "wobbled out there."

The intended receiver agreed.

"[Unitas's] arm wasn't good," Jimmy Orr remembered. "He had no arm at all, hardly."

That's the way Namath saw it, too. "Johnny's arm was not 100 percent," he said. "Johnny did not have the speed on the ball that he normally had."

Namath feared Unitas, injury or not. On the sideline he watched

Johnny U take the field, and his first impulse was to look up at the clock and beseech the Almighty to bend time.

"There was six minutes and some change left, and I do remember speaking to my spiritual leader, and I said, 'Please, God, let that clock run,'" Namath remembered.

Namath was a realist. He knew the Jets had an almost insurmountable lead. But every football fan in America viewed Unitas as a miracle worker. Week after week they saw him pull out victories that were implausible, if not impossible.

Namath was no different from the fans in the stands. "Having seen Johnny over the years, we knew that it wasn't in the bag," Namath said. "We were on edge. Johnny U coming into the game added a lot of concern."

Just as the sight of Unitas worried Namath, it inspired the Colts. "There was an uplift when he came in," right guard Dan Sullivan remembered. "We thought, 'Now that we have John, we're going to be okay.'"

Unitas understood the calming effect he had on others. He walked into the huddle and told his team, "We can still win this thing."

Everybody's expectations notwithstanding, Unitas's first drive looked a lot like Morrall's craftsmanship. The Colts went three and out.

Namath returned to the field good as new and enjoyed one more big moment. He targeted Sauer three straight times. On the first pass George dropped what should have been an easy reception. On the second Namath hit him with a quick slant that went for 9 yards. That one almost ended in tragedy for the Jets when Lenny Lyles held Sauer and Colts safety Jerry Logan came running in and smashed the receiver in the breadbasket. The ball was jarred loose, and Logan recovered it and began to run. But the referees frantically blew their whistles and said the play was dead before the fumble. The Jets retained possession.

Namath stubbornly went back to George, who put a burst of speed on Lyles. Sauer was in the clear, deep downfield, and Namath delivered a 39-yard pass of such perfection, he may as well have handed Sauer the ball. That put the Jets on the Colts' 10. The Colts' defense stiffened, and Joe refused to gamble further. And as the fourth quarter began, the Jets gladly settled for another field goal.

The score was now 16–0, New York. The Colts hadn't gotten a single first down in the third quarter or crossed the 50 even once. The situation was getting dicey for Baltimore. The Colts now had less than a quarter left, and they needed three scores.

Everyone knew that Unitas was the only hope for victory. The problem was his game was really built upon two factors: Number one, he used play calls over the course of a game to "set up" defensive players so that they would make a mistake at a crucial moment. Number two, Unitas also prospered by the threat of the big play, the bomb that he could launch at any moment with perfect accuracy. Defenses were forced to dread the possibility, though they never exactly knew the moment when he might heave it.

Because of the situation on the ground, however, those factors were limited. It was so late in the game, setting up the defenders for three scores was highly unlikely. And the big play didn't seem too plausible either, thanks to Unitas's aching arm. In contrast to Namath's guided missiles, Unitas's passes looked like overinflated dirigibles with drunk pilots. His throws were full of helium, soft, light, and off-target.

Even so, Unitas moved the ball well. Mackey caught a short toss for 5 yards. Matte dashed into the line for 7. When Unitas got more comfortable he became more ambitious and attempted to hit Willie Richardson on an out pattern, but the ball fluttered hopelessly away. So he let Matte and Hill take turns toting it, and together they gained 31 yards. Courtesy of those two fine runners, Unitas had the ball on the Jets' 25 with a first and 10. After another blown pass to Richardson, Johnny U took matters back into his own hands. He decided it was time to go for the end zone. He looked for his reliable old battery mate Jimmy Orr near the goal line and then released what could only be described as a nauseous goose. The ball barely seemed airworthy as it slowly hovered in the ether. Randy Beverly easily stepped in front of Jimmy and plucked the pass out of the air like it was ripe and hanging on a vine. If that wasn't humiliating enough, Johnny Sample ran up to Johnny U and expelled one of his toxic messages.

"Not today, John. It's not your day," Sample said.

"Where's my watch?" Johnny U responded, reminding Sample that he'd been a locker-room thief back in Baltimore.

Skirmishes and fights were starting to break out all over the field as the Colts' frustration mounted. Curiously, Curt Gowdy, NBC's play-by-play announcer, noted the bellicose Sample's role in the fracases and referred to the African American as *"the boy who stirred the pot."*

In 1968 that was an uncontroversial use of language, as it never would be again.

Namath, the height of cool, continued to grind the clock with conservative calls. He utilized big Matt Snell and the superb line and never risked a thing. He didn't throw a single pass in the fourth quarter.

Unitas had no such luxuries. When he got the ball he went to the air three straight times and missed three straight times. On fourth and 10 with just under six minutes remaining, he faded back again and hit Orr with a 17-yard shot for the first down. But that was only the opening salvo in a 15-play drive that sucked about three minutes of life out of the dying game.

When the long, exhausting drive finally resulted in a Colts touchdown, a Jerry Hill dash across the goal line, everyone enthused about that old Unitas magic. It also put a scandalous spotlight on Shula's decision to leave Johnny U on the bench so long. But Joe Namath, who idolized and feared Unitas, was a realist about what really happened on the field.

"Your defense might be playing a little different ball with a 16–0 lead and it's six minutes left in the game," Joe said. "Our defense wasn't giving up any big gamers. No one got behind anybody for long plays at that time."

In other words, the Jets were content to let Unitas move in small bursts so long as the clock continued to tick. That was a somewhat risky strategy, and things got a little tense for the Jets. After the Colts scored their touchdown they attempted an onside kick. The kick was recovered by Colts safety Rick Volk at the New York 44 with more than three minutes left. Volk had only lately returned to action after being knocked out cold by Matt Snell in the opening minutes of the game. Volk had recovered his senses and almost the kick, but in doing so was knocked out again and suffered his second concussion of the afternoon, a highly dangerous development. Volk looked morgue-worthy, as it took four of his massive teammates to drag his inert body from the field.

When play resumed Unitas quickly fired off three straight completions for 20 yards and briefly created the illusion that he had a hot hand, but his last-ditch drive was useless and ended moments later, after three straight incompletions. The only good throw of the bunch was spectacularly batted away by Johnny Sample. With the last misconnection, a clueless fourth-down pass that landed nowhere near Jimmy Orr, everyone in the stadium could hear the piper beckoning the Colts.

A few moments later the game was over. Jubilant Joe Namath, in the camera's eye as always, exited the field shaking his right index finger as he went. It was a sign of number one but also a "shame on you" for everyone who had doubted his legitimacy and his league. Matt Snell had played as complete a game as anyone in championship history. He rushed for 121 yards, hauled in four receptions for 40 yards, and even made a thumping tackle on special teams. Yet regardless of statistics, everyone knew the most valuable player just had to be Namath. His refusal to be intimidated all week had unnerved the Colts and electrified the Jets.

The Jets seemed like the height of glamour and modernity, but their victory was almost identical to stodgy Cleveland's championship win against the Colts in '64. Like Cleveland, the Jets ran effectively and passed sparingly. In fact, the Jets' and Browns' championship-game statistics against Baltimore were amazingly similar. Cleveland's quarterback, Frank Ryan, threw for 206 yards against the Colts; Namath threw for 208 yards. Jim Brown rushed for 114 yards against Baltimore in '64; Matt Snell went for 131 yards in the Super Bowl.

New York's game plan was especially compelling because it was such a complete departure from who the Jets really were. Namath threw the ball twenty fewer times against Baltimore than he did the Raiders just two weeks before. Snell ran it eleven more times against the Colts than he did Oakland. The Jets avoided their own strengths and instead focused on Baltimore's weaknesses, wisely, as it turned out.

Of course, the Jets could not have really planned for the five turnovers they got from the Colts. That was simply a gift. Few football teams could recover from that many turnovers, especially with championship-game pressure mounting against them. The Colts, with all of their gaudy statistics and press clippings, were no exception.

The man who received the least attention but deserved the most credit for the Jets' stunning victory was Weeb Ewbank. In defeating his former Baltimore employers, he settled the score with them. He was also utterly vindicated in New York, where he started the season on the chopping block. He had now conquered two leagues to win three world championships. He never lost a championship game, something even Lombardi couldn't say. He won the two most important games in football history, the '58 championship game and, now, Super Bowl III. He built both franchises from the ground up, including finding and developing two Hall of Fame quarterbacks. He coached both players so that they were self-sufficient and brilliant play callers. What was even more impressive was the fact that Ewbank's achievements came by and large at the expense of the most successful coaches in the history of the game. To win his titles Ewbank had to defeat coaching staffs that included Vince Lombardi, Tom Landry, Don Shula, Chuck Noll, Don McCafferty, Jim Lee Howell, Bill Arnsparger, and Allie Sherman. This collection of talent won a combined fifteen world championships as head coaches. But they all lost to Weeb.

So why did the Colts really lose?

Joe Namath still believes they did themselves in.

"The Colts in Super Bowl III, they had kind of a catch-22 situation," he said. "Why would they change anything for us? They lost only one game that year, and they turned around and beat that team in the championship game thirty-four to nothing. Why would they change anything for the New York Jets? They were totally overconfident. Their team was overconfident. The Colts weren't ready. The players, I've got to believe, were so overconfident, they weren't ready to play that day."

"That's absolutely true," Jimmy Orr said.

Namath said that the Colts' conceit harmed their chances in

practical terms by making them predictable on the field. With the kind of success Baltimore had, "you keep doing what got you there," he said. "They didn't change anything for us."

Some of the Colts' defenders lavished praise on Namath and accepted the blame. "We let down our teammates and the entire National Football League," Billy Ray Smith said after the game. "My pride is bent."

Though the Colts were too experienced and professional to descend into public sniping, they had their theories about what happened.

"Weeb Ewbank outcoached Shula," Tom Matte said. "I don't think there was any question about it. [Ewbank] knew where our weaknesses were, and the Jets attacked them."

Dan Sullivan agreed. "Weeb Ewbank never got the credit he deserved for beating us in Super Bowl III. He [had been] our coach. He knew most of the players on the team. He knew [our] tendencies. He knew what was good and what was bad. I would say Ewbank outcoached Shula; he probably did."

Shula might've been blamed for a lot of things, but the one decision that stuck to him like a bad smell for many decades was the one to leave Unitas on the bench to start the second half.

"Shula made a mistake," Matte said. "Earl Morrall played the worst fucking game in the world. He was a space cadet. He was nervous as shit. He wasn't himself."

Morrall wasn't much better in the locker room after the game. The man who had waited so long for professional success agonized about his poor performance and relived his disastrous decisions and missed opportunities for reporters.

Johnny U didn't show any emotion at all. "I've been in football a long time," he told reporters. "You always hate to lose. But a football player can't feel sorry for himself."

Bill Curry sat nearby and listened as the reporters pressed Unitas for a more genuine response to the day's unthinkable events. They wanted to know how painful it was to lose to the Jets.

"I don't feel any pain," Johnny U said. "I've been through too many of these games. It's not a big deal. We lost a game. It's a game!"

"Does anything upset you?" one disbelieving writer asked.

"Yeah," Johnny U said. "It'd upset me if somebody'd steal my beer. Then I'd cry."

If only Morrall could be so carefree. In a sense no one personified the topsy-turvy year like he did. Earl went from the depths of being unwanted to the pinnacle of the MVP, only to plummet again, humiliatingly, in the Super Bowl. Despite his inherent dignity, he wore the stain of ignominy hard. After the game he dutifully spoke to reporters. But then he went home, and he never breathed a single word to his wife, to his children, or to any other living soul for an entire week.

# SIXTEEN

## Denouement

On the bus ride back from the Orange Bowl Rick Volk, the defensive back who was knocked out cold twice in Super Bowl III, began to vomit into a cardboard box. Volk's wife, alarmed, alerted the team doctor. The good doctor's diagnosis: "We all feel sick to our stomach after that game," he said. Back in his hotel room Volk's condition worsened, and he went into seizures. Don Shula, who had put Volk's life at risk by reinserting him into the game after the first head trauma, came racing into the room and prevented the convulsing man from swallowing his own tongue. Rick was taken to the hospital, where he sat in a tub and vomited the night away under the supervision of both a doctor and his coach. So on the night of the day when his heavily favored team lost the Super Bowl to a supposedly inferior team in a lesser league, Don Shula kept at least one of his players from choking.

Meanwhile, Jimmy Orr, the sprightly receiver, was back at the hotel, lingering, hoping to avoid Carroll Rosenbloom's stillborn "victory party" for as long as possible.

"I said, 'Listen, let's not be the first ones there,'" Jimmy said. "I didn't want to catch his wrath. Turns out I'm the first [player] there. And I waited about an hour [before going]. Rosenbloom's there, [Senator] Teddy Kennedy's there, and a few other [celebrities]."

Jimmy's worst nightmares were realized. The boss was extremely unhappy and looking for answers. "Rosenbloom takes me out back and asks me, 'What the hell's going on?'" Orr said. "I softballed as best I could, but he didn't like getting beat. He thought we should have won. 'Did we come down here too early? What have we done wrong?' Hell, at that point I was still in shock. I was trying to get out of there. I was the only guy there! If I'd known that, I would have been later."

As time wore on the owner's frustration anger and embarrassment at the Jets' loss came out in passive-aggressive ways. For instance, instead of giving his Colts a ring, the traditional gift from an owner for a team that won the NFL Championship, Rosenbloom gave them each a defective timepiece.

"He had given us these watches after Super Bowl III, and [they] promptly fell apart," Bill Curry said. "I thought that was interesting."

Unitas's feelings after the terrible loss were more complicated. While he typically put on a controlled public face that echoed team messaging, he was seething beneath the surface. John Steadman, a longtime Baltimore sports columnist and editor, asked the quarterback in private the one question that was on everyone's mind.

"Why didn't you get in the game earlier?"

Unitas answered candidly: "I would have if Shula's big ego hadn't gotten in the way."

According to Steadman, Johnny U believed Shula wanted to "win with Morrall to show he didn't need Unitas." Of course, if anyone in the organization should have been paranoid, it was Shula himself. His relationship with Unitas had been bad for years, and now his ties to the owner were also crumbling. Carroll Rosenbloom was furious with his coach for losing the Super Bowl.

Like a man who regretted his bad second marriage, C.R. pined for his first spouse. He sought out Weeb Ewbank to come clean about the past.

"Carroll told Weeb the whole story of his firing," Charley Winner remembered. "[Carroll] said, 'Weeb, it was the biggest mistake I ever made.'"

"Carroll Rosenbloom said later that he realized it was a huge mistake" to fire Weeb Ewbank, Raymond Berry acknowledged.

C.R.'s nephew Rick Rosenbloom also knew about the struggles between his uncle and Shula. "It was common knowledge that [Rosenbloom's] relationship with Shula completely changed after they lost the Super Bowl," Rick Rosenbloom said. "That was the most shocking and humiliating loss in the NFL. It was a complete disappointment, okay, and a complete failure. It was also tremendously embarrassing."

Shula had a big ego, but he knew he was now under a nega-tive microscope. He could see that his relationship with Rosen-bloom was destroyed beyond repair. "Before Super Bowl III it was all laughs and respect," Shula remembered. "Afterwards it was something else."

Despite C.R.'s frustrations, there were no easy solutions. Fir-ing Shula would have made sense to no one. Whatever his fail-ures in the big games, Don Shula was widely hailed as the best coach this side of Vince Lombardi. His overall winning percent-age was higher than Lombardi's. In just six seasons leading the Colts, Shula had been named the Coach of the Year three times. He had lost only two games since 1966. He had already been to two championship games, and his team had just won the NFL title. Letting him go would be ludicrous. Yet with so many rela-tionships in Baltimore at the point of mutual embarrassment (the owner wasn't even speaking to the coach), keeping Shula didn't seem quite right either.

With nothing but bad choices, Rosenbloom held his nose and retained his coach. Meanwhile, Chuck Noll, a man who might have ably replaced Shula, resigned to take the head coach's job in Pittsburgh.

Though Shula remained, his status and prestige within the organization were waning. "What I heard was that after we lost to the Jets, Don went in looking for a raise," Dan Sullivan said. "And [Rosenbloom] says, 'A raise? I ought to cut your salary after you embarrassed me, losing to a coach that I fired.' To me that was the death knell for Don Shula."

Shula admitted it was true. "My relationship with Rosenbloom was never quite the same after that," he said. "He was very upset. You could just sense the tension."

Rosenbloom didn't even make a pretense about hiding his disdain for Shula from the players. At the start of the 1969 sea-son, when he made his annual address to the team, he picked at some painful scabs.

"Mr. Rosenbloom walked into the team meeting," Bill Curry remembered. "He had Shula standing right next to him. He said something like, 'Men, you know I already fired one world cham-pionship coach. I didn't come here to be humiliated like I was last January in Miami. I didn't come here to be second place.' He made it very clear, and Shula stood right there and took it."

It was all very humiliating for a proud man like Shula, but he knew how to deal with it. "I had to move on with my life," Shula remembered. "One thing I learned a long time ago was you can't change the score. When the game is over, you have to live with what that score says."

With so much negative baggage hanging over them, the Colts were under a cloud.

One positive omen was the return of Unitas. Presumably, he was healthy and ready to go, though even he acknowledged that Earl Morrall deserved to be the number-one man to start camp. Don Shula wholeheartedly agreed with him. By the time the season started, however, Unitas was back in the saddle and Morrall was back on the bench.

The Colts faced the Rams in the first game of the 1969 season. Unitas threw for almost 300 yards, but he also gave away three interceptions in a Colts defeat. After only one game Baltimore had already matched its loss total for all of 1968.

In week two the Colts traveled to Minnesota. Vikings quarterback Joe Kapp, a rough-and-tough Mexican American with a Canadian Football League pedigree, put on a clinic. He threw for almost 450 yards and seven touchdowns against the Colts. Baltimore's defense was powerless to stop him, though it employed every tactic in the toolbox—zones, man coverages, and blitzes. Nothing worked. The inartistic Kapp put up 52 points on the Colts' defense. In the entire 1968 season Baltimore had given up only 144 points.

Despite the total collapse of his defense, Shula saw something wrong with his quarterback. He benched a healthy Unitas in the second quarter and went with Morrall the rest of the way. Earl heaved up two interceptions of his own to add to the Vikings' rout of the Colts.

"It is the first defeat since I came here from Detroit that I'm ashamed of myself and the football team," Shula angrily admitted to reporters.

After that the Colts were never quite right. They ripped off three victories in a row against lesser teams, but then lost to winless

San Francisco. Young Steve Spurrier threw a touchdown against the Colts, while Unitas gave up a 57-yard interception for a touchdown to the 49ers.

Interestingly, the Colts then beat the Redskins and Packers in successive weeks. As Washington's new head coach, Vince Lombardi cast a long shadow over both franchises. In what would prove to be the last-ever head-to-head matchup in the hot rivalry between the great coach and Shula and Unitas, Baltimore destroyed the Redskins, 41–17. It was an odd game in that the Colts and Lombardi seemed to switch roles. Lombardi's Redskins took a page out of Unitas's book and attempted to win with the pass, while the Colts controlled the clock and the ball. Redskins quarterback Sonny Jurgensen put up more than 300 yards in the air, while Baltimore's Tom Matte ran for 117 yards and three touchdowns. It was the worst loss Lombardi had suffered in almost a decade.

That game brought the curtain down on one of the most intriguing, intense, and long-lasting rivalries in the history of the league. Only about ten months later Lombardi was dead at age fifty-seven, colon cancer defeating his indomitable will as no man could. His passing was a mournful sign that the '60s were truly over.

After the victories over Washington and Green Bay, things spun out of control for Baltimore. In the second game against San Francisco Unitas got off to a slow, ineffective start. He had completed only two of eight passes when Shula pulled him and inserted Morrall. The Colts lost anyway, and San Francisco's only two victories of the entire season so far were both against Baltimore. The Colts' record stood at 5-4, while their division rivals, the Rams, were still undefeated at 9-0. Even Shula admitted the Colts were out of the race for the postseason.

Though his team was eliminated, Shula made it clear he still expected to win on Sundays. His strategy for doing so was to put John Unitas on the bench. Morrall was listed as the Colts' starter for the upcoming Chicago game, marking the first time since his rookie season of 1956 that a healthy Unitas was not the Colts' starter. Johnny U didn't take it well.

In Baltimore he gave a terse "No comment" to the local press, making his displeasure evident without actually stepping out of line. But one small-town sports editor scooped everyone and created a minor stir when he scored an interview with the disgruntled quarterback. Dean Eagle, of the *Louisville Courier-Journal*, the newspaper in Unitas's old college town, quoted Johnny in a near rage.

"[Shula] hasn't told me why he benched me," Unitas said. "I didn't have a good first half last Sunday against the San Francisco 49ers but I don't think I was that bad. This is the last year of my playing contract. I might consider playing for another club. I thought I could play about three more years of pro football, but I won't play under these circumstances."

It appeared as though Unitas was threatening to demand a trade or retirement. But when asked about the remarks back in Baltimore, he denied everything. Speaking to a more familiar reporter from the *Sun*, he slammed the Louisville newspaperman and the press in general. "I never told the man I was going to retire or that I would play somewhere else. I don't know where you guys get these things. This is one of the reasons I am reluctant to talk to you [the press]."

Unitas admitted he didn't like sitting on the bench, but denied he harbored any special resentment. So what did he really say to Shula about being shelved?

"Okay, you're the boss," Unitas claimed he said. "I might not like it, but I'm not bitter about it."

Shula corroborated that Unitas took it well. Yet the tumult and the losses both hinted at big problems. The Bears game would only intensify the embarrassment that was brewing between the two men. Morrall, rusty from a lack of use, threw two interceptions that both led to Bears scores. With only about seven minutes remaining in the fourth quarter, and the Colts losing 14–7, Shula called on Unitas.

Johnny U baffled the Bears, who expected him to light up the skies. But when Unitas noticed that Chicago's tackles were cheating wide, probably to bring a more forceful pass rush from the outside on him, he crossed up Chicago and pounded the ball inside. Utilizing running backs Tom Matte and Terry Cole over and over, his only pass of note was a 21-yarder to Matte, a dagger that moved the Colts into scoring position. The tying touchdown came on a 16-yard trap play, right up the gut, where center Bill Curry took out Dick Butkus to enable the score.

After the game reporters stirred the pot. They wanted to know if Unitas felt any special motivation to succeed, given that Shula had benched him.

"All I did was my job," Unitas said.

Unlike Johnny U, Dick Butkus, the Bears' All-Pro linebacker, had no reason to be circumspect. He was effusive in praising Unitas. "He sure moved the ball when he got in there," Butkus said. "Just as he always does, John called the right plays. We didn't do it when we had to, but Unitas did."

Benching Johnny U, only to have him come off the bench and save the day, made Shula look indecisive, or worse.

As it turned out, the most notable absence from the game wasn't the superstar, Unitas, it was the Bears' backup halfback Brian Piccolo. Piccolo had recently lost energy on the field and asked to be removed from a game. He was also suffering from a mysterious cough. All these factors led him to the hospital where he was under observation.

Doctors eventually diagnosed the cause of Piccolo's distress. The halfback was suffering from testicular cancer that had spread to his lungs. Less than a year later, in June 1970, he died from the disease and its complications. He was only twenty-six, and he left behind a wife and three young daughters.

Piccolo was a fine college player at Wake Forest, where he led the nation in rushing and touchdowns his senior year, but he was considered too small for the professional game at six feet and 200 pounds, and he went undrafted. George Halas saw something in him and signed him to the Bears. But Piccolo, unlucky, came to Chicago the same year they selected Gayle Sayers. Piccolo managed to stick with the team and made the roster, but he mostly rode the bench and stayed in the shadow of the great superstar. Piccolo would get his chance to play when Sayers was felled by a serious knee injury, and he performed admirably.

Though he was, in truth, an inconsequential player on a bad team, Piccolo played an enormously important role in the unfolding epic of professional football. His impact on the game was long lasting anyway, as the circumstances of his life and death were later dramatized in a made-for-television movie that detailed his special friendship with Sayers.

One out of every two television sets in the United States tuned in for the film that vividly brought to life the game's virtues. Both Piccolo and Sayers were depicted as clean-cut and moral young men. Though they competed with each other for roster spots and playing time, they selflessly helped each other succeed. They became roommates, highly unusual for a black and a white player in the era. Piccolo was presented as a martyred, almost Christlike figure who pushed Sayers to overcome a catastrophic knee injury, even though Gayle's return would be a career setback for Piccolo.

Sayers and Piccolo were depicted as courageous and generous. These traits seemed endemic to their involvement in football. The positive aspects of the relationship were magnified by their racial differences. Broadcast just a few years after the nation's cities were aflame in race riots, *Brian's Song*, in its own melodramatic way, returned Americans back to Huckleberry Finn's raft, where black and white were set adrift together on the very same quest for freedom.

In Baltimore, it seemed, there was no harmony on the field. Despite his heroics in the Chicago game, Unitas seemed a shell of his former self, throwing only twelve touchdown passes on the year and a whopping twenty interceptions.

Sam Havrilak, a fine rookie who had emerged from Bucknell with superlative and diverse skills as a runner, passer, receiver, and even defender, saw Unitas and Shula grating on each other.

"There seemed to be a lot of friction between Shula and Unitas, more than normal," Havrilak said. "You would see them . . . kind of discussing things in a more animated way than you would normally see. I think that had an effect on the team."

Unitas wasn't the only one losing his tolerance for the head coach.

"I think everyone was kind of fed up with Shula," Havrilak said. "And for a couple of reasons. Number one, he liked to take credit for everything. Number two, he would jump on you for no apparent reason at all in front of everybody else. You don't do that. You don't belittle someone in front of everybody else. Take them in your office and do it in private. [The players] kind of got fed up with his ego."

According to Havrilak, the Colts also noticed lingering bad feelings between the owner and the coach. "This was never proven, but Rosenbloom was an inveterate gambler, and supposedly he lost millions of dollars on the Super Bowl. He didn't take too kindly to Shula because he thought Shula's coaching could have been better during the game."

The Colts finished 1969 with an 8-5-1 record, respectable in many cities but a disaster in Baltimore, where "dominance" was the expectation by both the owner and the fans. The Colts were one of the most stable organizations in the game, but it was clear that big changes were coming.

After the season Rosenbloom left for an overseas vacation. While he was away Shula was approached, through a Miami newspaperman, about a potential opening in the Dolphins' head-coaching position. Shula expressed his interest, and members of the Miami organization reached out to the Colts for permission to speak with him. With Rosenbloom away the owner's son Steve, a young Colts executive, supposedly granted that permission.

The Dolphins were primed for a man of Shula's skills. Much like Green Bay when Lombardi arrived, the Miami organization was overflowing with excellent but undeveloped talent. The Dolphins, who had not yet been winners on the field or at the box office, were eager to change their fortunes and believed that Shula could do the job, and owner Joe Robbie personally handled the negotiations with the coach. Robbie was known as a skinflint, but he pulled out all the stops for Shula. He offered the coach a dream position in which he would be far more powerful than just about any other head coach in the game. His titles would include general manager and minority owner. He got a raise from $60,000 per year to $75,000. The real money was in the ownership stake, which was said to be 3 percent of the team's worth, which at that time equaled $450,000. He didn't go to Miami for a raise or a better job. He went for life-changing money. Beyond the cash, the accord was also a show of extreme respect, a deal similar to the one bestowed upon Vince Lombardi in Washington. It was guaranteed to stoke the envy of every other coach in the league.

Needless to say, Shula jumped.

In an era when coaches and players were welded to their cities unless terminated, Shula stood apart. He exhibited the boldness to grab the reins of his own future, but still felt the need to answer charges of disloyalty or naked greed, so he explained his motivations for breaking his Colts contract and abandoning his city.

"Immediate and substantial interest in the Dolphins caused me to leave the Colts," Shula told the *New York Times*. And who could blame him? In truth, the Dolphins contract was a coup. It was a masterful career stroke, negotiating unprecedented rewards from a new team, even while he was teetering on the brink of being fired by his old team. It was a death-cheating comeback that could only be described as Unitas-like.

In a moment of perfect karmic justice, Rosenbloom, who had sent Weeb Ewbank on vacation seven years earlier to secretly interview and hire Shula, was enraged to learn that Shula had signed elsewhere while he was away on vacation. C.R. cried foul. With Shula still under contract to him, he wasn't about to give the coach away without some sort of compensation. The league, as always, saw things his way. Without reversing or nullifying the deal, Commissioner Rozelle ordered Miami to compensate the Colts with its number-one draft pick as restitution for the crime.

Meanwhile, the players who had played so hard and so well for Shula over the years lined up to bad-mouth him in the pages of *Sports Illustrated*.

Bubba Smith said, "Shula went crazy. He had this thing about Vince Lombardi. He wanted to be better than Lombardi. So he did a lot of screaming."

John Mackey agreed. "[Shula] became more and more of a dictator," the star tight end said.

Even Mike Curtis, who respected the chain of command and appreciated a strong sense of authority, said, "Maybe everybody hated Shula and maybe that's what he wanted. Maybe he felt it would translate into making a close team, pulling us together because we hated him. It was a bad situation."

Shula's oldest and most bitter antagonist, of course, was Unitas. Yet the quarterback was curiously more evenhanded than his teammates were in assessing the old boss. "Don made a lot of enemies among the players. He was a good coach, always a good coach. But the way he handled some players left a lot of bad taste around here," Johnny U said.

And then, for good measure, Unitas added a little fiction to his story: "I never let [Shula] bother me," he said.

The new sun-drenched Shula was cool behind his shades. Basking in the rewards and wealth of his new job on the beach, he didn't say a word in his own defense. He had no reason to respond.

It took the Colts a little while to move on. Rosenbloom and his new general manager, Don Klosterman, interviewed twenty-eight applicants for their open coaching job. Unitas eventually joined the owner and the GM in Hawaii, where they met to discuss their various options. But in the end they didn't reach far for their man, as they chose their own longtime offensive coordinator, Don McCafferty. "Mac" was a man whom Unitas knew well and liked very much. The players called McCafferty "the Easy Rider," due to his calm and demeanor, and Mac knew the Colts as well as any man, since he had been an offensive assistant under both Ewbank and Shula going all the way back to the '50s.

As head coach McCafferty ran essentially the same offense that the Colts had worked since 1954, the year Ewbank emerged from the Midwest with Paul Brown's playbook. It was an incredibly long run of consistency, and McCafferty made but two key changes. First, he restored Unitas's autonomy, allowing the quarterback to call his own plays without interference from the bench, and, second, he simplified the playbook and pared down the nomenclature that was so incredibly ponderous under Shula. In other words, the names of the plays and formations were greatly shortened, much to the relief of the huddle.

Other than that most things stayed the same. The *New York Times* reported that McCafferty would retain most of Shula's staff but that he would also need to hire as many as three new coaches. "At least one," the paper of record reported, "might be a Negro."

Even without Shula, the mystique of the Colts continued unabated. Unitas was no longer at his physical best, and he had to deal with the presence of the capable Morrall behind him. But he was still Johnny U, which is to say that he still had that incomparable football mind that could solve inscrutable problems in the split seconds before he was clubbed, slammed, or throttled by huge and menacing men.

In their first year without Shula, Unitas and the Colts lost only two games. One of those defeats was to the Dolphins, which Shula had improved from a three-win club the year before he got there to ten victories in 1970. But in the end Baltimore had the last laugh. In the first round of the playoffs, Unitas completed six passes, two of them for touchdowns, as the Colts beat Paul Brown and his Cincinnati Bengals assistant Bill Walsh, 17–0. In the first-ever AFC Championship Game, Unitas turned in yet another masterful performance in a historic contest. Johnny U defeated future Hall of Famer George Blanda in that one. Blanda entered the game after Oakland starter Darryl Lamonica was injured. Blanda had started his NFL career while Johnny U was still at St. Justin's High School in Pittsburgh. Unitas was spry by comparison. He also still had his uncanny accuracy; he completed a 63-yard touchdown pass to Ray Perkins to ice the game and send the Colts back to the Super Bowl. Meanwhile, Blanda and his teammates, so sure they were going to the Super Bowl, had already packed trunks for Miami. Instead, they went limping back to Northern California.

The Colts were slated to play the Dallas Cowboys in the big game. Dallas coach Tom Landry, a notorious micromanager, called all of the offensive plays from the sideline. Unitas was asked his take on that system, and he embraced the opportunity to take a direct shot at Shula.

"They wouldn't be getting the best out of me [if they called the plays]," Unitas said. "They could just use a mechanical man, a dummy."

Unitas followed that up with a blatant lie when he said, "I have never refused to run a play any coach has sent in. Don Shula used to send in several in a series, but I guess he didn't think I was getting the job done."

That point was mostly moot in the Super Bowl, where Unitas had only three completions against the Doomsday Defense before leaving the game for good in the second quarter after a brutal shot to his rib cage. One of his completions, however, was a 75-yard touchdown pass to John Mackey. It was the Colts' only touchdown in the air all day, and a crucial score, as Baltimore squeaked past the Cowboys, 16–13, in a mistake-laden game.

In his first year without Shula, Unitas accomplished something he couldn't do in seven years under the famously brilliant Shula: he won the Super Bowl.

If Shula felt envy or bitterness at seeing the team he'd built finally win it all without him, he took it out on his opponents. In 1971 Miami went 10-3-1 against the league, but one of those losses was to the Colts. Unitas began the year convalescing an off-season Achilles tendon tear, but his first start of the season was against Shula's Dolphins. Johnny U was in the saddle, but McCafferty warned him that if he was rusty or couldn't get the job done, he would be yanked in favor of Morrall. And that is what happened.

Unitas could put up only 78 yards against the Dolphins. He threw two interceptions. Morrall tried to rescue the Colts in the second half. He threw for more yards than Unitas did, but failed where Johnny U typically excelled, in the clutch. Down by only three, Earl threw an interception in the end zone with three minutes left in the game.

Enjoying the 17–14 victory, Shula told the press it was the "best win ever" for his ascending franchise. But the coach didn't have long to revel in the glory of it. The next match between the two teams was only three weeks later, and Unitas was back on his game. He outplayed young Bob Griese, the AFC's leading passer, by utilizing the Colts' running backs and pounding the Dolphins into submission. Unitas hogged the ball so effectively in the first half that Miami had run only six total plays with four minutes remaining in the first half.

Overall, Unitas was superb. He completed sixteen of nineteen passes, for 142 yards. The Colts skated past the Dolphins 14–3.

"They just kicked the heck out of us," Shula admitted after the game.

But there would be a third meeting between the two star-crossed franchises. In the AFC Championship Game, just a few weeks later, it was a far different story. Shula had a plan for Johnny U's wizardry. He adjusted his defense and shut down Baltimore's running game. The Dolphins limited the Colts to just 89 yards on the ground. On the game's climactic play, fourth and 2 from the Dolphins 9-yard line with only six minutes left before the half, McCafferty decided to go for it instead of kicking a field goal. Unitas handed off to powerful fullback Don Nottingham, but the great

Nick Buoniconti, the Dolphins' undersize but tenacious middle linebacker, met Nottingham in the hole and squelched the drive. Without an effective running game to aid him, Unitas threw three interceptions on the day.

The Dolphins and Colts were so similar, shared so many common connections, were so focused on one another, it was inevitable that a loss of composure would eventually emerge. "Mad Dog" Mike Curtis, a star linebacker drafted and developed by Shula, was penalized 15 yards when he slammed Bob Griese to the ground. Later in the game Curtis made another tackle, this time near the Miami sideline, and got an earful from his old coach.

"He called me a [bleeping] cheap-shot artist," Mad Dog said.

When it was all said and done the Colts were the crucible for the emerging Dolphins dynasty. Miami and Shula shut out Johnny and shut up Rosenbloom with a 21–0 victory to go to the Super Bowl. For Shula it was an incredibly satisfying victory, but it still did not exorcise his demons. The Dolphins lost the Super Bowl in embarrassing fashion to Dallas, 24–3. It was Shula's third loss in a row in a world championship game.

But in 1972 everything changed. It started in April when the Colts waived Earl Morrall. McCafferty felt so bad about releasing a player of such sentimental importance to the franchise, he flew all the way to Earl's home in Michigan to tell him in person. In his four seasons with Baltimore the so-called journeyman quarterback had a 22-3-1 record as a starter and appeared in two Super Bowls.

That was far from the most stunning news, however. In July, right near the beginning of training camp, Carroll Rosenbloom announced that he had traded the Colts franchise to Robert Irsay, an air-conditioning magnate from the Midwest, in exchange for the Los Angeles Rams. Irsay had only just acquired the Rams for $19 million, then the largest sum ever dished out for any professional sports franchise.

The transaction was vintage C.R. It was complex, brilliant, and, of course, calculated for Rosenbloom to come out on top. It allowed him to divest his holdings in Baltimore and acquire a far more valuable property, in a much larger market, without paying a penny in capital gains taxes. Irsay, the dupe in the scheme, came across as a rube, fleeced by a more sophisticated man.

Rosenbloom enjoyed many benefits from the deal, but perhaps the biggest one was shedding himself of Baltimore without looking like a latter-day Walter O'Malley, the demonized owner of the Dodgers who bolted Brooklyn for Los Angeles a generation earlier. Though Baltimore had offered Rosenbloom's immigrant family safe harbor and succor, though it played a key role in building his considerable fortunes, he was eager to leave it behind. For many years he had spent most of his time in New York anyway, returning home on weekends for Colts games.

Rosenbloom found his provincial hometown confining to his expansive ambitions. He had been a critic of Memorial Stadium for many years and regarded it as a charming dump, which in fact it was. The Thirty-Third Street structure was built in haste in just six months in 1922 and had significant structural issues. He offered to build a new stadium and finance it with $15–$20 million of his own money. But local politicians propounded Memorial Stadium to him as though it were a sacred site. They rebuffed him at every turn and offered public funds only to refurbish the old structure on Thirty-Third Street.

Rosenbloom complained loudly. No stranger to exerting leverage, he threatened to move the Colts, first to Columbia, Maryland, a planned community about halfway between Baltimore and Washington, and then to Tampa, Florida. He conducted several training camps in Tampa just to drive the point home. C.R. quickly got fed up with these cat-and-mouse games.

Rosenbloom wasn't only disenchanted with Baltimore's politicians; his relationship with the fans was also deteriorating. Though Baltimoreans of the '50s and '60s were celebrated in books and movies for their intense love of the Colts, they drew the line with Rosenbloom in a way that fiercely irked him. C.R. expected the fans to pay full price for preseason-game tickets. Baltimoreans were adamant that it was an unfair practice. It became a hot point of contention between the team and town, and in 1971 the defending world champions averaged only about sixteen thousand fans per preseason game. Rosenbloom, justifiably proud of the product he had given Baltimore, took it as a slap in the face.

With C.R. in Los Angeles and Shula in Miami, it was clear that the Colts' changes were affecting the entire league. Shula employed the old Colts playbook in Miami, and the Dolphins were quickly recognized as the best-run franchise in football. In Los Angeles the Rams' front office operated with the same efficiency and excellence that had once characterized the Colts' operation. With Rosenbloom running the show, the Rams instantly became Super Bowl contenders. C.R. hired Weeb Ewbank's old assistant coach Chuck Knox, and LA posted a 12-2 record in only his second year of ownership. The Rams won six consecutive division titles in the 1970s, though they never won the Super Bowl.

In Baltimore a horror show set in. Unitas had his last big day as a pro in a September shoot-out with Joe Namath and the Jets. Unitas threw for almost 400 yards and two touchdowns, but he was outdueled by Namath, who had almost 500 yards in the air and six touchdown passes in the Jets' 44–34 victory. Just two weeks after that thrilling and masterful performance, the Colts' front office pressured coach McCafferty to bench Johnny U and start the young backup Marty Domres. McCafferty refused. The following week, before the Dallas game, owner Robert Irsay personally demanded McCafferty sit Unitas. Again the coach refused to comply.

So before the second Jets game McCafferty was summarily fired.

In his two full years as head coach Mac had the best winning percentage in football. He guided the Colts to the championship his first season (the only rookie coach to ever win the Super Bowl) and the AFC title game the next. Despite his many years of loyal and excellent service to the Baltimore franchise, he was, to put it delicately, out on his can.

Mac was replaced by his best friend, Colts defensive coordinator John Sandusky. Sandusky did what McCafferty refused to do and benched Unitas, even though Johnny U was leading the league with eighty-five pass completions at the time.

Unitas accepted the decision but let everyone know he wouldn't be available for mop-up duty. Speaking to Dave Anderson of the *New York Times*, he said, "I'm not a clock runner outer."

The game against the Jets at the end of the long and bizarre week was incidental to the farcical show going on in Baltimore, but it had its own twists and turns. Namath produced an important but unlikely score late in the game when one of his passes was deflected into the hands of a Jets receiver for an 83-yard touchdown.

After the game one of the Jets attempted to honor the legend on the other bench when he said that he was "glad Domres was in there, not Johnny Unitas."

"They better be glad I wasn't in there," Unitas said, laughing. "I might've gotten lucky like Joe did."

Despite the show of humor, it was apparent that Unitas was more and more out of step, not only with the team and its ownership but also with the new breed of players around him. The young men in the helmets weren't fighting for respect and a paycheck anymore, like he and Raymond Berry and Shula were back in the '50s. For the young generation it was strictly about *la dolce vita*, the sweet life. Johnny U asked one young Colts quarterback what the kid was hoping to get out of professional football.

"A Corvette and a German shepherd," the aspiring player said.

Of course, the impertinent remarks of a veritable child were just a symptom of Baltimore's problem. The Colts' new owner was the disease. Robert Irsay clearly did not know how to run a team. Worse than that, he revealed himself as a man with serious emotional issues. His apparent substance abuse was a point of derision among the players and, eventually, found its way into the news media. The owner's lack of sobriety was evident to all and resulted in impulsive firings, calling plays from the owner's box, and public tantrums. When he traded for the team Irsay cited his admiration for Unitas as the key reason. But now, with Johnny U clearly on his way out the door, Irsay's regime refused to honor a ten-year, $300,000 personal-services contract Unitas had signed under Rosenbloom. After an ugly and public spectacle, NFL commissioner Pete Rozelle summoned the Colts' lawyers and Unitas to New York and attempted to broker a settlement of the unseemly dispute.

Rozelle asked Unitas what he would take to walk away. "I'll take $200,000 and you'll never hear from me again," Johnny U said. The team offered him only $50,000, and he had no real choice but to accept it. The Colts eventually unloaded Unitas on San Diego, forcing the venerable old player to uproot himself and relocate across the country. It was a terrible way to treat a man who, it could be rightly said, did more than any other to advance the entire enterprise of professional football. In a similarly crude manner, the team soon parted ways with many of its other stars. Tom Matte, Bill Curry, Mike Curtis, Bubba Smith, and Dan Sullivan, among others, were all soon Colts casualties.

It was unnecessary and debilitating to the franchise. In 1972 the Colts won just five games. It was their first losing season since 1956, the year before Unitas was the full-time starting quarterback. The next year was even worse: Baltimore won only four games. Sandusky and his entire coaching staff were fired days before Christmas. One of Shula's assistants in Miami, Howard Schnellenberger, took the job next. It was, however, a short and unhappy marriage. Colts GM Joe Thomas fired Schnellenberger's assistants at will. Irsay ultimately had an altercation with Schnellenberger during a game. After shouting at his coach behind a closed door, but within the hearing distance of both the players and the press, Irsay fired him on the spot and replaced him with Thomas, a man who'd spent the past fifteen years in front offices. Before Robert Irsay came on the scene, the Colts had four coaches in their entire history. In roughly two years under Irsay's control, the Colts also had four head coaches.

But it was the departure of Unitas, of course, that caused the most stir. When he involuntarily left the Colts, it was treated as momentous news. The *Sun*'s fine editorial writer Theo Lippman Jr., usually preoccupied by politics, turned his pen to the tawdry spectacle and sad ending of the great quarterback in a signed editorial entitled "Sic Transit Unitas."

Before Johnny U, "[Baltimore] was not well known in the nation at large and was, in fact, the butt of jokes where it was known," Lippman wrote. "In the 1950s Baltimore was the Colts, and the Colts were Unitas."

Earl Morrall resurfaced in Miami. Shula claimed him on waivers for the Dolphins and gladly paid the $100 waiver fee for him. The ancient Morrall contrasted sharply with his youthful teammates, yet he was a perfect fit for the team. When Bob Griese, the Dolphins' brilliant young starting quarterback, suffered a serious knee injury in the season's fifth game against the Chargers, Morrall trotted in from the sidelines, finished the victory, and then started the rest of Miami's remaining nine games. The Dolphins won every single one of those, too. Morrall quarterbacked the team all the way to the AFC Championship Game against Chuck Noll's Pittsburgh Steelers. Morrall started the game, while a completely healthy Griese sat on the bench and watched. The Dolphins looked listless in the first half, leaving Shula with an agonizing decision. He pulled Morrall at halftime of the 7–7 game and reinserted Griese. The future Hall of Fame quarterback sparked his teammates to a close 21 17 victory. The quarterback drama and the presence of Shula and Morrall made it all reminiscent of Super Bowl III, only this time with a happy ending. The key was that Griese was brought in early enough to make a difference and, of course, Griese was healthy.

Two weeks later Shula kept Morrall on the bench and started Griese in the Super Bowl against the Redskins. The Dolphins won that historic game and capped off the only "perfect season" in NFL history. Morrall, a striking contrast to how Unitas once handled a similar situation, demonstrated perfect comportment. He put the team ahead of his own legitimate claims and never made a stir.

Joe Namath once ticked off the names of several quarterbacks he said were better than Morrall. But when it was all said and done, and all the careers were over, Earl was statistically equal or superior to Namath in many respects. Although Joe threw more career touchdown passes, Earl threw seventy-two less career interceptions and outdistanced Joe in yards per attempt. Earl was a bigger winner, too. Morrall was 33-4-1 as a starting quarterback for Baltimore and Miami *after* he was "washed up." He went to four Super Bowls and was on the winning team three times. In '68 and '72 Morrall was the key man on two of the most memorable and important teams the league has ever seen.

Joe Namath, for all his star power, never returned to the big game again after his scintillating performance in Super Bowl III.

As Johnny U waned in Baltimore, Shula ascended in Miami. His achievement of a perfect 17-0 season has never been matched. The singular accomplishment made Shula a media rock star, and the newspapers couldn't attach enough superlatives to his name. None of this was lost on Unitas, who couldn't believe all of the hype. Every time he heard the name of his old nemesis, he'd say, "Oh, you mean the geeeeniussss." He'd play out the key word for an impossibly long time to enhance the comedic effect.

While the Colts franchise collapsed, its executives, coaches, and players from the 1960s dominated the NFL for many years to come. In the 1970s Shula, McCafferty, or Noll was the head coach in eight of the ten Super Bowls. They won seven of them. Red Miller, a line coach under McCafferty and Sandusky, was the losing coach in Super Bowl XII when the Cowboys defeated his "Orange Crush" Broncos. Later on the New York Giants named George Young general manager. Young, once a Colts assistant hired by Shula, hired former Colts receiver Ray Perkins to be his head coach in New York. Perkins's staff included future head coaches Bill Parcells, Bill Belichick, and Romeo Crennel. When Perkins left to take the head-coaching position at the University of Alabama, Young promoted Parcells to his first head-coaching job, drafted Lawrence Taylor, and assembled a squad that won two Super Bowls. In 1985 Johnny U's favorite target and his best friend, Raymond Berry, coached the New England Patriots to a victory over Shula's Dolphins in the AFC Championship Game before losing to the Bears in the Super Bowl. Colts center Bill Curry became a head coach at his alma mater, Georgia Tech; later on he succeeded Perkins at Alabama and then took the top job in Kentucky. Curry finally ended his career back in Atlanta as the inaugural coach at Georgia State.

The Colts' talent diaspora was incredibly long lasting and influential. It brought success to corners of the league where it had never existed before, even as it drained and depleted Baltimore's terminal franchise.

In 1979 Carroll Rosenbloom drowned while swimming in the Atlantic Ocean near his home in Florida. C.R. was by all accounts an excellent swimmer, and he was known to prefer the surf to a pool for exercise and relaxation. The official story was that he was caught in the undertow on a day when the water was unusually choppy and rough. There was, of course, speculation that his drowning was not an accident. The life he led made the nefarious plausible. He gambled on football and associated with underworld figures. He abandoned Baltimore and the Colts to a lout. He threatened to move the Rams' franchise in search of a better stadium. He used women. He bullied adversaries. He was said to have stolen the Colts' Super Bowl trophy, requesting to borrow it for an event and then never returning it. He left behind a fortune and a complicated estate. His primary heir, his wife, Georgia, remarried only a little more than a year after his death. Her next husband, Dominic Frontierre, went to jail for selling the Rams' allotment of Super Bowl tickets and then pocketing the cash. Soon after Georgia assumed control of the team, she fired C.R.'s son Steven Rosenbloom, who had long been his father's right hand in the football business.

Had C.R.'s death been a crime, there certainly could have been a long line of suspects and motivations. Carroll died with a lot of money, but he couldn't take any of it with him where he was going.

Whatever wealth Unitas and Shula amassed out of football, the greater assets were the legacies they earned. The excellence with which they practiced the craft, the innovation that they brought to the field, their work ethic, and the red-hot competitiveness raised the game to an impossibly high level of play. What they created was so compelling, it quickly disappeared, giving way to something that was more processed and manufactured. The game soon went from grass to "synthetic turf." It went from crumbling old baseball stadiums to publicly financed football palaces. It went from being a longed-for treat every Sunday to a Monday- and Thursday-night TV show. It went from a championship game played in front of real fans in the snow and the rain and the mud and the blood to a Super Bowl, a neutral-field warm-weather extravaganza wrapped around a sometimes obscene halftime show. The football players and owners of the '60s created plebeian theater, a stage where the ending was never scripted. But so much interest, power, and, especially, money came spilling into that theater, it soon became a toy for oligarchs.

Professional football in the 1960s took a short, unsentimental journey from authentic to decadent. The players became rich even as the game broke their perfect bodies and its skull-cracking intensity robbed them of their souls. "Our helmets," Browns receiver Gary Collins lamented many years later, "were nothing more than tomato cans with chinstraps." Earl Morrall, who survived twenty years in the league, was returned to an almost childlike state in his old age. At the end of his life the magnificent athlete could barely walk, shuffling along with the aid of his loving wife. His thoughts and memories were much quicker than his legs, but only as they flew away from his mind.

"My recall button don't work too well," Earl would say over and over as a pat reply to any question about his life.

Carroll Rosenbloom's disturbing legacy is swept out of sight in Baltimore and in the rest of the NFL. He is the owner with the highest winning percentage in league history, but he is not in the Hall of Fame. His many brilliant business maneuvers on behalf of the league go unnoticed.

Unitas and Shula built legacies that were bigger and stronger than any of the wealth they generated. One went on to recognition among the elite coaches of the game; the other sits atop most lists of the greatest players ever. Unitas and Shula gave football a facade of grim importance. During their watch the NFL became a potent force in entertainment, fashion, and even serious political discourse. Shula's inability to win the big game in Baltimore, his hasty departure, and his huge success at his next destination all buried his name in the city that first brought him to national attention. There are no Baltimore memorials to his incredible legacy, no tangible signs of the extraordinarily driven young man who achieved so many great and unprecedented things.

Unitas is entirely different. Johnny U was a national hero before anyone even knew Shula's name. In Baltimore he is accorded more civic respect and name recognition than the heroes of Fort McHenry who saved America from foreign invasion. The football stadium at Towson University in North Baltimore bears his name. At the NFL stadium, downtown, there is a statue of Johnny U that greets football fans at the main entrance. A few years ago the Ravens, Baltimore's successor team, removed Unitas from his pedestal and pushed him aside to make room for a likeness of Ray Lewis, the Ravens' great linebacker. It stands side by side with Unitas. Lewis, a mixed bag of a man, was once the subject of a murder investigation. The contrasts between Unitas and Lewis and the way they are depicted are striking. Unitas is frozen in the throes of battle, his helmet snuggly on his head, the ball cocked behind his ear. His eyes peer downfield, searching for the open man. In Lewis's sculpture the linebacker does not wear his helmet. He is not in a ballplayer's stance. He isn't tackling anyone. He is instead memorialized in game introductions, doing a dance. His impossibly muscled body is contorted as he thrusts his hips and pelvis toward the sky. Lewis isn't playing; he's posturing.

The contrast is a reminder of ever-changing tastes and mores, but it also says a lot about where the game went, and went wrong, in the half century since Unitas walked away from it.

When Baltimore lost its team, the Irsay family stealing it away to Indianapolis one freezing and sleeting night in 1984, it was apparent just how unsparing and unsentimental the league was. The city clung to the belief that its passion for the Colts and its place in the history of the league were enough to sustain it. It was an incredibly naive, almost laughable notion. In the twenty-first century the league regularly chooses stadium deals over its fans. For years it has considered strategic relocations from stalwart cities like Oakland, Buffalo, and Minneapolis to glitzy international venues like Toronto, London, Las Vegas, and Mexico City.

Eventually, almost everyone and everything connected to the Colts' great legacy packed up and took off. Weeb retired to Ohio. Charley Winner and Earl Morrall both settled in Florida. Chuck Noll went to Pittsburgh. Raymond Berry, after coaching around the league, relocated to Tennessee. Jimmy Orr golfs every day in St. Simons, Georgia, the beautiful southern hamlet where Jim Brown was born into segregation.

Carroll Rosenbloom, an individualist to the end, flouted Jewish proscriptions and was cremated and then scattered to the winds like a thousand unanswered questions.

Only Johnny U regarded the compact between city and team as inviolable. "He never wanted to leave Baltimore," his daughter Jan said. And he never did. After his short, embarrassing stint in San Diego, he quickly returned to Maryland and lived out the remainder of his life. He died on September 11, 2002, the victim of a heart attack. Today the man so associated with the air mingles with the soil in the town he loved so deeply.

Baltimore has moved on in every conceivable way since Unitas's era. It's a different place than the segregationist "Charm City" where the old Colts played, but it's still on the cutting edge of American racial mistrust. The people root for a new team in a different stadium. There isn't a lot of recognition for the old Colts in the new venue.

In his decision to permanently settle in Baltimore, Unitas bequeathed the city an eternal connection with his indomitable spirit. Even Shula, sitting in his gilded manse in Miami, could peer through the gauze of time and clearly see just how much that meant.

"Unitas was the toughest guy mentally and physically I ever coached," Shula said. "Griese was a great field general, and Marino was the best pure passer I think who's ever played the game. But Unitas was just so tough. They'd knock him down, and he'd get up bloodied and battered and throw the next pass for a touchdown.

"He was that kind of a competitor," Coach Shula said. "He was that kind of a warrior."

# Afterword

inding Unitas and Shula's Colts was like going back to the Creation. These men played in the 1960s when the game came of age. At the start of their decade pro football was a highly risky business proposition and a distant second to baseball as America's favorite sport. By the close of the '60s pro football was big business and a national obsession.

To a large extent Unitas and Shula were at the center of this transition. Despite their inability to take the title, they were excessive in the cause of victory and together created an organization that was the very hardest one to beat.

When I traveled the country to find and converse with their colleagues and cronies, it wasn't only to unlock the mysteries of their tense, maybe hateful, relationship. It was also to understand the forces of their era and the professional football phenomenon that they certainly created and that continues to this day.

One thing I found out is that old football players all have two things in common. One is an unusually large and strong pair of hands. The other is that they all have wives who may have a few accumulated years but who still pack a glamorous wallop.

Just about every Colt I spoke to expressed an affection and loyalty for both Shula and Unitas. But their personal effects told a different story. Every single player or former coach I visited had a picture displayed somewhere in his home or office of himself with number 19. It was clear that even these men, each one an idol to countless others, felt a certain amount of veneration for Johnny U, and him alone.

It's not too often in any line of work that men revere one of their own contemporaries. But all of the Colts I spoke to felt that way about Unitas. He gave even them the aura or mystique of being connected to someone or something transcendent.

I went to New England, where I found the magnificent old guard Dan Sullivan. Sully, as his teammates called him, lives a happy life not far from Walden Pond. He spends his days with his wife, and the two of them care for their daughter, a very sweet young lady who happens to be mentally challenged.

After his playing days Dan was an executive with Mrs. Filbert's Margarine, a Baltimore-based business. He did well in that career, and today he enjoys a comfortable retirement. Belying the stereotype of the big, brutish lineman, Sully is an extremely thoughtful and articulate man. He speaks with a New England accent. Among his memorabilia are two photos of Unitas. One, a large print, shows Johnny U's last great moment as a Colt. The quarterback had just thrown his final touchdown pass for Baltimore, and he and Sullivan are shaking hands.

Sully also has a snapshot of Unitas on a tractor cutting his grass.

"He came here for a visit once and got bored, so he went out and cut my grass," Sullivan remembered. With a great deal of affection he also recalled the quarterback's rapport and kindness with his disabled daughter.

When I met Bill Curry in his downtown Atlanta office, he was getting ready for his last season at Georgia State. Curry was the Panthers' founding head coach. In his playing days Curry had been a magnificent and technically sound football player. He was also unusually connected to football history. He played for both Vince Lombardi *and* Don Shula. He played in the first-ever Super Bowl with the Packers and the most famous Super Bowl, the one against Joe Namath and the Jets. He protected Bart Starr and Johnny Unitas. He went head-to-head with guys like Ray Nitschke and Dick Butkus. He seemed too gentle, too refined, to tangle with those kinds of animals. But he did, and he usually came out on the winning side to boot. When he was a Packer he beat the Colts every single time he played them. And when he was a Colt he beat the Packers every time.

The best and happiest years of Curry's career were undoubtedly in Baltimore. He liked and admired Shula but had only a grudging respect for Lombardi. Nevertheless, when I saw him, he wore his Green Bay ring from Super Bowl I.

As a boy Curry decided he didn't even want to be a football player, but his father made him play and the game somehow became his life. He played and succeeded at the highest levels. He coached it. He talked about it on TV as an analyst. And he even wrote about football in two books. Curry was a mature man the day I saw him, but he still had a youthful and trim appearance and was still excited as ever by his own memories.

In many respects the most fascinating man I met with was coach Charley Winner. In an earlier age Winner could only be described as a "dear person." He was extraordinarily polite, likable, funny, and intelligent. As a coach and front-office man for so many decades, he was connected to just about everyone and everything from football's golden age. He worked for Paul Brown, Weeb Ewbank, and Don Shula. He was professionally connected to Otto Graham, Johnny Unitas, and Joe Namath. He personally coached Don Shula. He was also the mastermind behind some legendary defenses. In the '60s he had an easy job. All he had to do was shut down the Packers' sweep, contain Jim Brown, solve Bobby Layne and Y. A. Tittle, and outthink George Halas. If he could do all of that, he could survive.

He must have accomplished all that because when I met him, he was relaxed and happy and near the age of ninety. He was still possessed of a keen mind and a body so trim and athletic that he still played tennis every day in the broiling Florida sun.

Winner told me quite a bit about how the great Colts teams of the '50s were formed and what it was like the day Johnny U showed up on the scene. He told me all about the forces that sunk his father-in-law, Weeb Ewbank, and the transition to Shula's bellicose reign.

Tom Matte, the great Colts running back, offered me more candor than any man I met. He inveterately told the truth, no matter how painful, and did everything he could to get you to a deeper understanding of personalities and root causes. He was also extremely profane and funny.

Matte was so dedicated to film study as a player, his old projector and reels of game film were still sitting at the ready in his library.

Tom and I conversed out back on the patio of his rustic home.

He was under no illusions; nevertheless, he was somewhat distressed about his reputation as a player. He felt it was unfairly fading away with time, as evidenced by the fact that the *Baltimore Sun* had just written a series about the "175 greatest Baltimore-area athletes" and Matte was left off the list.

It was, in fact, a terrible injustice and a sign more about how the city had moved on from the old Colts than it was about Matte's ability. Tom was, in fact, a superb football player who was probably the Colts' best offensive weapon in the late '60s. His performance as the emergency quarterback who almost defeated Lombardi with barely any preparation time still stands as one of the gutsiest and most compelling performances in all of football history. There is simply nothing else to compare to it. His team failed in Super Bowl III, but had Matte been on the winning side, he could have easily been considered the MVP of the game.

The wide receivers I spoke to were an interesting contrast in styles and personalities. The first one was Raymond Berry, the great Hall of Famer and my own father's idol. Raymond agreed to speak to me only because Jan Unitas, Johnny U's daughter, implored him to do it. Our interview was on the phone, not in person, and my subject matter irritated him. He was a best friend with Unitas, and he admired and respected Shula. He felt that exploring their relationship was an inherently negative exercise, and he didn't want any part of it.

"Don't ask me questions about that," he said, "because I don't want to be on your tape recorder saying 'No comment' twenty times." With that rule in place we carried on and had a cordial and educational conversation. I learned a lot about Don Shula, the athlete and teammate, from Berry. And I learned a lot about what made the old Colts tick as a brilliant team.

I went all the way to Jimmy Orr's house in St. Simons, Georgia, to interview him. St. Simons is a beautiful part of the United States, and it seems to sit on a shelf that juts out into the Atlantic Ocean, where it is kissed by the salty waves. Jimmy played golf every single day in that beautiful setting. When he wasn't playing golf, he watched it on TV. Fun and friendliness and manly companionship come naturally to Orr, and he invited me to sleep over at his house. I accepted.

The Orrs and I went out for dinner and drinks at two different country clubs. Jimmy lived with his wife, a beautiful woman,
in their magnificent home. Mrs. Orr was sweet, and, like Jimmy,
she spoke in a thick southern vernacular.

Going out for drinks with Jimmy was cool. In the opulent set-
tings he frequented, it was like going out with the Great Gatsby.
Because he was a famous and old-school carouser, I enjoyed the
feeling of being out with Mickey Mantle or Joe Namath in their
prime. Jimmy hadn't played ball in forty or so years, but he still
had the swagger of a big timer.

When I visited Gary Collins, the Cleveland pass catcher who ate
up the Colts in the '64 championship game, it was as opposite to
the Orr experience as it could be. I met up with Gary in his ordinary middle-class home in suburban Harrisburg, Pennsylvania.
Jimmy golfed his days away, while Collins cut grass every day for
his son's landscaping business. If that seems undignified for a
former championship-game MVP, Collins doesn't care. He loves
to stay in shape, and he enjoys hard work. He still loves sports
and watches football, basketball, and baseball obsessively in the
rare moments he is relaxing in his plush easy chair.

Collins is an utterly unsentimental man and doesn't dwell on
his football accomplishments. He sees them as part of a distant
past. "Am I pissed off that nobody knows anyone from the Browns
but Jim Brown? No," he said.

As a former Cleveland Brown living on the outskirts of Steelers country, he takes some abuse but doesn't care. "My neighbor
who lives down the street, who is a Steelers fan, every time the
Steelers beat the Browns, which is all the time, he puts Steelers
shit all over my mailbox. I don't follow the Browns. I don't give a
shit about the Browns. It's something I did, it's gone, and I have
no loyalties. It was ten years' quick bullshit."

The most famous men I spoke to, of course, were Joe Namath
and Don Shula. Namath, as you can imagine, was fun to talk to.
He is witty and feisty. He's a modern man, but also a relic from
the '60s. He kept saying to me, "Jack, Jack, Jack, you have to
remember I'm a Gemini." That was his way of explaining a particular behavior or point of view. Throughout our conversation I
got on his nerves a few times, but it quickly passed. Incredibly,

he still held an old AFL grudge for the NFL. In recounting the stories of Super Bowl III, and especially explaining his criticisms of Earl Morrall, he pointed to the fact that the two leagues were hot rivals. I told him I knew that and that some of the Colts I spoke to still held a grudge for him. His answer: "Yeah, I still kind of hate all the guys who beat me, too."

Coach Shula was extremely kind to me. He immediately took my call and set up a face-to-face interview in his home. I was surprised when I saw him. He had aged, obviously, and had white hair and used a walker. His memory alternated from excellent to a little forgetful. He could remember with perfect clarity a catch his son made for the Colts in a preseason game thirty years earlier, but had a little trouble recalling Bubba Smith and whether drafting Smith had been a success or failure.

In his long career Shula matched wits with Vince Lombardi, Paul Brown, George Halas, Chuck Noll, Bill Walsh, George Allen, Tom Landry, Bill Parcells, and Bill Belichick. In all he went to seven NFL Championship or Super Bowl games. He developed three Hall of Fame quarterbacks—Unitas, Griese, and Marino. The list of historic games he coached in is almost unbelievable: the '64 championship game, the '65 playoff game against Lombardi in which Matte played quarterback, Super Bowl III, the "Sea of Hands" game, the "Snow Plow" game against New England, and on and on. His work with Earl Morrall ("All he did was win for me"), elevating a journeyman to a four–Super Bowl quarterback, is one of the great accomplishments in the history of the game by any coach.

My visit with Earl Morrall was the most poignant I made. He passed away not long after I interviewed him. His infirmities were evident, as the once magnificent athlete walked and spoke slowly. He could have been a poster child for the damage an NFL career does to the mind and the body. Robbed of many of his faculties, he was still abundant in character. It was obvious how much love he had for his wife and also what a good-natured and decent man he was. Imagine that. Earl Morrall was the toughest of men and he played the most violent of games, but as the memories of it had all faded away, the one thing he retained was love.

## ACKNOWLEDGMENTS

Writing a book is long, hard, and extremely difficult work. It requires deep concentration and a sense of well-being to succeed. It was only thanks to the encouragement and support from my family and friends that I was able to achieve my objective with this project.

The first person I should thank is my agent, Emily Williamson. Her faith and enthusiasm for my work and her advocacy meant a great deal to me, as did her judgment. She is a first-rate literary professional who became my friend and confidante as well as my agent. Her husband, Greg, is also owed my thanks, as he pulled my manuscript from a pile and passionately advocated for it to his wife.

Of course, the University of Nebraska Press and its team of editors and marketers are at the top of my list, too. I owe the biggest gratitude to Robert Taylor, the acquisitions editor who has shepherded my manuscript and handled it with so much sensitivity to my vision. My copyeditor, Annette Wenda, was pleasant and thorough and completely dedicated to the task of polish, and I can't thank her enough. Sara Springsteen and Anna Weir were also exceptional people who enhanced my experience.

My children, Max and Iliana, were the people I worked for and the people I hoped to please. They are both readers and writers. When my son was just a few days old, back in 2002, he sat on my lap and we watched the Ravens versus the Steelers in a postseason game together. It was one of the happiest memories of my life: watching football for the first time with my very own son. A few weeks after that I wrapped his little infant body in a blanket, and he braved the January air to go to a pub with me and watch the Super Bowl, which he did strapped into a rocking car seat sitting on the bar. No one carded him. My daughter has endured more football than she ever hoped to just to be near me. She is the most wonderful girl in the world, and I love her more than anything.

Two other special people who made this project possible are my sister, Juliet Gilden, and my friend Gerry Frank. Both were there to help me in a way that few friends are. They called to check on me and made sure I stayed afloat mentally, physically, and financially while I wrote. Some guys have no use for their friends' wives, but Gerry's wife, Margie, is a special kind of person. She was patient and kind to me also, especially in sharing her husband with me when I needed him.

The main source of literary advice for this project came from Michael Olesker, a man who could only be described as a Baltimore treasure. A very fine journalist and author, Olesker is to Baltimore what Jimmy Breslin was to New York or Mike Royko and Studs Terkel were to Chicago. His unique writing voice, an eloquent English with Yiddish inflections, has intrigued me since I was a child reader of the *Baltimore Sun*. His heart is always in the right place, and he has a genuine care and concern for the people of his hometown. His zeal for football and the old Colts and his brilliant storytelling ability are not the least of his many fine qualities.

My friends Larry Lichtenauer and Beth Blankman Keyser made the book possible in their own ways. Larry also wrote a book, an inventive novel about ice hockey and wish fulfillment aimed at ten- to fourteen-year-olds. Larry gave me a brotherly voice to talk to when I needed one. Beth, a professional librarian, first with the Enoch Pratt Free Library and then later with the state of Maryland, is my old school friend from Chestertown, where we both went to Washington College. She took a shine to my project early on and gave me invaluable assistance in so many ways, I can't list them all. Suffice to say that she has a feel for literature and the business of literature. Every writer should be lucky enough to know someone like Beth.

Barry Gogel is a lawyer and also a very fine writer. He read my contracts for me and gave me valuable business advice. He also happens to be my drinking buddy. He is always up to meet me at one of our favorite local watering holes, where we sit, eat, drink, and talk endlessly about baseball and football and our sons.

Amir Kahn is my auto mechanic and also my friend of nearly twenty years. Knowing I was writing a book, he did everything he could to keep my car going without putting me in the poorhouse. He also lent me his home in Miami, which served as my home base as I conducted my many Florida-based interviews. He's one of the nicest and most decent men I have ever known.

Dika Seltzer is an elegant woman and a psychotherapist in the Towson area. She met me for dinner several times a month to discuss my book and to assure me it would be completed someday. If I called her with any problem, she always answered the phone.

My old friend and high school football teammate Evan Davis talked to me endlessly about my ideas and about our mutual passion for professional football. Bob Morrow is also one of my oldest friends and was always there for me. He regularly called me to check in on the progress of this book and to help me through any and every problem. My good friend Dr. Joseph Layug, brother of my buddy Tommy Layug, explained the complex medical issues described in this book to me.

The very first person (besides Jan Unitas) to assist me in this project was Denise Purgold. She helped me arrange travel plans to Atlanta and was a good friend to me throughout the long process.

Jan Unitas, Johnny U and Dorothy's eldest child, is a very special friend of mine. She acted as a source for this book and provided me my first Colts interview when she asked Raymond Berry to speak to me. Jane Morrall and Mary Anne Shula were also very helpful in assisting me in getting to the heart of the matters I wanted to know and understand. Coach Shula was extremely generous with his time and attention and forthrightly answered some questions that must have been uncomfortable for him.

I wanted to say a special thanks to all of the football players and coaches of the Baltimore Colts: Charley Winner, Dick Bielski, Bobby Boyd, Bill Curry, Dan Sullivan, Tom Matte, Jimmy Orr, Earl Morrall, Jane Morrall, Dr. Sam Havrilak, Jim O'Brien, and Pert Mutscheller.

The great journalist and author Gay Talese made time for me to tell me everything I wanted to know about the '60s, the sexual revolution, men's fashion, sports, and his friend David Halberstam. John Unitas's friend Richard Sammis, the beloved car dealer known to everybody in Baltimore as "Mr. Nobody," told me all about the man he knew. John Ziemann, the leader of the marching band and also a Unitas confidant, is a walking encyclopedia of Baltimore football information. He shared it all with me, as he gave me the green light to call him any time of night or day. John is a real gentleman.

The Colts' enemies also provided me with their perspectives: Frank Ryan and Gary Collins from the Cleveland Browns and Joe Namath from the New York Jets.

The Enoch Pratt Free Library in Baltimore provided me invaluable one-of-a-kind information. Much of this manuscript was written in Elkton, Maryland, at the Cecil County Public Library, one of my favorite work spaces.

Waitresses and bartenders were my staunch allies in the project, as I worked quite often at the Bagel Works in Timonium, Maryland, owned by members of the Bielski family. Waitresses Lita Thepsuwan and Sharon Brown and their manager, Jenny Young, became an everyday familial presence in my life. At the La Cakerie Bakery on Allegheny Avenue in Towson, owner Jason Hisely and manager Ciera Stewart let me hang out and write all day long.

If I look good in the author photo, it is only due to the miraculous efforts of Steve Belkowitz, a Philadelphia-based photographer. Steve and I have been friends so long, I was an invited guest at his bar mitzvah. My favorite barber in the world, Judy Durank, also did what she could to keep a sinking ship afloat.

Finally, I want to thank the great journalists of the 1960s. John Steadman offered me the catalyst for this book when I was fifteen years old. No one knew the Colts better than he did. His writing and insight provided me valuable information. The Colts' beat writer for the *Sun* was Cameron Snyder. Snyder was a fun writer and good storyteller who had a talent for the offbeat anecdote. Bob Maisel, Bill Tanton, Phil Jackman, and Alan Goldstein, all of the *Sun* or *Evening Sun*, were also great writers whose material yielded much. Dave Anderson and William N. Wallace of the *New York Times* were also particularly helpful, as was the greatest sports journalist of them all, Red Smith.

# BIBLIOGRAPHY

Research for this book includes a combination of both primary and secondary resources. The points of view offered by and large come from the extensive personal interviews I conducted, but books, newspaper reports, and magazine articles also contributed to painting the picture of the Colts, Baltimore in the 1960s, Johnny Unitas, Don Shula, and the many people who populated their profession and world.

### PERSONAL INTERVIEWS

Raymond Berry
Dick Bielski
Bobby Boyd
Gary Collins
Bill Curry
Dr. Samuel Havrilak
Phil Jackman
Dr. Joseph Layug
Michael MacCambridge
Tom Matte
Earl Morrall
Jane Morrall
Pert Mutscheller
Joe Namath
Jim O'Brien
Michael Olesker
Jimmy Orr
Peter Platten
Rick Rosenbloom
Frank Ryan
Richard Sammis

Joseph Sheppard
Don Shula
Dan Sullivan
Gay Talese
Bill Tanton
Jan Unitas
Charley Winner
Nancy Winner
John Ziemann

PUBLISHED SOURCES

Bagli, Vince, and Norman L. Macht. *Sundays at 2:00 with the Baltimore Colts.* Centerville M D: Tidewater, 1995.

Berry, Raymond, with Wayne Stewart. *All the Moves I Had: A Football Life.* Lanham M D: Lyons Press, 2016.

Bowden, Mark. *The Best Game Ever: Giants vs. Colts, 1958, and the Birth of the Modern NFL.* New York: Atlantic Monthly Press, 2008.

Brown, Paul, with Jack Clary. *PB: The Paul Brown Story.* New York: Atheneum, 1979.

Callahan, Tom. *Johnny U: The Life and Times of John Unitas.* New York: Three Rivers Press, 2006.

Curry, Bill. *Ten Men You Meet in the Huddle: Lessons from a Football Life.* New York: ESPN Books, 2008.

Dylan, Bob. *Chronicles.* Vol. 1. New York: Simon and Schuster, 2004.

Greenfeld, Karl Taro, ed. *Muhammad Ali: The Tribute.* New York: Sports Illustrated Books, 2016.

Halberstam, David. *The Best and the Brightest.* New York: Random House, 1969.
————. *Summer of '49.* New York: Avon Books, 1990.

MacCambridge, Michael. *America's Game: The Epic Story of How Pro Football Captured a Nation.* New York: Random House, 2004.

Mackey, John, with Thom Loverro. *Blazing Trails: Coming of Age in Football's Golden Era.* Chicago: Triumph Books, 2003.

Maraniss, David. *When Pride Still Mattered: A Life of Vince Lombardi.* New York: Simon and Schuster, 2000.

Moore, Lenny, with Jeffrey Jay Ellish. *All Things Being Equal: The Autobiography of Lenny Moore.* Champaign IL: Sports, 2005.

Morrall, Earl, and George Sullivan. *Comeback Quarterback: The Earl Morrall Story.* New York: Tempo Books, 1970.

Olesker, Michael. *Front Stoops in the Fifties: Baltimore Legends Come of Age.* Baltimore: Johns Hopkins University Press, 2013.

————. *Journeys to the Heart of Baltimore.* Baltimore: Johns Hopkins University Press, 2001.

Pietila, Antero. *Not in My Neighborhood: How Bigotry Shaped a Great American City.* Chicago: Ivan R. Dee, 2010.

Plimpton, George. *One More July: A Football Dialogue with Bill Curry*. New York: Berkley, 1977.

Roberts, Randy, and Johnny Smith. *Blood Brothers: The Fatal Friendship between Muhammad Ali and Malcolm X*. New York: Basic Books, 2016.

Sahadi, Lou. *Johnny Unitas: America's Quarterback*. Chicago: Triumph Books, 2004.

Smith, Red. *American Pastimes: The Very Best of Red Smith*. Edited by Daniel Okrent. New York: Library of America, 2013.

Steadman, John. *The Baltimore Colts Story*. Baltimore: Press Box, 1958.

———. *Football's Miracle Men*. Cleveland: Pennington Press, 1959.

Towle, Mike. *Johnny Unitas: Mr. Quarterback*. Turner ME: Turner, 2003.

# INDEX

City College, Baltimore, 99, 181

civic sports, 75

civil rights movement, 65–66

Civil War, 63

Clay, Cassius Marcellus, 211, 219. *See also* Ali, Muhammad

Clifford, Clark, 208

Cole, Terry, 286

College of William and Mary, 116

Collier, Blanton, 264; and Carroll Rosenbloom, 11; as coach of the Browns, 91; and Don Shula, 25, 112; and Frank Ryan, 97; and integration, 90; and John Unitas, 94; and Paul Brown, 91; and University of Kentucky, 93

Collins, Gary, 11, 97, 114, 118, 309

Colts, Baltimore: and Andy Nelson, 20; and Carroll Rosenbloom, 7, 28, 47, 283; and championship (1958), 25; and championship (1964), 87–88, 107, 113–27, 160; and championship (1968), 240; and Charley Winner, 9; and death of Big Daddy Lipscomb, 66–69; disbanding of, 297–98; and Don Shula, 2, 7, 14, 16, 37, 77, 286; and draft, 12–14, 28–30; and fans, 31, 56, 98, 112, 222; and 49ers, 57; and game formations, 15, 122, 171, 291; and Giants, 60; and the "Greatest Game Ever Played," 60; and the horseshoe, 34, 160; and John Unitas, 77, 157–58, 286; and Memorial Stadium, 98; move of, from Baltimore to Indianapolis, 303; and Packers, 2, 79, 84, 86, 184–85, 196–97; public image of, 2–3, 5, 7–8; and race relations, 58–60; and revenge tour, 235; and Robert Irsay, 297; and special tryouts, 9; and Super Bowl III, 239–40, 264–82; and Weeb Ewbank, 7, 11, 15, 34, 84; and winning seasons, 160

Colts Marching Band, 112, 271

Columbia Broadcasting System. *See* cbs

Constam, Rose, 48

Corso, Lee, 117

Cosell, Howard, 105, 243

Cowboys, Dallas, 30, 187, 198–99, 201, 231–32, 292, 294

Crennel, Romeo, 300

Cronkite, Walter, 215

Cuba, 4, 43, 209

Cuozzo, Gary, 161–68, 171–72, 186, 188–89, 223

Currie, Dan, 83

Curry, Bill, 9, 140, 174, 190–93, 234, 298

Curtis, Mike, 257, 264, 290, 298

Dallas tx, 60

Davis, Al, 243

Davis, Ernie, 38, 90, 92–93, 117

Davis, Milt, 58, 60

Davis, Willie, 83, 186

Dawson, Leonard, 94–95, 225–26, 260

Democratic National Convention, 50, 216

Diehl, John, 107, 111

DiMaggio, Joe, 207, 236–37

Ditka, Mike, 38, 45, 250

Dodgers, Brooklyn, 90

Dolphins, Miami, 3, 14, 298–99

Domres, Marty, 296–97

Donovan, Arthur "Art," 20–21, 57, 68

Dos Passos, John, 50

draft: and afl, 28, 158, 182, 245, 257; and caliber of athletes, 256–57; and expansion, 189; and league rivalry, 158; and nfl, 83, 90, 106, 108, 119, 164, 190–94, 223, 225–26, 257; and restitution, 290

Dundalk Marine Terminal, 49

Dupre, "Long Gone," 23

Dylan, Bob, 66

Eagles, Philadelphia, 39, 81, 162–63

East Conference, 187

Eastern Division, 127

Edwards, Dave, 198

Eisenberg, John, 44

Elway, John, 105

Emerson Hotel, 65

Enoch Pratt Free Library, 50

*Evening Sun. See Sunpapers*

Ewbank, Weeb: and Charley Winner, 11, 33, 40, 137, 282; as coach of the Baltimore Colts, 11, 33–35; as coach of the Browns, 14–15; as coach of the Jets, 278; and draft picks, 9–14, 30, 38; and John Unitas, 8–11, 53, 79, 136; and press conferences, 11, 157; and Super Bowl III, 268; and Vince Lombardi, 34

expansion teams, 30, 37, 187

a social force, 252; and Super Bowl III, 264–70

narcotics, 69

Nash, Ogden, 50, 237

National Collegiate Athletic Association (NCAA), 33

National Football League (NFL), 1, 30, 57; and championships, 120, 141, 185, 187, 198, 201, 226, 240, 258–59, 282–83, 310; coaches in, 35, 95; commissioners of, 42, 44, 258, 297; and draft, 30, 90, 119, 164, 190, 225; and expansion teams, 30, 189; history of, 30, 34–35; and rival leagues, 92, 158, 250–51, 261, 310; and standardization of goalposts, 176; and televised games, 14

Nelsen, Bill, 264

Nelson, Andy, 19, 102, 109

Newton, Helmut, 148

New Yorker, 150

New York Times: and championship (1964), 124, 131; and Colts vs. Jets, 296; and David Halberstam, 205, 211; on Don Shula's move to Dolphins, 290–91; and Giants, 228; and Hattie Carroll, 66; and William Wallace, 222

NFL. See National Football League (NFL)

Ninowski, Jim, 25, 94, 96

Nitschke, Ray, 83, 166, 192, 306

Nixon, Richard, 215–16

Noll, Chuck, 35, 278, 300, 310; and Baltimore Colts, 182–83, 185, 195, 201, 235, 264; and Chargers, 182; and Steelers, 283, 299, 303; and Super Bowls, 300

Nolting, Frederick, 205

North Carolina State, 82

Notre Dame, 22, 89, 117, 194, 224, 249

Nowatzke, Tom, 257

Nugent, Tom, 116–17

Ohio State, 91, 168, 170

Oilers, Houston, 28

Oklahoma State, 108, 244

Olesker, Michael, 59–62, 68, 312, 315–16

Olsen, Merlin, 103, 200

Olympics, 217–19

Orange Bowl, 108, 201

Orioles, Baltimore, 7

Orr, Jimmy, 2, 162–63, 240, 270–71, 308–9

O'Sullivan, Chester, 74

Oswald, Lee Harvey, 216

Owens, Luke, 60

Owens, R. C., 109, 119

Packers, Green Bay: and Baltimore Colts, 2, 166, 184, 263; championships of, under Vince Lombardi, 2, 79, 201; and Ice Bowl, 83, 201; and Paul Hornung, 22, 83; and public ownership, 84; and Super Bowl, 201

Page, Alan, 194

Parcells, Bill, 181, 300, 310

Parilli, Babe, 260

Parker, Buddy, 226

Parker, Jim, 60, 86, 98, 133, 222

Parrish, Bernie, 113

Patriots, New England, 106, 300

Pellington, Bill, 8, 27, 40, 85, 158

Peppler, Pat, 82–83

Perkins, Don, 29–30, 198

Perkins, Ray, 195, 292, 300

Peter Lane Motel, 61

Petty, Charles S., 73–74

Piccolo, Brian, 287

Pikesville Armory, 45

Platten, Peter M., III, 82

Playboy, 147–48

Plimpton, George, 192

Plum, Milt, 25, 94, 163, 227

Plunkett, Sherman, 60

Poe, Edgar Allan, 50

press conferences, 8, 11, 157, 205

Pro Bowl, 20, 83, 118, 126–27, 129

professional football, 5, 14, 18–19, 25, 37, 104, 218, 243, 254, 287

Provident Hospital, 73

Pugh, Jethro, 198

Quinlan, Bill, 83

quota system, 59

Rabbit Run, 151

race relations, 6

racism, 5, 62, 90, 216, 220

Raiders, Oakland, 201, 265